LEARNING TO WRITE "INDIAN"

LEARNING TO WRITE "INDIAN"

The Boarding-School Experience and American Indian Literature

AMELIA V. KATANSKI

UNIVERSITY OF OKLAHOMA PRESS : NORMAN

Library of Congress Cataloging-in-Publication Data

Katanski, Amelia V., 1970–
    Learning to write "Indian" : the boarding-school experience and American Indian literature / Amelia V. Katanski
        p.   cm.
    Includes bibliographical references and index.
    ISBN 0-8061-3719-3 (cloth)
    ISBN-13: 978-0-8061-3852-7 (paper)
    ISBN-10: 0-8061-3852-1 (paper)
    1. American literature—Indian authors—History and criticism. 2. Indians of North America—Intellectual life. 3. Indians of North America—Education. 4. Boarding schools—United States. 5. Boarding schools in literature. 6. Indians in literature. I. Title.

PS153.I52K38 2006
810.9'8997—dc22

                                                                2005043933

The paper in this book meets the guidelines for permanence and durability of the Committee on Production Guidelines for Book Longevity of the Council on Library Resources, Inc. ∞

2 3 4 5 6 7 8 9 10

In memory of my father, Frank W. Katanski,
the finest storyteller I have ever known.

And for Jonathan O'Brien and Rose and Vittoria Katanski.
Your love, support, and patience have made this book possible.

CONTENTS

Illustrations

Preface and Acknowledgments

This project began many years ago with a seminar paper on Zitkala-Ša for a graduate course on American Realism taught by Elizabeth Ammons at Tufts University. I was immediately drawn to Zikala-Ša's powerful voice, but I was also puzzled about her choice to teach at the Carlisle Indian Industrial School, given what little I knew of the goals of this institution. I was intrigued and perplexed at the complicated, multiple rhetorical strategies and identity positions Zitkala-Ša used strategically in her writing and I began to explore the connections and disjunctions between her educational experiences and representational strategies. My inquiry into Indian boarding-school literature broadened when I was earning my Masters in American Indian Studies at UCLA. I was lucky to be able to work with Paula Gunn Allen, Paul Kroskrity, Greg Sarris, and a host of extremely talented scholars and teachers, and I began to realize the extent of the impact the boarding schools had made on American Indian literature.

Contemporary American Indian scholars such as Robert Allen Warrior and Craig Womack have urged, with good reason, that criticism and theories of American Indian literature written by Native people must be the central focus of scholarship on Native people. Warrior and Womack join a host of other Native scholars who further assert the importance of reading Native literature as the production of members of tribal nations. My work attempts to follow these guidelines, though this book necessarily differs, in its approach, from a work like Womack's *Red on Red*, which deals with a specific, Creek literary tradition, because the Indian boarding-school experience is explicitly pan-tribal. I have carefully scrutinized my position as a non-native scholar working with this material, and I have come to recognize that there is an intellectual and moral imperative for non-native scholars to acknowledge and understand the Indian boarding schools and their legacy. As a white woman educator, it is my obligation to be certain that I do not reproduce the ideological contortions of social evolutionary thought, with its rigid categorizations of Indian identity and denial of tribal sovereignty. This book is my effort to think through these issues and articulate a critical praxis that avoids those (still too common) pitfalls.

I owe a large debt of gratitude to the many people who have read parts of this manuscript and offered their expertise and assistance, including Elizabeth Ammons, Paula Gunn Allen, Tara Browner, Ellen Caldwell, Duane Champagne, Jane Elizabeth Dougherty, Stephanie Fitzgerald, Paul Kroskrity, Elisabeth Lavin-Peter, Dan Littlefield, Elizabeth Manwell, Deborah Mix, Barbara Rodríguez, Greg Sarris, and Siobhan Senier. Barbara Rodríguez has been especially gracious in mentoring me as I have worked my way through the (sometimes tortuous) publication process. I am grateful as well to Ruth Spack and Jane Hafen for sharing their outstanding scholarship on Zitkala-Ša. Jane Hafen has had a significant impact on the way I think about scholarly integrity in Native Studies. All of these individuals have helped to make this manuscript much stronger, though any limitations or errors are my own.

My deepest thanks as well go to Barb Landis at the Cumberland County Historical Archives for her wisdom and assistance over the years. The library research staff at Tufts University, UCLA, Michigan State University, Kalamazoo College, the Sherman Institute, and the Newberry Library have provided invaluable aid. I greatly appreciate the efforts that Alessandra Jacobi, Pippa Letsky, JoAnn Reece, Marian Stewart, and a host of others associated with the University of Oklahoma Press have put into the polishing and production of this book. My current and past colleagues in the English Department at Kalamazoo College have been wonderfully supportive during the many stages of this project. In particular, Bruce Mills has provided invaluable mentorship and has always taken time out of his busy schedule to talk through ideas or concerns with me; and Cari

Carpenter's too-brief presence felt like a rare and wonderful gift—the opportunity to work and teach alongside another scholar of American Indian literature in a department that had only three Americanists! I am also indebted to Erin Ashmore, my final-stage research assistant, because this book would never have made it to press without her sharp mind and hard work.

This project, from start to finish, would not have been possible without the tireless support of my family, especially my husband, Jonathan O'Brien, who has been research assistant, confidant, and morale booster. Special thanks, too, to my mother, Rose Katanski, and my sister Vittoria, for their patience. Neputo and Zuzu, who have both helped and hindered this project, provided unconditional love along the way.

LEARNING TO WRITE "INDIAN"

LEARNING TO WRITE "INDIAN"

D iné poet and scholar Laura Tohe begins *No Parole Today* (1999), her collection of poetry and prose memoir about Indian boarding schools, with a piece called "Letter to General Pratt." Tohe's addressee is Richard Henry Pratt, the army officer who founded the Carlisle Indian Industrial School in 1879. Carlisle was the prototype for federal off-reservation Indian boarding schools designed to destroy tribal nations and strip Native children of their cultures, languages, and religions. Tohe begins with an epigraph taken from a speech Pratt gave in 1883, in which he said, "In Indian civilization, I am a Baptist, because I believe in immersing the Indians in our civilization, and when we get them under holding them there until they are thoroughly soaked."[1] Tohe writes back in response not just to Pratt but to the "colonialist efforts of the Indian schools" he founded.[2] Writing as a Diné woman who, though she attended government boarding schools, speaks the Diné language, values her tribal culture, and sees herself connected to other boarding school students as a "survivor," Tohe proclaims, "I voice this letter to you now because I speak for me, no longer invisible, and no longer relegated to the quiet margins of American culture, my tongue silenced. The land, the Diné, the Diné culture is how I define myself and my writing. That part of my identity was never drowned; it was never a hindrance but a strength. To write is powerful and even dangerous. To have no stories is to be an empty person.

Writing is a way for me to claim my voice, my heritage, my stories, my culture, my people, and my history."[3]

In this compelling passage, Tohe links together writing, Diné tribal identity, and resistance to the assimilative, culturally genocidal policies of the boarding schools. Storytelling, in Diné or in English, guarantees personhood and tribal nationhood and provides the means of recovering all that the schools tried to strip away from their students. This assertion is an expression of power, in fact, dangerous to white American hegemony because it undermines the still-prevalent belief that tribal nations have been ingested and consumed by European American (in Pratt's term, "civilized") culture and, therefore, been rendered politically and culturally powerless. Tohe's voice speaks out against presumptions of the "inevitability" of Indian cultural death, presumptions that have attempted to disarm tribal claims to land and resources since 1492. In directing her remarks to Pratt, whose educational philosophy was to "kill the Indian to save the man," she pointedly discredits the aims and disproves the predicted outcomes of boarding-school policy.[4]

A century ago, even those who claimed to be "pro-Indian" in the debates over how to solve "the Indian problem" held the goal of eventually obliterating tribal culture and identity. These "progressives," a group of white, Christian policy makers and philanthropists known as the "Friends of the Indian," firmly believed that Indian people must completely assimilate into the European American population. In 1880, the Board of Indian Commissioners noted in its Twelfth Annual Report (with evident disappointment):

> The most reliable statistics prove conclusively that the Indian population taken as a whole, instead of dying out under the light and contact of civilization, as has been generally supposed, is steadily increasing. The Indian is evidently destined to live as long as the white race, or until he becomes absorbed and assimilated with his pale brethren. We no longer hear advocated among really civilized men the theory of extermination, a theory that would disgrace the wildest savage. As we must have him among us, self-interest, humanity and Christianity require that we should accept the situation and go resolutely to work to make him a safe and useful factor in our body politic. As a savage we cannot tolerate him any more than as a half-civilized parasite, wanderer or vagabond. The only alternative left is to fit him by education for civilized life.[5]

The board proceeded to advocate establishment of off-reservation industrial boarding schools, patterned after Richard Pratt's Carlisle Indian Industrial School in Carlisle, Pennsylvania. Pratt, the most prominent advocate of Indian assimilation through education, developed his philosophy through an "experiment" educating a group of Kiowa, Comanche, and Cheyenne prisoners at Ft. Marion, Florida. Pratt cut the prisoners' hair, dressed them in army uniforms, drilled them like soldiers, and began to teach them to speak and read English to test his long-pondered theory that "wild Indians could be transformed into peaceful, enlightened citizens."[6] Carlisle, established in 1879, was based on Pratt's Florida experience and on the Hampton Institute's program of industrial training for former slaves.[7] The Indian boarding schools, led by Carlisle, brought together children from many tribes, who were forbidden to speak native languages, wear traditional clothing, or practice ancestral religions. The Pan-Indian nature of the boarding-school student body, enhanced by the method of taking children away from their families when they were very young and keeping them away for years at a time, separated these children from their tribal traditions. Pratt fully reveals the philosophy behind this system of education in his ironically titled autobiography, *Battlefield and Classroom:*

> I suppose the end to be gained, however far away it may be, is complete civilization of the Indian and his absorption into our national life, with all the rights and privileges guaranteed to every other individual, the Indian to lose his identity as such, to give up his tribal relations and to be made to feel that he is an American citizen. If I am correct in this supposition, then the sooner all tribal relations are broken up; the sooner the Indian loses all his Indian ways, even his language, the better it will be for him and for the government and the greater will be the economy to both. . . . To accomplish that, his removal and personal isolation is necessary.[8]

By 1889, 10,500 of an estimated Indian student population of 36,000 attended facilities patterned on Carlisle.[9] They were subject to Pratt's philosophy, which, as his rhetoric indicates, was shaped by social evolutionary thought. Social evolutionism imagined a linear, hierarchical relationship among races. The ideology was accompanied by a "replacement" model of identity, which claimed that education would totally transform students as they "progressed" from tribal "savagery" to Western "civilization" because they would lose their Indianness as they gained knowledge of English and other elements of "civilized" culture. Each "civilized" trait they gained would eliminate the corresponding "savage" trait. These theories implied that the creative expression of students would likewise be transformed. If Indians successfully mastered European American expressive forms they would no longer represent themselves as Indians.

In a piece called "Our Tongues Slapped into Silence," Tohe targets the keystone of the boarding school's "transformative" curriculum—English-language literacy. As the U.S. commissioner of education told the Friends of the Indian in 1895: "Education has become a great potency in our hands."[10] His message for Indian parents demonstrated the primacy of English literacy to that "potent" source of power and control—"Give us your children. We will give them letters and make them acquainted with the printed page. . . . With these comes the great emancipation, and the school shall give you that."[11] Tohe contests the "emancipatory" effect of cruelly enforced English-only classrooms. "The taking of our language was a priority," she explains, and she demonstrates the linguistic violence perpetrated against students who "had no choice in the matter," through her rewriting of a Dick and Jane reader—here entitled "Dick and Jane Subdue the Diné."[12] While Dick, Jane, Father, Mother, Puff, and Spot "introduced us to the white man's world," the lessons taught along with the English language insist that Diné culture and language have no place in the classroom and that students should "feel shame for the crime of speaking Diné."[13] Instead of seeing Dick run or seeing Spot jump, the Diné boarding-school students who attempted to converse in their ancestral language were more likely to *"See Eugene with red hands, shape of ruler. / oh, oh, oh / See Eugene cry. oh, oh, oh / See Juanita stand in corner, see tears fall down face."*[14] The results of the suppression of Diné language in the classroom is clear: *"Oh see us draw pictures / of brown horses under blue clouds. / We color eyes black, hair black. / We draw ears and leave out mouth."*[15] Boarding-school students, as Tohe's poem shows, were supposed to be receptacles for the language of the colonizer, voiceless and powerless, tongues "drowned in the murky waters of assimilation."[16]

Alongside the pain and humiliation of the classroom experience, Tohe charts the student culture—a purposeful conglomeration of school and home languages, values, and customs that helped students to navigate the harsh disciplinary authority of the classroom. Tohe herself is the fourth generation from her family to attend the schools, and her placement of her school narratives next to the boarding-school story told her by her grandmother, Julia Barton, "in Diné storytelling fashion" stresses that students found ways to survive the schools and return home.[17] Tohe, like her grandmother and many other former boarding-school students, has been able to redraw her mouth, to find her voice, making use of the English language to bear witness to the anguish of the school experience and to hold the memory of student negotiation of that dangerous space. Her tongue, held under the waters of the "civilizing" institution of the schools, has, in the words of a recent anthology of American Indian women's writing, "reinvented the enemy's language" to express the complexity of student response to and survival of the boarding schools.[18]

This process of literary reinvention of the representational tools of assimilation, staking a claim to continued tribal identity and connection to land, history, and language through the telling of boarding-school stories, is the subject of this book, which examines how American Indian boarding-school students developed complex self-definitions and turned their ability to read and write in English to their own uses despite a curriculum that made English literacy the marker of lost tribal culture and achievement of "civilization." The schools attempted to shape how their students used English, and they succeeded in this to a certain degree, cowing students into obedience or voicelessness. But as linguist William Leap has shown, "Indian student varieties of English" were *codes under construction*, codes that students were creating, as individuals and as a group, on the basis of the knowledge of language they had acquired in their home/tribal communities, were learning from their teachers, and were learning from each other. This, of course, was not the school's plan for English language development."[19] These constructed, heterogeneous codes reflected ancestral language patterns, embedding tribal cultural continuance into the colonial language thought to "[plant] treason to the tribe" deep within Native students.[20] Making use of such codes, and of a similarly heterogeneous collection of literary forms culled from tribal literatures, the Anglo-American literary tradition, and pan-tribal emergent narratives, boarding-school students generated a wide-ranging literary response to their educations, writing back to the institution to claim, as Tohe does, their voices, cultures, nations, and history. I call this dialectic "learning to write 'Indian.'"

This phrase has several interrelated meanings that structure my inquiry into the impact of boarding-school education on American Indian literature. Learning to write "Indian" refers most basically to the process by which American Indian people were taught literacy in English at the boarding schools, literally learning to write the word "Indian" in English. William Leap's work *American Indian English* discusses language acquisition from a linguistic perspective, and Ruth Spack's monograph *America's Second Tongue* engages the topic through ESL theory and practice. This book, however, approaches the subject from the perspective of literary and cultural criticism, arguing that implicitly and strongly connected to English language education in the schools was educators' belief in their control over how (and if) their students textually represented themselves as Indian people. The controlling pedagogy of the anti-tribal schools was to monitor and restrict representations of Indianness so that students would affirm their assimilative project and embrace a sense of tribal culture as inferior and "savage." Educators attempted to achieve this goal by producing scripts of Indianness for their students to follow. I interrogate the narratives of domination that were created by boarding-school educators and distributed in venues such as the school newspapers in order to provide an understanding of the way the schools attempted to define what it meant to write "Indian." As Tohe's book illustrates, boarding-school students continually engaged in a complex process of self-definition and self-representation—but frequently couch their writing as a response to the copious and often vicious articulations of the schools' racist philosophy of language education.

Learning to write "Indian" also refers to the boarding schools as generators of a pan-tribal identity, where students from different tribes met one another, recognized shared values and experiences of injustice crossing the boundaries of tribal nations, and developed a sense of themselves as "Indian" that did not cancel out their tribal affiliation but cultivated instead what linguistic anthropologist Paul Kroskrity has termed a repertoire of identities.[21] Off-reservation boarding schools such as Carlisle, Chilocco, and Haskell consciously and purposefully brought together children from different tribal nations to make it difficult to speak tribal languages, practice religious rituals, or maintain any aspect of tribal culture at school. As Pratt insisted, "The solution of the Indian problem hinges upon . . . the devising of means that will disintegrate the tribes."[22]

Instead of losing their tribal identities, however, students explored and inhabited diverse identities that contradict both nineteenth-century social evolutionism and our contemporary understandings of "biculturalism." Students deployed identities within their repertoires situationally to deny a simple, linear (and therefore genocidal) assimilative process. Although they did not possess unlimited freedom to self-identify, or to be simultaneously utterly traditional and utterly assimilated, most of these students had some degree of agency to choose when and how to exercise various identities within their repertoires.[23] The boarding schools were closely linked to the rise of a Pan-Indian identity at the turn of the twentieth century, as Hazel Hertzberg and other scholars have demonstrated.[24] In fact, even as late as 1944, long after the boarding school fell from favor among U.S. policy makers, Ruth Muskrat Bronson (Cherokee), a former student and teacher at the Haskell Indian Institute, included boarding schools such as Haskell, Sherman, and Chemawa on her map of "Indians of the U.S.A." (see Figure 1), which was reproduced on the inside cover of her treatise *Indians Are People, Too* to chart contemporary as well as historical Indian communities and occupations. For Bronson, as for many other Indian people, the boarding-school experience had become part of the way in which they mapped their identities as Indians.[25]

Just as this growing repertoire of identity options denied simplistic social evolutionary binaries, representations of the boarding school in American Indian literature, too, prove that despite the schools' deep, lasting, and often destructive impact on tribal communities, students were not passive victims, crushed and destroyed by their contact with European American culture. Their spirited and generative narrative creativity is at the heart of our understanding of learning to write "Indian." As Kathryn Shanley has defined the term, "writing Indian" is a recognition of "Indianness as a politic and a poetic,"[26] and it is my contention that both American Indian politics and poetics shape—and have been shaped by—Indian boarding-school narratives. Historian Frederick Hoxie contextualizes the connection between boarding schools and Indian politics when he writes:

> Among the first generation of native young people educated at boarding schools were hundreds of graduates who used their facility with English, their "civilized" appearance, and their understanding of American institutions to enter political life. They participated in

tribal and village councils, circulated petitions attacking the policies of the Office of Indian Affairs, and employed the American legal system to pursue community objectives. Through such actions, the political leaders of a supposedly vanishing race began to define the legal limits of federal and state intrusion into their communities. This effort produced the insight that certain "rights" set Native Americans apart from other residents of the United States. That insight inspired tribal leaders to launch a campaign to defend their rights and to use existing political and legal institutions to reclaim control of community government and communally owned resources.[27]

Clearly writing "Indian" and Indian rights have more than a homonymic relationship. The combination of verbal skills and group identification developed in Indian boarding schools produced a range of texts—from legal briefs to congressional testimony to autobiographical narratives, poetry, fiction, and plays—that explicitly concern themselves with tribal and indigenous sovereignty. Representations of the schools and their students have always been politically charged, whether they were deployed by the educators or by current or former students. This study reads each of the texts examined as articulations situated within a sociopolitical context. These narratives do much more than reflect that context. They actively seek to transform the discourses into which they enter.

In learning to write "Indian," boarding-school students transformed the English language itself by telling their stories of boarding-school life— building literary forms and tropes that signify in what we know today as the American Indian literary tradition. In doing so, they achieve what Scott Lyons has termed "rhetorical sovereignty," or "the inherent right and ability of *peoples* to determine their own communicative needs and desires in [the pursuit of self-determination], to decide for themselves the goals, modes, styles, and languages of public discourse."[28] Paula Gunn Allen points to the centrality of the schools to American Indian literary history when she states that "the Indian boarding school and its effects form a major subtext in Native American narrative," a subtext that is present throughout twentieth-century American Indian literature because writers were "either [the schools'] products or were raised by parents and grandparents who were."[29] This centrality is ironic, since the schools' agenda was to eradicate Indian cultural identity, which would include the elimination of any sort of identifiable American Indian literature. And yet, many American Indian

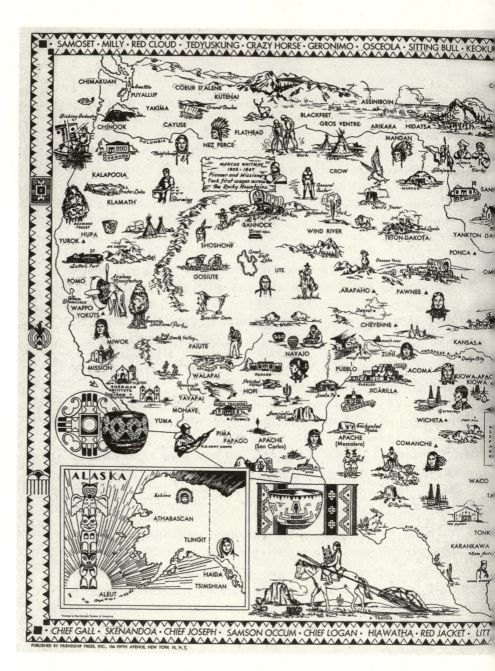

Fig. 1. "Indians of the U.S.A.," by Louise E. Jefferson, printed on the endpapers of Ruth Muskrat Bronson, *Indians Are People, Too* (New York, NY: Friendship Press, 1944). The map does not mark the location of the Carlisle Indian School, which closed in 1918, but does include the Sherman, Haskell, and Chemawa schools as well as the Santee Normal School.

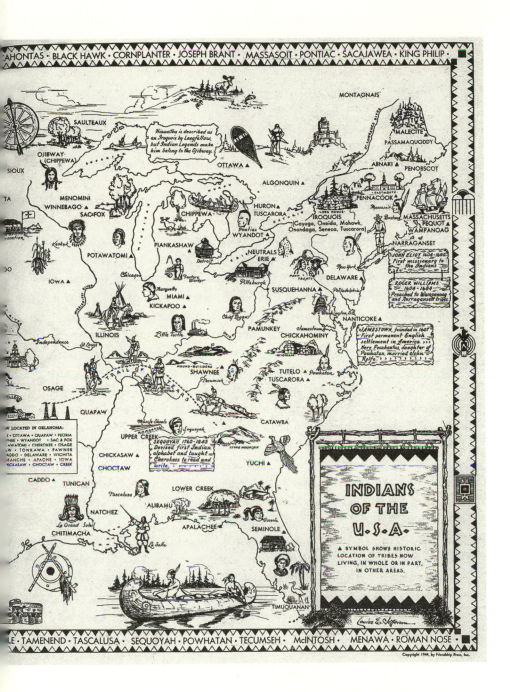

MONTAGNAIS

SAULTEAUX

Hiawatha is described as an Iroquois by Longfellow, but Indian Legends make him belong to the Ojibway.

OJIBWAY (CHIPPEWA)

SIOUX

MALECITE

PASSAMAQUODDY

ABNAKI

PENOBSCOT

OTTAWA ▲

ALGONQUIN ▲

DARTMOUTH

PENNACOOK

MENOMINI

WINNEBAGO ▲

SAC·FOX

CHIPPEWA

HURON ▲

TUSCARORA

IROQUOIS
(Cayuga, Oneida, Mohawk, Onondaga, Seneca, Tuscarora)

LONG HOUSE

Massasoit

Boston

MASSACHUSETTS ▲

PEQUOT

WAMPANOAG ▲

NARRAGANSET

Keokuk

POTAWATOMI

Pontiac

WYANDOT ▲

Detroit

NEUTRALS
ERIE ▲

New York

DELAWARE ▲

JOHN ELIOT 1604-1690. First missionary to the Indians.

IOWA ▲

Chicago

Factory Worker

Pittsburgh

Philadelphia

ROGER WILLIAMS 1604-1684 Preached to Wampanoag and Narraganset tribes.

Independence

St. Louis

Marquette

MIAMI ▲

KICKAPOO

Chief Logan

Little Turtle

ILLINOIS

PIANKASHAW

SUSQUEHANNA

NANTICOKE ▲

PAMUNKEY

CHICKAHOMINY

Washington D.C.

JAMESTOWN, founded in 1607. First permanent English settlement in America. Here Pocahontas, daughter of Powhatan, married John Rolfe.

Jamestown

WIGWAM

OSAGE

TRAIL OF TEARS

MOUND·BUILDERS

Daniel Boone

Tecumseh

SHAWNEE

TUTELO

Powhatan

TUSCARORA

QUAPAW

NOW LOCATED IN OKLAHOMA:
OTTAWA · QUAPAW · PEORIA
... · WYANDOT · SAC & FOX
...AWATOMI · CHEROKEE · OSAGE
... · TONKAWA · PAWNEE
...ADDO · DELAWARE · WICHITA
...RANCHE · APACHE · IOWA
...ICKASAW · CHOCTAW · CREEK

Muscle Shoals

Sequoyah

SEQUOYAH 1760-1843 Devised first Indian alphabet and taught Cherokees to read and write.

UPPER CREEK

CATAWBA

STONE MOUNTAIN

CADDO ▲

CHICKASAW

CHOCTAW

YUCHI ▲

TUNICAN

Tascalusa

LOWER CREEK

NATCHEZ

ALIBAMU

Osceola

Le Grand Soleil

CHITIMACHA

APALACHEE

SEMINOLE

La Salle

TIMUQUANAN

INDIANS
OF THE
U·S·A·

▲ SYMBOL SHOWS HISTORIC LOCATION OF TRIBES NOW LIVING, IN WHOLE OR IN PART, IN OTHER AREAS.

Louise E. Jefferson

writers were able to wrest control of both the content and the form of their self-representations and fictional literary productions out of the hands of the schools in acts of rhetorical sovereignty. In their representations of the boarding-school experience, moreover, these writers—from the 1880s to the present—generate a repertoire of shared ancestral, hybrid, or Western representational forms, connecting intertextually to form a significant part of the discourse of "American Indian literature."

Laura Tohe's poem "The Names," for example, meditates on boarding-school educators' eagerness to rename, and hence redefine, the children who entered their classrooms. The children in the poem hear the teacher change the sound and sense of their names as she mispronounces the Diné words. After hearing her name mispronounced as "Laura Toe," the narrator is filled with dread. She reports, "Suddenly we are immigrants, / waiting for the names that obliterate the past."[30] By revisiting this moment, the poem resonates not only with other Diné literature, through its explanation of the meaning of Diné names, but also with other boarding-school narratives that describe the process of student renaming, such as Luther Standing Bear's depiction of his first day in a classroom at Carlisle when his teacher, Marianna Burgess, wrote English names (that none of her students could read) on the board and made each of them come up to "pick" one to replace their own. Standing Bear explains, "When my turn came, I took the pointer and acted as if I were about to touch an enemy," counting coup on his English name in an assertion of Lakota identity in a threatening moment.[31] Likewise, Tohe's poem ends with the Diné names of each of the students in the class, moving from English transliterations to Diné words (among them the name Tapahonso—surname of another Diné author, Luci Tapahonso; see Chapter 5). Individually, each text comments meaningfully upon student experience and resistance; together, they illustrate a shared literary history united by the iteration of common experiences.

When Tohe writes pieces such as her "Letter from the Indian School" series, she signifies on the many, many letters boarding-school students wrote home.[32] In the several "Letters from the Indian School" included in *No Parole Today*, students recount to their families how they negotiate the system in order to circumvent the school's surveillance and control, learning from one another "all the dos and don'ts at Indian school."[33] Ojibwe historian Brenda Child, who wrote a history of Indian boarding schools based primarily on student letters, notes that many student letters, uncensored and speaking of everyday minutia, are texts that "reflect Indian opinions, emotions, and experiences before, during and after government boarding school." The letters, she says, are "Indian writings."[34] When Tohe makes use of the genre of the letter home in her collection of poetry and memoir, she emphasizes that the letters not only are historical artifacts but also constitute an Indian literary form—recognized by and available to other writers in a repertoire of formal choices that serve as the building blocks of the poetics of writing "Indian."

There is already a vibrant scholarly interest in the Indian boarding-school experience. My work's contribution is to make this distinction between boarding-school narratives as historic documents and boarding-school narratives as elements of an Indian poetics. The rich historical analyses of books by David Adams, Brenda Child, Amanda Cobb, Michael Coleman, K. Tsianinah Lomawaima, and Devon Mihesuah, among others, make use of the literature produced by boarding-school students as "documentation" for a "new Indian history."[35] Ruth Spack's *America's Second Tongue* is particularly attentive to what the narratives reveal about English language education, "approach[ing] these works as *autoethnographic* texts."[36] While these scholars have a great influence, a consideration is still very much needed of the artistry of the texts coming out of the boarding-school experience. My work seeks to examine how boarding-school students learned to adapt and manipulate both tribal and European American literary forms in the service of communicative goals that were often pro-tribal or politically Pan-Indian.

Through their literary production, Native writers demonstrate a response to boarding-school education that complicates not only the educators' understanding of how assimilatory education should work but also the contemporary literary critical tendency to group texts as "resistant" or "capitulating." One must respect the complexity of students' responses and recognize their authorial agency in order to understand fully the Indian boarding-school experience and its impact on the American Indian literary tradition.

To focus on boarding-school student agency is not to suggest that students escaped unscathed. Many students lost their lives as the result of intense physical abuse and neglect, infectious diseases that attacked them in their dormitories, or severe emotional battery and trauma. Even more students experienced a psychic death at the schools, driven away from their families and toward the harmful cycles of alcoholism and violence.[37] Even the Yankton Dakota writer and activist Zitkala-Ša, who spoke out against the boarding-school agenda, described her own removal to school as a silencing.[38] Some students could not find a way to speak and be heard in the schools' racist, culture-killing environment. Others chose silence— especially a refusal to write in English (primarily experienced today as "silence" even if they were vocal in their tribal languages)—as resistance, as refusal to reproduce the words of the educators. As Zitkala-Ša's and Tohe's writings prove, though, many students were able to find a voice to speak about the institution.

A sizable body of work exists by those American Indians who did have a way, and a desire, to speak for and about the students. N. Scott Momaday remarks, "In the Indian world, a word is spoken or a song is sung not against, but within the silence." This book considers the Indian boarding-school-student voice that reverberates within the silence like a song inside a drum, without forgetting or ignoring the distress of those who were voiceless.[39] The path these writers took to expression was neither painless nor easy, but they fought for the means to articulate their complexity in print and to subvert and dismantle the representations of Indian boarding schools and their students that were written and circulated by the white educators.

Some literary critics have found it easy to discount or erase student agency—to execute what Greg Sarris calls more generally a literary "removal" of the Indian from the text, which amounts to the perpetuation of stereotypes and fallacies about American Indian people—by focusing on narrowly defined, restrictive definitions of authenticity and identity in relation to literary production.[40] As Sarris's term suggests by its allusion to the Indian "removals" of the nineteenth century, which were designed to push tribes out of their territories so land could be claimed by the colonizing force of the United States, such critical praxis has anti-Indian political implications. The years around the beginning of the twentieth century for many American Indians were extremely painful and necessitated complex responses in order to survive. Too often in today's discourse on turn-of-the-century American Indian literature, scholars focus on obvious statements of resistance and view the slightest sign of accommodation as "selling out." Boarding-school students—especially those considered "successful" by white standards—are particularly vulnerable to this type of criticism. In a desire to make sense of this difficult period, scholars replicate the tenets of social evolutionary theory, reproducing the savage/civilized binary by proclaiming "no longer Indians" those who seem to have mastered their European American education. Or, worse, scholars proclaim them "trapped between two worlds" if they fail to fall easily into either side of the binary, thus stripping writers of personal or rhetorical power in order to position them solely as victims. When we pay attention to the intricacies of boarding-school students' identity formation and expression, carefully reading the ways they controlled and complicated their responses to their education (even within an oppressive, restrictive institution), we can see the multiplicity of identity options that allowed many students to escape the linear, "progressive" model of assimilation enforced by turn-of-the-century social evolutionist thinkers. Working to understand such multivalent identities, critics can develop a praxis that sanctions contemporary American Indian survivance on its own terms.

Chapter 1 begins the process of articulating this critical praxis by providing historical and theoretical grounding for the close readings later in the book. It begins with a historically located reading of Leslie Marmon Silko's *Storyteller* (1981), which enacts the link between historical analysis and literary and cultural criticism. This chapter provides background on social evolutionary thought and the philosophical positioning of Richard Pratt and the Friends of the Indian. It concludes with a theory of representation that is based on the model of the repertoire of identity, which deconstructs the binary categories that eliminate student agency by simplifying the complexity of student identity development to being "trapped between two worlds." This model of the repertoire of representation resists the reproduction of social evolutionary tenets in its approach to literary criticism. Instead it focuses on situational deployments of authors' rhetorical sovereignty.

Chapters 2 and 3 work in tandem to explore the tension between two competing stories of identity—representations *of* and *by* boarding-school students at the turn of the century. The focus is on Carlos Montezuma, Dennison Wheelock, Francis La Flesche, and Zitkala-Ša, whom boarding-school educator Jessie Cook, in an article published in 1900, identified as "representative Indians." Cook selected these "representative Indians" because they appeared to fit her assimilative and restrictive definitions of identity. But they possessed their own tools for representing themselves.

Primarily by using the English literacy they had acquired at the boarding schools, these writers, scholars, and activists rewrote the oppressive narratives of the schools from their own perspectives.[41] These writers were not mere pawns in the construction of the story of assimilation, as told by educational reformers of their time. Instead, they actively challenged assimilationist representations of Indians and Indian identity. Not traditional, yet not assimilated, the "representative Indians" attempted to represent themselves and their identities through their creative work in far more complicated ways than the assimilative model touted by the Friends of the Indian would suggest.

Chapter 2 demonstrates how the Carlisle Press attempted to regulate representations of Indian identity in its school newspapers by creating an "Indian voice" that ventriloquized the social evolutionism of Pratt and his cohorts. The focus is on the construction of this voice (what I call the "represented Indian," echoing Cook's term) in Carlisle's student newspaper, the *Indian Helper*. Carlisle used this paper to produce an image of the Indian student as subservient and grateful, amenable to the assimilative goals of the schools, utterly transformed by contact with the "light of civilization." Stories such as "Home Difficulties of a Young Indian Girl" presented fictional Indian students who perfectly represented—and enacted in writing—Pratt's ideology. So did the fascinating *Stiya: A Carlisle Indian Girl at Home* (1891), a novel written by Marianna Burgess, the editor of the *Indian Helper*. Burgess's and Pratt's "paper Indians" unabashedly declared their preference for white civilization over their tribal savagery in order to establish and reinforce white hegemony over the students. Published selections from letters the students wrote to those "back home," as well as student essays, like Dennison Wheelock's prize-winning tract that supported banning tribal languages at the schools, indicate the impact of the "represented Indian" on Indian self-representation. The *Indian Helper* and its "creator," the Man-on-the-Band-stand, a persona that stood in for the school's disciplinary power, served as a form of surveillance over student self-representations, and the newspaper acted as rhetorical panopticon, encouraging student self-colonization through writing.

While Pratt was able to exert considerable control over his young students' representations of themselves, he was not as successful at regulating the voices of the adult "representative Indians," most of them either former Carlisle students, former Carlisle employees (most often teachers), or people somehow associated with Carlisle. In Chapter 3, Indian voices break out of the roles assigned them. The Carlisle newspapers respond to the literary self-representations of representative Indians La Flesche (Omaha) and Zitkala-Ša (Yankton Sioux), who in 1900 both published autobiographical texts that dealt with their experiences in the boarding schools and that contradicted Pratt's image of the metamorphosed student. Pratt willfully misread La Flesche's *The Middle Five* as a narrative of assimilation, when, in fact, La Flesche showed how students used the boarding school as middle ground—a generative space in between cultures where they could develop new systems of meaning and new situational identities to add to their repertoires.

Pratt was unable, however, to formulate such a misreading of Zitkala-Ša's intensely angry portrayal of her boarding-school experiences in her autobiographical essays, "Impressions of an Indian Childhood," "School Days of an Indian Girl," and "An Indian Teacher among Indians," and in her short story, "The Soft-hearted Sioux." Pratt clearly sought to use Zitkala-Ša's literary success as proof of her "representative" acculturation (much as he did with La Flesche), but her fierce anti-boarding-school prose defied his attempt to control her presentation of herself and of her educational experience. This struggle over representation exploded in a series of fascinating exchanges in the *Red Man* and the *Red Man and Helper*, which illuminate the high stakes involved in controlling Indian self-representation at a time when anything less than a fully assimilated Indian was an intolerable "half-civilized parasite," simultaneously dangerous and useless.[42]

Chapter 4 concentrates on autobiographical narratives written by Sioux authors Charles Alexander Eastman and Zitkala-Ša. These narratives exhibit repertoires of identity and repertoires of representation that challenge prevalent critical assumptions about the relationship between form and authenticity in American Indian autobiography. Literary critics' readings of boarding-school-era Indian autobiographical self-representation actually reproduce repressive elements of the social evolutionary ideology behind the boarding-school education. I argue against critics' tendencies to equate form and identity, which thus "fix" an autobiographer with a static identity by assessing the Indianness or Europeanness of the autobiographical form. I attempt to de-center critical fascination with authenticity in Indian autobiography by examining how these writers use various literary forms—to suit their rhetorical and political ends and not to reveal uncritically their degree of Indianness.

The final chapter canvasses contemporary Indian authors' representations of boarding-school students and provides readings of Luci Tapahonso's short story "The Snakeman" (1978), N. Scott Momaday's play *The Indolent Boys* (c. 1992), Hanay Geiogamah's play *Foghorn* (1973), and Leslie Marmon Silko's novel *Gardens in the Dunes* (1999). These contemporary authors portray boarding-school students as being both resistant and in possession of a remarkable degree of power and agency. These representations are set in context by focusing on the explicit connection the texts make between writing and tribal survivance. I argue that representations of the boarding-school experience in late twentieth-century American Indian literature express a complex combination of tribal nationalism and Pan-Indian solidarity, clear acts of rhetorical sovereignty. These contemporary retellings elucidate the ongoing centrality of the boarding-school experience to the American Indian literary tradition, writing "Indian" into the twenty-first century in echo of Laura Tohe's defiant declaration that "to write is powerful and even dangerous."[43]

CHAPTER 1

STORYTELLERS AND REPRESENTATIVE INDIANS IN A THEORY OF BOARDING-SCHOOL LITERATURE

Laguna Pueblo author Leslie Marmon Silko's writings attest to the health of post–boarding school Indian representations of Indian and tribal cultural continuity. A century ago, Silko's proud, positive assertion of Indian and tribal identity in her autobiographical collection *Storyteller* (1981) would have been distasteful and dangerous to the Friends of the Indian. For Silko, as for many other Indian authors, storytelling is strongly tied to identity since, as she recounts, "From the time we are very young, we hear these stories, so that when we go out into the world, when one asks who we are or where we are from, we immediately know. . . . We are the people of these stories."[1] In *Storyteller,* Silko blends fiction and poetry with family stories, historical episodes, and photographs, creating a text that celebrates and defines her complex identities as a woman, a Laguna Pueblo tribal member, an Indian, a person of mixed racial heritage, an American, et al. Arnold Krupat explains, "Silko's book would seem to announce by its title . . . the familiar pattern of discovering who one is by discovering what one does, the pattern of identity in vocation. . . . In Pueblo culture, however, to be known as a storyteller is to be known as one who participates, in a communally sanctioned manner, in sustaining the group; for a Native American writer to identify herself as a storyteller today is to express a desire to perform such a function."[2] Silko's storytelling, then, both describes and feeds cultural vitality. She explains that her own "dreadful" Bureau of Indian Affairs (BIA) schooling actually had the result of encouraging her to maintain life-giving tribal narratives: "Whatever literature we were exposed to at school (which was damn little), at home the storytelling, the special regard for telling and bringing together through the telling, was going on constantly. And as the old people say, 'If you can remember the stories, you will be alright. Just remember the stories.'"[3] *Storyteller's* late-twentieth-century denial of Indian cultural death through assimilation and its assertion instead of tribal and Pan-Indian continuance make it a text that Indian boarding-school ideology would never have wanted and could never have predicted.

STORYTELLING AND SURVIVAL

From the very beginning Silko recognizes the impact of the off-reservation boarding schools on her family, on the stories, and on herself. Silko makes her first reference to Indian boarding schools on the first page, as she informs us that her Grandpa Hank, Henry C. (Anaya) Marmon, attended the Sherman Indian School in Riverside, California.[4] The photograph obviously predates Henry Marmon's return from Sherman, since it displays Silko's great-grandmother, Maria Anaya Marmon, and her great-grandfather, Robert G. Marmon, holding her infant Grandpa Hank. Maria Anaya Marmon, Silko's Grandma A'mooh, wears the Victorian clothing that served as the marker of the boarding-school-educated Indian. In fact, Silko tells us that both Grandma A'mooh and her daughter-in-law, Silko's great-aunt Susie, attended the Carlisle Indian School. This first image of Maria Anaya Marmon and her son—representing two generations of Marmons who would attend federally run, off-reservation, Indian boarding schools—illustrates the multigenerational involvement of the schools in Silko's family.

We can immediately see the effect of the boarding schools on Silko's storytelling, since she learned her trade primarily from Grandma A'mooh and Aunt Susie. Through the stories she tells about her mentors, Silko complicates our understanding of how the boarding-school experience functions in her work. She reports that Aunt Susie was sent away to Carlisle in the last years of the nineteenth century and continued her education at Dickinson College. Aunt Susie returned to the reservation to teach, a professional choice that might give the appearance she supported the anti-Indian sentiments of the boarding school by herself propagating its Eurocentric education (*Storyteller* 3). In fact, Aunt Susie was to become known for creating her own curriculum, which included both European American and Laguna knowledge and skills. The dedicators of the Susie Reyos Marmon Elementary School explained in 1990, "Mrs. Marmon exemplified the blending together of two cultures, retaining the old ways while learning the new."[5] Silko informs us that while Aunt Susie

> had come to believe very much in books
> and in schooling. . . .
> She must have realized
> that the atmosphere and conditions
> which had maintained this oral tradition in Laguna culture
> had been irrevocably altered by the European intrusion—
> principally by the practice of taking the children away from Laguna
>   to Indian schools
> taking the children away from the tellers who had in all past
>   generations
> told the children
> an entire culture, an entire identity of a people." (*Storyteller*, 4, 6)

Combining her belief in writing and in books with her commitment to passing down the oral tradition, Aunt Susie painstakingly wrote the stories in English, attempting to use her boarding-school education to maintain the legacy of the Laguna people for future generations. Silko does not, in fact, see Aunt Susie as a "white-educated scholar" but as a "scholar/ of her own making/ who has cherished the Laguna stories/ all her life" (7). In her scholarly practice, Aunt Susie blends languages and literary forms, as in the story of the little girl who wanted her mother to make her *yashtoah*, or "the hardened crust on cornmeal mush" (8). Silko explains that this is a "very old story," and in Aunt Susie's telling of it "you will also hear the influence of the Indian school at Carlisle."[6] The story instructs its audience about geography, culture, and Pueblo language, defining terms like *yashtoah* and *byn'yah'nah'* ("the west lake"). Alongside these markers of tribal identity, Aunt Susie uses "some English she picked up at Carlisle—words like *precipitous*." As Silko says, in this story "things are not separated out and categorized; all things are brought together."[7] Most of Aunt Susie's stories were passed on orally, since her poor eyesight made her writing progress very slowly, but Silko clearly sees herself taking up Aunt Susie's role as the one who will record the oral on paper, putting the skills gained at the boarding schools to work for the continuation of the people in an act of literary synthesis. Aunt Susie teaches Silko not Carlisle's assimilative curriculum but ways to preserve the old stories, and each time Silko uses the word "precipitous" in *Storyteller*, she invokes and continues the Laguna storytelling lineage.[8] Because she uses her literacy in English as a tool for tribal cultural survival rather than as a marker of her achievement of civilization, Aunt Susie disproves the educators' zero-sum theory of identity (the more familiar one becomes with European American culture, the less "Indian" one is), according to which her knowledge of and appreciation for her tribal language would be eliminated by learning English. (This theory placed English literacy as the gateway between "barbarism" and "civilization.")

Grandma A'mooh was the other storyteller who deeply affected Silko, representing Laguna tradition to her great-granddaughter despite her time at Carlisle. The name that Silko calls her, A'mooh, signifies this association: "I thought her name really was A'mooh. . . . I had been hearing her say/ *'a'moo'ooh'*/ which is the Laguna expression of endearment/ for a young child/ spoken with great feeling and love" (*Storyteller*, 33–34). Silko identifies Grandma A'mooh, then, with nurturing children and speaking to them in the Keres language. Silko also remembers watching Grandma A'mooh care for herself and her family in traditional ways, passing on her knowledge to the young through example—an important traditional tribal form of education.[9] She washes her hair with yucca root and informs the young Silko that this will keep white hair from yellowing; she makes red chili "on the grinding stone/ the old way, even though it had gotten difficult for her"; most important, she tells stories about her youth and about tribal customs and history (34).

This is not to suggest that she remained untouched by her years at Carlisle. One telling sign of the lasting impact of her boarding-school education was her continuing literacy in English. Silko relates that in addition to telling Laguna stories, Grandma A'mooh read a book about Brownie the Bear to Silko and her sisters, and to Silko's father and uncles in their youth. Grandma A'mooh's manner of reading the book shows how she was able to adapt her Carlisle education to her Laguna culture. Silko recalls, "she always read the story with such animation and expression/ changing her tone of voice and inflection/ each time one of the bears spoke—/ the way a storyteller would have told it" (*Storyteller*, 93). Grandma

A'mooh traditionalizes the contemporary and turns a Victorian storybook into a Laguna custom, a feat that works against the boarding-school educators' assumptions about the unidirectionality of the assimilative process.

Clearly, her education did not stop Grandma A'mooh from becoming a respected tribal elder, who filled the role of caring for and teaching the young. One of the most important lessons she taught Silko was that storytelling keeps people alive. Though able to live through her difficult years away at school, Grandma A'mooh, who was sent to Albuquerque to live with her daughter during her last years, "did not last long without someone to talk to" (35). Grandma A'mooh and Aunt Susie both teach Silko the vital importance of storytelling to the community, the family, and the individual. Their time at Carlisle does not keep them from telling the stories that ensure the survival of Laguna culture. While the separation of children from their families made it more difficult for traditional education to take place, storytellers like Silko's mentors did not lose the stories, as the educators hoped. They did, however, use the representational tools acquired at Carlisle, such as English literacy, to adapt new methods of telling and recording the ancient stories, developing repertoires of representation. Furthermore, as Silko's text exhibits, they added a new type of story to their repertoires—the boarding-school story. The stories of relatives' experiences at boarding school become just as significant a part of who the Laguna people are as the ancient stories about Grandmother Spider or Yellow Woman.

Silko's relatives not only acquired verbal representational tools at school. They also used photography, a European American artistic form, to pass on Laguna history and culture. Marmon family photography originated in the boarding schools, Silko explains, since "My grandpa Hank first had a camera when he returned from [the Sherman] Indian School" (*Storyteller*, 1). At Carlisle and its imitators, Indians were the subjects of photographs, but never the photographers. Within the schools, photographs signified much differently than they do in Silko's text. Carolyn J. Marr notes, "While the technology [of photography] itself is neutral, the manner in which it is used is imbued with issues of power."[10] Richard Pratt used photographs as propaganda to illustrate the supposed absolute transformation of Indian students from "savages" to "civilized Americans" in a series of "before" and "after" images, making photography an important sign of the boarding-school experience, and more specifically of the power that the schools exercised over representations of their Indian students. In Silko's text, however, Indians are behind the cameras as well as in front of them. Photography becomes a way for Silko to trace the threads of the stories she is telling, rather than an indicator of the loss of Indian culture. Silko discusses the apparent incongruity of Indian photographers in an essay called "The Indian with a Camera." In this essay, she maintains that the Indian with the camera directly disrupts the assimilating project of the boarding schools: "When the United States government began to forcibly remove Pueblo children to distant boarding schools in the 1890s, the Pueblo people faced a great crisis. . . . How would the children hear and see, how would the children learn and remember what Pueblo people, what Native Americans for thousands of years had known and remembered together?" Photography, Silko explains, served as an aid in this process of remembering. "The identification of the faces and the places in the photographs never failed to precipitate wonderful stories about the old days, which in turn brought out even older stories that stretched far beyond the confines of the snapshots."[11] A Western representational form, photography as it is used in Silko's work encourages the storytelling that keeps the community alive—demonstrating the ability of Indian people to use Western form as part of their repertoires of representation to promote goals not sanctioned by European American society.

Her father's photographs, most of the images in *Storyteller*, concretely illustrate the continuance and flexibility of Pueblo culture. In *Indi'n Humor*, Kenneth Lincoln uses Marmon's work as an example of "integrative wit." Speaking of Marmon's best-known photograph, "White Man's Moccasins"—an image of Laguna elder Jeff Sousea sitting in the sun wearing a traditional head wrap and jewelry paired with Converse high-top tennis shoes—Lincoln states, "The dissociative splits between Indian and white, Indian and Indian, Indian and individual tragically have left too many dysfunctional, schizoid, and undeniably dead natives between 'two worlds.' . . . Note, by contrast, the '-emic' snap of . . . Lee Marmon these days finding an elder smoking a cigar and wearing 'white man's moccasins' (Converse tennis shoes) by the Laguna road."[12] This "-emic snap" is the humor that, for Lincoln, enables Indian survival in the contemporary world. Through the humor, and yet the perfect sense, of this image—of a man who is simultaneously Indian elder and American consumer—that encourages cleansing, integrative laughter, Marmon posits a version of Indian identity that is far more complicated than the linear path of assimilation and "progress" would allow for. Silko explains that this syncretic blending of cultural elements strengthens Indian culture:

> Pueblo cultures seek to include rather than exclude. The Pueblo impulse is to accept and incorporate what works. . . . The Indian with a camera is frightening for a number of reasons. Euro-Americans desperately need to believe that the indigenous people and cultures that were destroyed were somehow less than human; Indian photographers are proof to the contrary. The Indian with a camera is an omen of a time in the future that all Euro-Americans unconsciously dread: the time when the indigenous people of the Americas will retake their land. Euro-Americans distract themselves with whether a real, or traditional, or authentic Indian would, should, or could work with a camera. . . . Hopi, Aztec, Maya, Inca—these are the people who would not die, the people who do not change, because they are always changing. The Indian with a camera announces the twilight of Eurocentric America.[13]

Rather than an "after" picture that proves total assimilation, the Indian with the camera is a powerful image—and image maker—that provides, through the Indian's resiliency, a radical sign of Indian resistance that was born, ironically, in the boarding-school experience. Through her use of photographs and the implicit presence of the Indian with a camera in her text, Silko controls her own representation of herself, her people, and her stories. She uses a representational tool introduced to the Marmon family by the Indian boarding schools for a far different purpose than the schools had intended. Silko's transformation of the Indian with a camera from a sign of assimilation to a sign of revolution also indicates the manner in which contemporary Indian writers re-create Indian boarding-school students and their experiences to serve as inspiration for and sign of political activism.

The syncretism of the figure of the Indian with the camera reflects Silko's understanding of the resiliency and complexity of her own identity. She explains:

> My family are Marmons at Old Laguna on the Laguna Pueblo Reservation where I grew up. We are mixed blood—Laguna, Mexican, white—but the way we live is like Marmons, and if you are from

Laguna Pueblo, you will understand what I mean. All those languages, all those ways of living are combined, and we live somewhere on the fringes of all three. But I don't apologize for this any more—not to whites, not to fullbloods—our origin is unlike any other. My poetry, my storytelling rise out of this source.[14]

This "mixed blood" identity also denotes a mixed cultural identity, which is not easily characterized as either assimilated or bicultural, as she makes clear. The various identities she lists are sometimes central and sometimes peripheral to the self she represents in her writing. This diversity does not suggest weakness or isolation. While she may at one time have felt the need to apologize for her multiplicity, she now claims it with pride. Silko's family history mirrors the history of Laguna Pueblo, which welcomed Pueblo and non-Pueblo immigrants nearly from its inception, defining itself as a hybrid community even in some versions of its origin story.[15] The constant influx of different people contributed to the flexibility that Silko posits as one of the hallmarks of Laguna culture. Silko's creative self-fashioning, the situational identities that are available to her, are the source of her literary (and cultural) creativity. Without this history of hybridity, adaptivity, and continuance, Silko claims, she would not be a storyteller, a keeper of Laguna, Marmon, Indian culture. Silko's multiform self-definition is an example of a repertoire of identity, a collection of identity options that can be deployed situationally.

The figure of Yellow Woman, prominent within both traditional Laguna storytelling and Silko's text, embodies this flexible construction of identity. According to Ruoff, "Yellow Woman becomes a symbol of renewal through liaison with outside forces."[16] Through Yellow Woman stories, Laguna people explain the survival of their culture in the face of outside influence, both friendly and hostile. Silko's adaptation, "Yellow Woman," explores the ability of "mythic" figures from the stories to exist in contemporary reality. In Silko's story, the protagonist experiences many of the same situations that Yellow Woman has always encountered. She has heard the stories of Yellow Woman running off with a *ka'tsina*, or with Buffalo Man, leaving her community and her family only to return with something that will aid them. When she meets Silva, a strange man at the stream who lures her away from her community, he calls her Yellow Woman, and she insists, "'But I only said that you were him and that I was Yellow Woman—I'm not really her—I have my own name and I come from the pueblo on the other side of the mesa. . . . [T]he old stories about the ka'tsina spirit and Yellow Woman can't mean us" (*Storyteller*, 55). As the modern Pueblo woman lives her adventure with Silva, she attempts to deny her own participation in the continuing reality of the stories, claiming:

> "What they tell in stories was real only then, back in time immemorial, like they say." . . . I will see someone, eventually I will see someone, and then I will be certain that he is only a man—some man from nearby— and I will be sure that I am not Yellow Woman. Because she is from out of time past and I live now and I've been to school and there are highways and pickup trucks that Yellow Woman never saw. (56)

Silva responds, "'But someday they will talk about us, and they will say, 'Those two lived long ago when things like that happened'" (57). As she comes to understand, neither material artifacts like highways and pickup trucks nor the experiences of a Eurocentric education mean that the stories have become static and have ceased to be real. In fact, she eventually realizes that she is indeed Yellow Woman, and even though she is a contemporary Pueblo woman who has contact with European American "civilization," she still experiences and appreciates the reality and continuing vitality of the stories as well. In her house, however, "My mother was telling my grandmother how to fix the Jell-O" (62), a detail that seems to suggest the "evolution" that boarding-school proponents anticipated, in which the cultural wisdom of elders is disregarded in favor of participation in European American consumer culture. The protagonist worries, too, that her family might not understand or believe that she is Yellow Woman. She decides "to tell them that some Navajo had kidnaped [*sic*] me, but I was sorry that old Grandpa wasn't alive to hear my story because it was the Yellow Woman stories he liked to tell best" (62). Despite the narrator's wistfulness at the end of the story, this is not a tale of lost culture. Grandma might be learning how to make Jell-O, but the protagonist still remembers Grandpa's stories and teachings. She learned from her adventure with Silva that the stories are still as vibrant and as powerful as they were in "time immemorial." This knowledge is the help that she brings back to the community. And by aiding the Pueblo, she fulfills her role as Yellow Woman, which further empowers her and strengthens her tribal identity. The stories continue, they are real, they are powerful, and they shape Indian lives and identities—even the lives of those who have attended school. Silko's Yellow Woman is "white-educated," and yet she is a culture hero as well. Her experience of the ritual world of the Laguna, the world of the stories, does not deny the circumstances of her contemporary existence. Instead, she embraces the simultaneous coexistence of a repertoire of identities, proving once more the inability of the schools' replacement model of identity to describe the way boarding-school education affected Indian people.

Silko's repertoire, as demonstrated through her stories, not only includes "Laguna, Mexican, and white" identities but also, in the title piece of the collection, the story of a Yupik woman living in a small Alaskan settlement. The story recounts the woman's development into a storyteller who comes to recognize her role in the community and her place in the ongoing narratives that structure and create her reality. The protagonist is a former boarding-school student, who chose to attend school "because she was curious about the big school where the Government sent all the other girls and boys" (*Storyteller*, 19). Her curiosity abates when she is whipped for refusing to speak English and feels isolated from the student culture. She rejects European American education and uses instead her knowledge of the river's currents and freezing patterns to lure onto the ice the "Gussuck" (white) man who killed her parents by selling them bad liquor. He falls through the ice to his death. While witnesses describe this as an accident, the protagonist insists that "the story must be told. There must not be any lies" (26). She tells the story of her premeditated revenge, from prison, insisting that "it must be told, year after year, as the old man had done, without lapse or silence," choosing storytelling over personal freedom (32). Though she will remain incarcerated, she takes her place within her community as a storyteller, creating reality by telling the story that empowers her people—the story of their resistance and revenge rather than a story of accident and victimization. The presence of this story—with a protagonist who is so clearly not Silko and who participates in a tribal culture and tradition far removed from Laguna Pueblo—within a book that many label an autobiography, signifies the presence of a Pan-Indian identity in Silko's repertoire. This identity is built upon shared experiences and values that reach across tribal boundaries, coalescing, in part, around abuses and injustices faced by Indian people across the continent.

Silko's incorporation of many voices and stories into what Krupat calls "Native American autobiography in the dialogic mode" articulates the intricacy of contemporary Indian identity. Possessed of a repertoire of identity options that are woven into a web of creative expression, Silko forces the monologic voice of social evolutionary rhetoric into a dialogue. As Krupat says, "the effort [in *Storyteller*] is to make us hear the various languages that constitute Silko's world and so herself." This "strongly polyphonic text" avoids a "single, distinctive or authoritative voice."[17] In doing so it derails the narrative of assimilationism. By demonstrating the continued presence and strength of Indian and Laguna identities in what she clearly understands as a post-boarding-school world, Leslie Silko's storytelling substantiates that Indian boarding-school students like Grandma A'mooh, Aunt Susie, Grandpa Hank, the contemporary Yellow Woman, the Yupik woman, and many others did not undergo an absolute metamorphosis; they did not replace their tribal culture with what they learned at school. Likewise, Silko's use of photography and the English language to tell these stories does not signify assimilation into white culture. These representational forms, though Western in origin, serve her overall goal of describing and sustaining Laguna and Indian culture and vitality. Her achievement of this goal in *Storyteller* is the collective achievement of Indian authors who have struggled to voice in print their own impressions of the boarding schools, during the one hundred twenty-five years since the opening of the Carlisle Indian school. As Zitkala-Ša wrote in defiance of the educators who insisted that her writing be interpreted through the lens of their social evolutionary ideology, "no-one can dispute my own impressions and bitterness."[18] Like other Indian people from her generation and from today, Zitkala-Ša, though embittered, was empowered by verbalizing her own representation of her encounters with the schools. Boarding-school narratives have a significant place in the American Indian literary tradition, and in their complexity they need to be read and understood through the paradigm of the repertoire that Silko enacts in *Storyteller*.

SOCIAL EVOLUTIONISM AND CULTURAL REPLACEMENT IN THE REFORMERS' IDEOLOGY

It is important, before going on to examine additional literary representations of the boarding schools, to sketch out more completely the ideology that shaped Indian–white relations and that animated the Friends of the Indian at the turn of the century. Evident in the boarding-school rhetoric is the language of social evolutionism, a doctrine with roots stretching back to eighteenth-century Enlightenment thought, which asserted that human culture and civilization constantly progress as the human mind develops and becomes capable of more complicated thought.[19] As Europeans colonized non-white people across the globe and came into sustained contact with their different cultures, nineteenth-century evolutionary ethnologists adopted Edward B. Tylor's "comparative method" for examining the progress of civilization. Tylor needed to "find a 'means of measurement' against which he could 'reckon progression and retrogression in civilization.'"[20] Confident of his own superiority, he believed that certain groups or races froze in various stages in their progression toward civilization; ethnologists could, therefore, simply compare European people (clearly, in their own minds, at the height of civilization) to the other groups and societies with whom they came in contact. As Tylor wrote:

> Civilization actually existing among mankind in different grades, we are able to estimate and compare it by positive examples. The educated world of Europe and America practically settles a standard by placing its own nations at one end of the social series and savage tribes at the other, arranging the rest of mankind between these limits according as they correspond more closely to savage or to cultured life. . . . Thus, on the definite basis of compared facts, ethnographers are able to set up at least a rough scale of civilization. Few would dispute that the following races are arranged rightly in order of culture: Australian, Tahitian, Aztec, Chinese, Italian.[21]

These absolute—and starkly Eurocentric—standards formed the basis for the burgeoning field of anthropology. As the nineteenth century progressed, social evolutionary ideas were supported by and served as support for Darwin's theories of biological evolution. Eventually, social evolutionists constructed a network of beliefs and theories that confirmed their own racial, social, and cultural superiority. George Stocking explains:

> Darwinian evolution, evolutionary ethnology, and polygenist race thus interacted to support a ratiocultural hierarchy in terms of which civilized men, the highest products of social evolution, were large-brained white men, and only large-brained white men, the highest products of organic evolution, were fully civilized. The assumption of white superiority was certainly not original with Victorian evolutionists;

yet the interrelation of the theories of cultural and organic evolution, with their implicit hierarchy of race, gave it a new rationale.[22]

These theories gained currency on both sides of the Atlantic. Lewis Henry Morgan, one of the "founding fathers of American anthropology," codified the stages of social evolution in his most widely read book, *Ancient Society*, breaking down the three major divisions of savagery, barbarism, and civilization into seven stages: Lower, Middle, and Upper Savagery; Lower, Middle, and Upper Barbarism; and Civilization. Morgan listed the characteristics, achievements, and limitations of each division and provided examples of ancient and contemporary races and tribes that fit each stage. He clearly felt that American Indian tribes should be placed in various stages of savagery and barbarism, with the Pueblos coming closest to civilization, their adobe buildings and irrigation systems moving them into the "Middle Status of Barbarism." No North or South American indigenous people attained even the highest stage of barbarism, which was marked by the manufacture of iron.[23] Morgan identifies the commencement of civilization with literacy: "The use of writing, or its equivalent in hieroglyphics upon stone, affords a fair test of the commencement of civilization. Without literary records neither history nor civilization can be properly said to exist."[24] Other achievements of civilization—signs of a highly evolved consciousness—include Christianity, industrial advancement, and a state founded on "the concepts of territory and the ownership of property."[25]

Such social evolutionary ideas dominated both scientific and popular American thought in the late nineteenth century. Adams reports, "It is not clear how many [of the Friends of the Indian] actually read Morgan's *Ancient Society*, but it is safe to say that the widespread publicity surrounding the book helped fortify the intellectual framework within which philanthropists operated."[26] The framework must have been particularly attractive to this homogeneous group of white Protestant reformers, since, according to Stocking, the "practical impact of evolutionism . . . was to confirm Western man in a belief that every aspect of his own civilization provided a standard against which all primitive cultures could be judged and found inferior."[27] Robert Bieder explains: "Ethnologists did not delude themselves into thinking that Indians as 'savage Indians' could retain a position in American society. The answer always seemed clear: 'civilization' or death."[28] This confirmation of their own superiority, wedded with a Christian Protestant imperative to convert and uplift the "lower races," formed the basis of the ideology of the Friends of the Indian and suggested their course of action.[29] As Tylor noted, "'That any known savage tribe would not be improved by judicious civilization, is a proposition which no moralist would dare to make. . . . [Therefore,] the science of culture is essentially a reformer's science.'"[30] Religious doctrine, combined with self-interest and supported by social scientific theories, mandated that the Friends of the Indian work to civilize and assimilate their savage or barbaric heathen brethren.

The civilizing program, in keeping with the Victorian reformers' high regard for education, relied on schooling. Through the first years of the twentieth century, social evolutionists believed that the progress of the "lower races" had been impeded at a point that made them "childlike," but they did possess the potential for advancement.[31] Though later iterations of social evolutionary thought would claim that Indian people were genetically marked as inferior, the reformers claimed that, if Indian children were placed in the midst of "civilization" before their progress was arrested by the limitations of savage or barbaric surroundings, their civilized environment would encourage further development.[32] As Pratt noted in a paper given at the Nineteenth Annual Conference of Charities and Correction in 1892:

> It is a great mistake to think the Indian is born an inevitable savage. He is born a blank, like all the rest of us. Left in the surroundings of savagery, he grows to possess a savage language, superstition and life. . . . Transfer the savage-born infant to the surroundings of civilization, and he will grow to possess a civilized language and habit. . . . The school at Carlisle is an attempt to do this.[33]

Ideologues like Pratt, who developed the curriculum at the boarding schools, embraced the language and ideology of social evolutionism, and their vision of their schools as civilizing institutions dictated the curricula, which they designed to provide the skills and "achievements" Morgan identifies with the attainment of civilization, especially industrial training, regard for private property, Christianization, and literacy in English. Industrial training (synonymous at the boarding schools with manual labor) formed an important part of the schools' curricula. Children spent only half of their day in the classroom or the chapel and worked in the fields or learned a trade during the other half. Each school sought to establish its self-sufficiency through the development of farms and the use of the children's labor to provide uniforms made by the sewing classes, furniture made by the carpentry classes, and even meals made by the cooking classes.[34] The role of manual labor in the "civilization" of the students is perhaps most clearly seen in Carlisle's "outing" program, in which students would live with and work for mostly rural white families for extended periods of time during school vacations or during the school year itself. Pratt saw the outing program as absolutely central to the civilizing agenda of the schools, since it simultaneously broke down tribal ties by isolating the students both from one another and from their homes and "immersed" them in civilized society.[35]

Related to the industrial training or manual labor aspect of the curriculum was the strict military discipline that held sway at most boarding schools. Military personnel established and ran many of the early boarding schools and instituted a military regimen that would persevere at Indian schools through the 1930s.[36] The students wore military-style uniforms, and their days were strictly regimented; they marched in formation from activity to activity and moved at the sound of a bugle or a bell. Coleman states that the educators believed this type of discipline and control "would develop 'civilized habits,' Western concepts of time, and a Christian respect for work." Though the schools were run by the federal government, Christianity was mandatory, and the only religious freedom the students had was the "freedom" to choose among Protestant denominations. "For most secular as well as missionary educators, 'civilization' was inconceivable if not grounded in Christian—especially Protestant—values," notes Coleman.[37]

Certainly the time spent outside of the classroom in industrial or religious instruction limited the academic achievements of the students. This was not, however, something that concerned most of the educators. Lomawaima states:

> The idea of an "appropriate" education for Indians fit educators' preconceived notions of racial minorities' "appropriate" place in American society, as manual laborers supporting America's agrarian economic sector. This educational philosophy emphasized the nuclear family as the basic economic unit and eschewed higher academic or professional training for Indians. . . . Industry meant instruction in the rudiments of civilized living, especially the hard labor necessary to serve the most civilized elite.[38]

A boarding-school education should, according to commissioner of Indian Affairs Thomas J. Morgan, "fit the Indians to earn an honest living in the various occupations which may be open to them," as well as teach them to value private property, nuclear families, individual income, and the "rights and privileges" of citizenship.[39] Such a curriculum not only reflected the ideas of social evolutionists like Lewis Henry Morgan but also worked to enforce policies that benefited whites, such as the General Allotment (Dawes) Act, which divided reservation land into individual parcels, supposedly to encourage advancement through the private ownership of farmland by individual families. Instead of advancing and enriching Indians, the Dawes Act and similar "civilizing policies" actively promoted Indian dispossession when the "surplus" tribal land that remained after allotment was sold off or leased to white settlers on extremely beneficial terms. By providing the type of education deemed necessary to farm an allotment successfully, boarding schools educated their students for material and cultural loss.[40]

While Commissioner Thomas Morgan stated in 1889 that a system of Indian education "should make ample provision for the higher education of the few who are endowed with special capacity or ambition, and are destined to leadership," collegiate or professional education was clearly beyond what the educators expected the boarding schools to provide— and beyond the level of education they intended most Indians to attain.[41] The generation of policy makers that followed Morgan would not even acknowledge the possibility of Indians "endowed with special capacity or ambition." They focused instead on what Hoxie calls "a curriculum of low expectations."[42] But if Indian students were not to achieve a college education in the Indian boarding schools (or even, in most, a complete grammar-school education), the reformers intended the students to leave the schools with a working knowledge of, and literacy in, the English language. Just as literacy was the "fair test" of civilization for Morgan, it served as a very real marker of assimilation in the boarding schools. J. D. C. Atkins, the commissioner of Indian Affairs from 1885 to 1888, pointed to the centrality of English-language training to the mission of the schools when he wrote, "the main purpose of educating [Indians] is to enable them to read, write and speak the English language and to transact business with English-speaking people."[43] Atkins, and other sources he references in his 1887 report to the Secretary of the Interior, firmly believed that knowledge of

English was necessary for Indian people to become assimilated as citizens of the United States. Atkins cites a report of the 1868 Peace Commission (made up of military leaders such as generals Sherman, Harney, Sanborn and Terry), which claims:

> by educating the children of these tribes in the English language these differences [between the tribes and the white settlers who lived near them] would have disappeared, and civilization would have followed at once. Nothing then would have been left but the antipathy of race, and that, too, is always softened in the beams of a higher civilization. . . . Through sameness of language is produced sameness of sentiment and thought.[44]

Furthermore, according to the Peace Commission, teaching all Indians how to speak English would weaken tribal ties and "blot out the boundary lines which divide them into distinct nations."[45] While the Peace Commission, in the 1868 report, could only offer suggestions for a future course of training, such suggestions were institutionalized in the Indian schools, which forbade students to speak in their tribal languages or to gain literacy in a "tribal vernacular" when that was possible. Atkins further cites "an Indian agent of long experience" among the Sioux, who writes:

> I desire to state that I am a strong advocate of instruction to Indians in the English language only, as being able to read and write in the vernacular of the tribe is but little use to them. Nothing can be gained by teaching Indians to read and write in the vernacular, as their literature is limited and much valuable time would be lost in attempting it. Furthermore, I have found the vernacular of the Sioux very misleading, while a full knowledge of the English enables the Indians to transact business as individuals and to think and act for themselves independently of each other.[46]

The English language itself apparently possessed qualities that individuated its speakers, removing them from tribal communalism and bringing them one step closer to individual civilization.

Learning to speak, read, and write English, then, would "immediately" civilize Indian students and change their very thought patterns. Since the reformers saw "civilization" as such a clear and moral improvement over traditional Indian lifeways, they came to expect that their students, once truly on the road to civilization, would appreciate the value of European culture as well. Amanda Cobb explains in her study of the Bloomfield Academy for Chickasaw Females that Indian schools developed several kinds of "literacy" curricula to meet their goal of assimilation: academic literacy (standard school classes covering "rudimentary" knowledge), social literacy (skills like art, dancing, and etiquette "considered necessary to be 'cultured,' 'refined,' and socially mobile"), religious literacy (the daily rituals of Christianity), and domestic literacy (including homemaking, farming, personal hygiene, and parenting).[47]

Cobb's categories are helpful in demonstrating the totalizing nature of the assimilative agenda of the schools. Proficiency in English, though, held a privileged place in the schools' curricula, functioning as a meta-literacy that would communicate and reproduce all of the schools' "civilizing" lessons. According to Noriega, "Education has been the mechanism by which colonization has sought to render itself permanent, creating the conditions by which the colonized could be made essentially *self*-colonizing, eternally subjected in psychic and intellectual terms and thus eternally self-subordinating in economic and political terms."[48] An essential step in colonization through education, then, is encouraging self-colonization by coercing the colonized to teach and impose the views of the colonizer on themselves and their peers, and language education was perceived to play a significant role in this process. The reformers expected that once fully indoctrinated into white culture, "successful" Indian boarding-school graduates would use their knowledge of English to promote the civilizing efforts of the school. This philosophy is reflected in a statement made by Mr. N. Konishi, a Japanese visitor to Carlisle in 1897. Though Konishi did not address the students themselves because he was "embarrassed" by his own unfamiliarity with spoken English, he was said to have provided a transcript of his thoughts to Pratt, who reprinted them in Carlisle's school newspaper, the *Indian Helper:*

> You graduates will write about yourselves rightly, but not boastfully and give good warning and advice to your next generation, thus improving your civilization more and more as all others in the world do. We will not care for our complexions, but we will try constantly to improve ourselves in civilization. I trust you all are thankful to your kind Superintendent and teachers for teaching, and also our statesmen for giving you such liberal instructions and supplying such fine buildings.[49]

This visitor, who was himself well versed in the language and ideology of social evolution (and who seemed to agree with its placement of Asians as "less civilized" than Europeans), firmly believed that, because graduates of the school were able to write in English, they would write in praise of the schools and would actively work to further the process of civilization and social evolution. Successful graduates of the schools would not be "half-civilized parasites," since the mission of the schools was to move their students the full length of the linear path from savagery to civilization.[50] No successful student, with proven competency in the civilizing curriculum of the schools, could resist total transformation. This model of evolutionary assimilation assumed a "cultural replacement" or "zero-sum" approach to identity formation: cultural evolution was progressive (the direction of the movement was always from savagery to civilization), and as one moved up the evolutionary scale one "would replace Indian ways with White ways." Indian ways and white ways of practicing religion, social organization, and literate expression would not and could not coexist, except among "transitional" or "marginal" groups that were doomed to a speedy extinction.[51] The "light and contact of civilization" would eradicate the darkness of savage ways.[52]

The centrality of language and the manner of its use by graduates of the schools points to the fact that student success was as much about representation as it was about mastery of a curriculum. Indian students, who were given the tools of representation, were expected to work to further the progress of the race—and were therefore expected to promote the actions and ideologies of the schools. Representations of the transformative and progressive (in the evolutionary sense) work of the schools became important to the reformers on two fronts: first, such representations of total transformation would (as Konishi suggests) enforce the ideology of the schools among their current students, showing them the inevitability of their own transformations; second, these representations would serve the purpose of proving the worth and the successes of the schools to the general public.

By 1900, when Jessie W. Cook, an educator at Carlisle and Sherman, published "The Representative Indian" in *The Outlook*, a New York–based magazine, a generation of Indian children had already passed through Carlisle and its fellow boarding schools.[53] Cook's article affirms the Board of Indian Commissioners' recommendation of the boarding schools as civilizing institutions. It identifies several Indians whom she thinks embody the ideal of the "progressive," educated Indian. Cook firmly believed in the necessity of Indian assimilation into white American culture and professed that "if [Indians are] placed in contact with other humans, equal development will follow."[54] Prominent among the "representative Indians" that Cook names are Zitkala-Ša/Gertrude Simmons Bonnin (Yankton Dakota), Francis La Flesche (Omaha), Charles Alexander Eastman (Santee Dakota), Carlos Montezuma (Yavapai), and Dennison Wheelock (Oneida).[55] According to Cook, these Indians, who will "pull their race up with them," in essence retained their racial identity as Indians but acquired a white cultural identity.[56] Although they came from different tribes, each of these individuals was educated in boarding schools (though most had additional higher education as well), and each was associated for at least part of his or her adult life with Pratt and/or the Carlisle Indian Industrial School. Together, they made up a white-educated, English-speaking Pan-Indian elite.[57] Reformers viewed them as the most successful and representative examples of what a boarding-school education could do for the Indian. As Cook makes clear, they were not numerically representative of the Indian population at the turn of the century, nor were they representative of the image of the Indian held in the minds of most white people at that time. As Cook suggests, and as Robert Berkhofer's study of images of Indians confirms, most white Americans at the turn of the century based their conception of Indians on western dime novels and Buffalo Bill's Wild West Show, imagining generic, feathered, "wild" Plains Indians as "representative."[58] In contrast, Cook's representative Indians are "a drop of water in the great ocean of the Republic. If [they desire] fame, [they] can get it far more quickly by starting a gentle insurrection and frightening a timid agent somewhere, who will call on the United States troops and make a great sensation."[59]

Despite, or perhaps because of their relative anonymity, the "representative Indians" are shining examples, for Cook, of the potential of assimilative educational institutions to kill off indigenous cultural attributes. As Cook insists, "There is *but one hope* for Indians as a whole, and that is to live with the people whose ways they *must* adopt. . . . Indians *must* by actual contact and actual competition attain to a higher form of civilization. The representative Indians are a proof of this."[60] Her language reflects the urgency with which educators worked to eradicate the dangerous, costly, "undigested, unassimilated part of the body politic."[61] Her essay is only one example of the "torrent" of writing of the Friends of the Indian, whom Prucha describes as "an articulate lot, who employed rhetoric as a weapon in their crusade."[62] Cook's rhetorical arsenal attempts to subsume her representative Indians and their creative work within the framework of social evolutionary thought, reading their identities by placing their self-representations on a linear scale that judged their "progress" toward "civilization."

The schools themselves also sought to manipulate representations of their current and former students. Most books on Indian boarding-school education, and especially those that deal with the history of Carlisle, contain before and after photographs of the students that were taken for the school.[63] These photographs, as Lonna Malmsheimer points out, "are iconic representations of the cultural transformation that was the central aim of the school."[64] The before photographs inevitably show the incoming students dressed in "tribal" clothing, with long hair, moccasins, and blankets, clearly representing the "wild Indians" who supposedly lacked culture, education, and even the rudiments of hygiene (see Figure 2). The after photographs, on the other hand, showed these same students with closely cut hair, often holding books or other accouterments of "civilization," and dressed in the school's military-style uniform (see Figure 3).[65]

As Malmsheimer's careful research indicates, however, this model of identity—and the representations Pratt and his cohorts used to support it—clearly does not show the whole picture. Malmsheimer reveals, for example, that "The 'before' versions [of the photographs] include little or no indication of prior acculturation."[66] Similarly, the "after" photographs reveal no lingering trace of "reservation dress." Only complete transformations are depicted in the photographs. Malmsheimer explains, "only those who arrived in 'reservation dress' were photographed," while those who arrived already wearing elements of "citizens' dress" were left out of the photographs; thus the evidence of assimilation that the photographs appear to provide was in fact distorted and rigged.[67] In order to display the transformative impact of the schools, Pratt had to falsify the photographic record. His model of total transformation or acculturation could not accommodate the complex constructions of identity that existed in Indian country and that Indian students created as a result of the boarding school experience.

Fig. 2. Tom Torlino (Navajo) as he appeared when he arrived at the Carlisle Indian School in 1882. Cumberland County Historical Society Archives.

STUDENT CULTURAL HYBRIDITY AND
THE DIALECTICS OF IDENTITY

A number of important recent studies of the Indian boarding schools expose as biased and inaccurate their official pronouncements that they utterly metamorphosed their students.[68] In addition to falsifying or selectively

Fig. 3. Tom Torlino in 1885, after three years at Carlisle. Cumberland County Historical Society Archives.

representing the photographic record and other evidence, the educators ignored or were unaware of much of the actual students' responses to their experiences. Lomawaima points out that, "Student experiences and feelings were not, as a rule, tributary to the stream of documents flowing between Chilocco [and the other boarding schools] and Washington, DC. Much of student life was unobserved by and unknown to school staff or administrators."[69] Scott Riney argues that "students did not necessarily see the school as a hostile institution with agendas wholly foreign to their own wants and needs," suggesting that "the model of action-response, with the school continually impinging on Indian lives and Indians responding, is not an accurate characterization."[70] Brenda Child states,

> In part [the history of boarding-school education] is the history of people who experienced forced assimilation, and who to varying degrees lost control over important aspects of their own lives. This was true for students in the schools, and it was also true for parents and other family members in the community who repeatedly clashed with school authorities and were forced to submit to the will of the bureaucracy governing Indian schools. At the same time, Native students and their families resisted and frequently triumphed over that bureaucracy, and they used government boarding schools for their own advantage."[71]

Child and Lomawaima summarize: "Students were resourceful and ingenious—they found ways and means, times and places, to speak their own languages, eat their own foods, and exercise religious practices. . . . Private moments knitted students together in shared joy, shared language, or shared mischief."[72] Both ignorance and ideology prompted the boarding-school educators to disregard or falsify the record of student response to the schools and to attempt to control how that record was interpreted by a wider audience, forcing student responses to be read as markers of assimilation instead of appreciating the complexities they revealed.

In fact, the boarding-school system was one aspect of several federal Indian policies that inadvertently encouraged an Indian ethnic resurgence. According to former student Ruthie Blalock Jones, the schools "were started to stamp out the Indian from the Indian, you know, make us all into white people, and you know, it didn't work. Actually . . . it was the exact opposite: It made us stronger as Indian people. It made us more aware of and more proud of who we were."[73] Joane Nagle explains:

> The apparent paradox of Indian ethnic resurgence in the face of assimilation can be resolved by challenging the assumptions underlying common-sense thinking about ethnicity and assimilation. I suggest that the post[-World War II] growth of the American Indian population did not occur *in spite* of increasing assimilation. Rather,

the rise of American Indian ethnic identification, Indian ethnic mobilization, and Indian cultural survival occurred *because* of assimilation processes. In other words, the very processes thought to reduce or destroy ethnic distinctiveness can, ironically, become the means by which ethnicity is generated and renewed.[74]

This irony is only visible and comprehensible when we discard the linear replacement model of ethnic identity, and view ethnic identity instead as "a dialectic between internal identification and external ascription. It is a socially negotiated and socially constructed status that varies as the audiences permitting particular ethnic options change."[75] Identity is situational, determined by choices people make—and by social constructs and attitudes that delimit those choices.[76] One's ethnicity is not static and singular, as proponents of Indian acculturation and assimilation believed at the turn of the century.

Rather than exemplifying a simple process of acculturation, boarding-school students were developing what Paul Kroskrity calls "the repertoire of identity," which "focuses on the interactional and communicated nature of social identity."[77] Arguing that one's ethnic identity is not a continuous, constant designation, Kroskrity's model examines the potential for moving among numerous identities. Although the identity options available to a particular person or group can be limited by power relations with other groups, the individual does actually have agency in selecting from among the repertoire of available options, switching among identities as is necessary or desirable.[78] Rather than emphasizing which single group an individual belongs to, or claiming that assuming a given identity necessarily means obliterating a prior identity choice, "the model naturally focuses attention on the *when*, *how* and *why* of switches within the repertoire of identity."[79]

Instead of indicating a sameness [read "whiteness"] of sentiment and thought, writing by boarding-school students or former students such as the representative Indians provides a rich source for examining the complicated identity constructions that the students produced, and for examining how they switched identifications based on their responses to particular situations. If the reformers had recognized the students' formation of repertoires of identity, they would have had to question the schools' ability to "solve the Indian problem" by eliminating Indian culture, language, traditions, and lifeways without physically killing Indian people. The schools did not "kill the Indian to save the man," as Pratt insisted they would, though they did deeply traumatize many students and gravely disrupt the practice of traditional tribal culture. But in order to make it appear that the schools did succeed in their mission of cultural genocide, Pratt and his cohorts needed to control representations of their students, by sanctioning or producing only representations of total transformation. A careful reading of the texts and representations produced by Indian people, however, reveals the formation of a complex, multivalent student culture and repertoires of identity that defy social evolutionary theory, and its accompanying "replacement model" of identity (trans)formation. Kroskrity's framework carves out a space within which we can acknowledge and study students' creative agency. This space is necessary if we are to read Indian writing about the boarding-school experience without reimposing binary-driven, racist, social evolutionary theory.

CHAPTER 2

THE MAN-ON-THE-BAND-STAND AND THE REPRESENTED INDIAN

Education theorist Paulo Freire, in his seminal work *Pedagogy of the Oppressed*, lists with almost uncanny accuracy the myth-enforcing agenda of the Indian boarding-school curriculum in his description of an oppressive educational curriculum:

> It is necessary for the oppressors to approach the people in order, via subjugation, to keep them passive. . . . It is accomplished by the oppressors' depositing myths indispensable to the preservation of the status quo: for example, . . . the myth that the dominant elites, "recognizing their duties," promote the advancement of the people; . . . the myth that rebellion is a sin against God; the myth of private property as fundamental to personal human development (so long as oppressors are the only true human beings); the myth of the industriousness of the oppressors and the laziness and dishonesty of the oppressed; as well as the myth of the natural inferiority of the latter and the superiority of the former; [and the myth of the model of itself which the bourgeoisie presents to the people as the possibility for their own ascent]. All these myths[,] . . . the internalization of which is essential to the subjugation of the oppressed, are presented to them by well-organized propaganda and slogans, via the mass "communications" media—as if such alienation constituted real communication![1]

Freire bases his text on his experiences with peasants in Latin America during the twentieth century, but his work provides important insights into the colonial power relationship present in most monological and oppressive pedagogical systems. The Indian boarding schools worked to incorporate an oppressive and culturally genocidal understanding of "civilization" into their programs of study, insisting that students internalize European American cultural norms—such as appreciation of private property, acceptance of a Christian God, adherence to military-style discipline, and acknowledgment of their tribal inferiority and of the need to "ascend" the scale of civilization in order to "progress." As Freire clearly states, though, this "progression" was itself a myth used to cover up, or justify, oppression. Indian boarding schools conformed closely to Freire's model of the "banking" concept of education, the pedagogical relationship between oppressor and oppressed in which students are viewed as depositories for the lessons deposited by the teacher. Freire explains, "The teacher issues communiqués and makes deposits which the students patiently receive, memorize, and repeat. . . . Knowledge is a gift bestowed by those who consider themselves knowledgeable upon those whom they consider to know nothing. Projecting an absolute ignorance onto others, a characteristic of the ideology of oppression, negates education and knowledge as processes of inquiry."[2] In the boarding schools, the role of the student was to be a passive receptor, or to use Pratt's words, to be a "blank" upon which would be imprinted the mark and values of a "civilized language and habit."[3]

(IM)PRINT(ING) CULTURE

Language, literacy, and writing were important to this process of education as imprinting. According to Freire:

A careful analysis of the teacher-student relationship at any level, inside or outside the school, reveals its fundamentally *narrative* character. This relationship involves a narrating Subject (the teacher) and patient, listening objects (the students). . . . [The teacher's] job is to "fill" the students with the contents of his [*sic*] narration—contents which are detached from reality, disconnected from the totality that engendered them and could give them significance."[4]

The Indian boarding-school teachers' narratives were purposely disconnected from any tribal system of meaning. In fact they actively denied all that engendered the students, such as tribal languages, religions, and cultural practices. Narratives of Indian students metamorphosing into white Americans were equally detached from the reality of the complex processes by which students were forming repertoires of identity. Nevertheless, by creating these narratives of assimilation the educators sought to fill the minds and bodies of their students with a curriculum based on the myths of social evolutionary thought, which the students would then repeat and reproduce. The educators maintained the belief that depositing these myths into their students would transfigure Indian people—remaking narrative as reality—and move them up the social evolutionary scale toward the "pinnacle" of civilization, that is, a value system more conveniently dealt with and managed by European America.

Freire links the dissemination of the mythos of oppression to a pedagogical moment that takes place outside the classroom—dissemination through the "mass 'communication' media." Such media, in the form of widely distributed boarding-school newspapers, became an important part of the pedagogical process at the off-reservation boarding schools. As Daniel Littlefield and James Parins assert, the government-subsidized Indian-school presses served the "essentially propagandistic purpose" of assisting the schools and the Indian agencies in "carrying out their missions." Boarding schools used newspapers as instruments of disciplinary power to control representations of Indians and Indian identity, and, in fact, to create their own representations—or narratives—of Indian students as subservient and receptive to the assimilative goals of the schools. Nowhere is this more evident than in the newspapers and other materials printed by the Carlisle Indian School Press, considered to be the most influential boarding school publications.[5]

Richard Pratt's administration attempted to regulate representations of Indian identity in Carlisle school newspapers by creating an "Indian voice," which ventriloquized the social evolutionism and assimilationism of Pratt and his cohorts. This voice was created in Carlisle's student newspaper, the *Indian Helper*, between 1885 and 1900, as if spoken by "the represented Indian"—the Indian identity most amenable to the school's goals. The represented Indian was constructed and narrated in the pages of the newspaper both by "paper Indians" (fictional Indian characters invented by the educators) and by appropriating the writing of Indian students (allowed into print under tight control so they would appear to vocalize the ideology of the educators). These represented Indians would serve to establish and reinforce hegemony over the students, who were expected to conform to a unified, assimilated, "American" identity without question or resistance. Indeed, the link between print culture and Carlisle's pedagogy of oppression is so strong that the printing metaphor displaces Freire's banking metaphor. At Carlisle, education was a process of imprinting, and those who controlled the printing process—who were also both literally and figuratively the educators—deeply believed in their power to edit and rewrite Indian identity through use of the newspapers as disciplinary tools and rhetorical weapons. "Hurrah for the printer! / Hurrah for his stick! / What fashions the world / Is its clickety click!"[6]

In 1880, not even a full year after the establishment of the Indian school at Carlisle, Richard Pratt introduced printing into the curriculum, publishing *School News,* a small newspaper intended mainly for the students at the school, as well as *Eadle Keatah Toh,* a higher-quality paper intended for larger circulation.[7] In 1885, the *Indian Helper* took the place of *School News* and was printed weekly until 1900, when it merged with the larger-circulation *Red Man* to form the *Red Man and Helper.*[8]

According to historian Everett Gilcreast, the printing program was of immediate importance to the curriculum and to the wider interests of the school: "The news issues served as another English lesson for the students and another incentive to school pride. And, more importantly, an issue went to every member of Congress, to all Indian agencies and military posts, and to most of the prominent American newspapers. It became a powerful weapon for Pratt to spread his ideas beyond Carlisle."[9] Gilcreast correctly identifies the dual mission of the newspapers, but the hierarchy he establishes between them is misleading. The internal and external missions of the Carlisle Press were equally important. The newspapers must act outwardly, as propaganda to move the Friends of the Indian to support the school financially and politically, and inwardly, to act as a potent agent of colonization, assimilation, and discipline of the student body. The *Indian Helper,* then, was a "school paper," in the sense that one of its primary audiences was the Carlisle student body, but its mission stretched far beyond that of most school papers, as did its weekly circulation. In 1893, this "school paper" was distributed to nine thousand individuals or households each week![10] The following poem, "The Song of the Printer," served as an epigraph to the May 19, 1899, *Indian Helper*

and illustrates the Carlisle administration's clear belief that the power of
the press worked to consolidate its institutional power:

> Pick and click,
> Goes the type in the stick,
> As the printer stands at his case;
> His eyes glance quick, and his fingers pick
> The type at a rapid pace;
> And one by one as the letters go
> Words are piled up steady and slow—
> Steady and slow
> but still they grow
> And words of fire they soon will glow
> Wonderful words, that without a sound
> Traverse the earth to its utmost bound;
> Words that shall make
> The tyrant quake
> And the fetters of the oppress'd shall break:
> Words that can crumble an army's might,
> Or treble its strength in a righteous fight.
> Yet the types they look but leaden and dumb,
> As he puts them in place with finger and thumb;
> But the printer smiles,
> And his work beguiles
> By chanting a song as the letters he piles,
> With pick and click
> Like the world's chronometer, tick! tick! tick!
>
> O' where is the man with such simple tools
> Can govern the world as I?
> With a printing press, an iron stick,
> And a little leaden die,
> With paper of white and ink of black
> I support the Right, and the Wrong attack.
> Say, where is he, or who may he be,
> That can rival the printer's power?
> To no monarchs that live the wall doth he give:
> Their sway lasts only an hour;
> While the printer still grows, and God only knows
> When his might shall cease to tower!

This children's poem confirms and celebrates the printer's power to re-create the world to conform to his or her image of righteousness—a power bounded only by the might of God. Furthermore, the poem ascribes the attributes of Western civilization—order, efficiency, growth, and expansion leading to world domination—to the process of printing. Marianna Burgess, Carlisle's superintendent of printing, who possessed particular responsibility for the content of the *Indian Helper*, probably authored the anonymously printed poem.[11] Burgess shared Pratt's conviction that the power of the press should be harnessed and used to propagate the Carlisle philosophy. She saw herself and the school as the defenders of the Right, as defined by the Friends of the Indian. It is important to note, from the outset, that definitions of "right" and "wrong" in the *Helper* were not subject to debate; nor were any cultural differences recognized or tolerated in such value-laden terms. The paper's editorial staff was content with—and even reveled in—its definition of white cultural superiority and native inferiority and insisted that assimilation was the right route for the Indian. Indeed, the newspaper defined itself as the defender of the Indian, who was oppressed by tribalism and traditions.[12] As "the world's chronometer," the timepiece that would keep track of the sequence of events marking the passage of time (an image certainly linked to the reformers' beliefs in the passage of evolutionary time, which marks the "progression" of humankind), the newspaper would help "liberate" Indian people. It would be the weapon that "crumbled" the chains of tribal culture. Simultaneously, the news-paper would "treble its [army's] strength in a righteous fight" by "civilizing" Indians through its pedagogical force, mustering them into the righteous, progressive army. By marking the passage of time, by tracking the evolu-tionary progression of the Indian students, the Carlisle Press would create and affirm the narrative content of the Indian school's myth-enforcing curriculum.

Because the Carlisle Press produced the *Indian Helper* for a primary audience that included current and former students, Pratt and his staff controlled the content of this newspaper very closely and consequently used the paper as a medium to control students. Each masthead of the *Indian Helper* proclaimed, "*The Indian Helper* is PRINTED by Indian boys, but EDITED by The-Man-on-the-Band-stand who is NOT an Indian" (emphasis in original) delineating the division of labor between "Indians" and "helpers" in this publication. The Indian boys could learn the trades of copy-setting and printing as part of the school's industrial training program, but editorial control over the contents of the newspaper would be out of Indian hands. This division of labor problematizes the explanation of journalistic power that Burgess provides in "The Song of the Printer." Power rests with typesetters only if the words they compose are their own. While printers could theoretically subvert the process of textual production by altering and manipulating the words of the editor or author, such a model of print power does not appear in Burgess's poem, and it is certainly not a model she intends to encourage.[13] Instead, the distinction the newspaper made between "Indians" and "helpers" reflects not only Freire's ideas about the role of the teacher as narrator—where the teacher (here also the editor) produces narratives of white domination that must be reproduced by the student "printer boys"—but also Michel Foucault's understanding in *Discipline and Punish* of the role of writing in the disciplinary web created by such institutions as schools and prisons. Burgess's elision of the distinction between typesetter and author implies that the typesetter has fully agreed to the validity of the story and has chosen to accept and to reproduce the narrative of social evolutionism and Indian transformation—a myth of their consent to their own subjection.

Michel Foucault's study of disciplinary institutions helps illuminate how the *Indian Helper* and its creator, the Man-on-the-Band-stand (a persona invented by Burgess to embody the disciplinary ideology of the school), served as a form of surveillance over student self-representations. The newspaper acted as a rhetorical panopticon, encouraging student self-colonization through writing. If we bring together Freire's concept of the narrativity of pedagogy with Foucault's understanding of surveillance as constitutive of the pedagogical relationship, we are allowed an understanding of how the boarding school press embodied and expanded disciplinary power, especially in the carefully controlled, monologic *Indian Helper*. The implications of the disciplinary power associated with the boarding-school publications can also be seen in Burgess's 1891 novel, *Stiya: A Carlisle Indian Girl at Home*. The Carlisle Press consolidated narrative and disciplinary power to teach students to adopt and replicate social evolutionary ideology and the practical policy goals associated with such thought, especially the eradication of tribal languages, religions, and gender roles, and the encouragement of allotment (in short, a program of cultural genocide). Selections from student writing printed in both the

Indian Helper and in the Hampton Institute's *Southern Workman* confirm the impact of these "represented Indians" on Indian self-representation by demonstrating how the writing of "good students" ought to display the marks of discipline and surveillance.

DISCIPLINE AND NARRATIVITY

In his history of the birth of the prison, *Discipline and Punish*, Michel Foucault discusses the composition and function of power: "We must cease once and for all to describe the effects of power in negative terms: it 'excludes,' it 'represses,' it 'censors,' it 'abstracts,' it 'masks,' it 'conceals.' In fact, power produces; it produces reality; it produces domains of objects and rituals of truth. The individual and the knowledge that may be gained of him belong to this production."[14] Foucault focuses specifically on disciplinary power, a form of power that "defined how one may have a hold over the other's bodies, not only so that they may do what one wishes but so that they may operate as one wishes, with the techniques, the speed and the efficiency that one determines" (138). His study details the way disciplinary power functions in a series of related disciplines. He states, in a footnote to his section on discipline, "I shall choose examples from military, medical, educational and industrial institutions. Other examples might have been taken from colonization, slavery and child rearing."[15] Since the Indian boarding school was a unique combination of school, prison, factory, and barracks, set within the context of colonialism and informed by the experiences of slavery, it represents a concentrated locus of disciplinary power and control.[16] The schools' use of disciplinary techniques was no accident. Significantly, Foucault aligns the rise of disciplinary power with the advent of evolutionary thought. Because disciplinary power relies on breaking down tasks or goals into a series of levels, so that progress can be carefully monitored,

> The disciplinary methods reveal a linear time whose moments are integrated, one upon another, and which is oriented towards a terminal, stable point; in short, an "evolutive time." . . . But it must be recalled that, at the same moment, the administrative and eco-nomic techniques of control reveal a social time of a serial, orientated, cumulative type: the discovery of an evolution in terms of "progress." The disciplinary techniques reveal individual series: the discovery

of an evolution in terms of "genesis." These two great "discoveries" of the eighteenth century—the progress of societies and the geneses of individuals—were perhaps correlative with the new techniques of power. . . . "Evolutive" historicity, as it was then constituted—and so profoundly that it is still self-evident for many today—is bound up with a mode of functioning of power. . . . With the new techniques of subjection, the "dynamics" of continuous evolutions tends to replace the "dynastics" of solemn events. (160–61)

The boarding schools relied on this "dynamics of continuous evolutions"—on disciplinary power—to structure and control the student population. By structuring the school experience as a graduated series of "lessons" and "exercises" in civilization (thus reflecting the ideological position of social evolutionism), the school officials could closely monitor each step the students took up the social evolutionary ladder. In fact, the educators collapsed the distinction between disciplinary and evolutive progress. As students moved up the disciplinary ladder, contained ever more completely within the schools' subjecting power, they simultaneously moved up the evolutionary scale. This explains, for example, the correlation the educators sought to make between physical change and internal mutation. The physical change, which suggested compliance to the disciplining of the students' bodies, "proved" the corresponding change in identity, the movement into "civilization."

Each small movement up the ladder needed to be monitored constantly in order for the system of power to work, so surveillance was an important part of the disciplinary process. Foucault claims, "A relation of surveillance, defined and regulated, is inscribed at the heart of the practice of teaching, not as an additional or adjacent part, but as a mechanism that is inherent to it and which increases its efficiency" (176). Just as narration was constitutive of the teacher-student relationship for Freire, surveillance is a necessary part of the pedagogical process for Foucault. Disciplinary power seeks to normalize, to fix, to individuate, and to rank according to an absolute (and absolutely ethnocentric) concept of progress, so educators sought to generate and maintain a field of disciplinary power over their students to assure that their pedagogical narrative was appropriately received and acted upon. In the *Indian Helper*, this is most clearly seen in the figure of the Man-on-the-Band-stand, who signified both the disciplinary gaze and the enforcing voice of Carlisle's student newspaper. Littlefield and Parins contend that the Man-on-the-Band-stand was almost certainly Richard Pratt himself.[17] The sensibility and beliefs of the Man-on-the-Band-stand may indeed reflect the ideology and charismatic force of Pratt, but the voice of this figure is the voice of the *Indian Helper*'s editor, Superintendent of Printing Marianna Burgess. Combining the beliefs of the school's founder with the voice of its press, the Man-on-the Band-stand embodies the power of discipline at Carlisle; he expresses the collective voice of the pedagogy of oppression practiced by the school. Explaining his title, the Man-on-the-Band-stand wrote, "The Band-stand commands the whole situation [at Carlisle]. From it he can see all the quarters, the printing office, the chapel, the grounds, everything and everybody, all the girls and boys on the walks, at the window, everywhere. Nothing escapes the Man-on-the-Band-stand."[18] The persona of the Man-on-the-Band-stand represents—and exerts—absolute institutional and charismatic control over every aspect of student life at Carlisle.

The Man-on-the-Band-stand emphasized the ability of the written word to serve as constant surveillance over the student body. Features such as a regular column by "Mr. See-All" reported on the day-to-day activities of the children, drawing both their successes and their failures to the attention of the entire school and interpreting their every action as evidence for or against their progress toward civilization. In one issue Mr. See-All observes, for example: "Who is that leaf-sweeper who takes three sweeps to the other boys' one? Why, if he goes through life in that fashion, obstacles will fly before him, and he will reach a place worthwhile."[19] Even such a tedious chore served as a measure and predictor of evolution. Surveillance helped the educators engage in what Foucault calls "infra-penality" or "micro-penality"—watching, evaluating, and punishing behavior that is not usually covered by laws, such as "the slightest departures from correct behavior" in the areas of speech, sexuality, time, and the body. Thus, "idle chatter," "inattention," "lateness," and "irregular gestures" became violations subject to censure and humiliation (178). All of these categories described by Foucault were important in the boarding schools' system of punishment. Added to them was a layer of punishment for indigenous cultural practices, including language, religion, clothing/grooming, and so on. This system of micro-penalities enforced adherence to the school's definition of the normative. Such surveillance works because of a "network of relations"— those at the top of the hierarchy watch those beneath them—but surveillance also works from bottom to top, and laterally. Because everyone constantly watches and monitors everyone else, surveillance generates a "permanent and continuous field" of disciplinary power (177).

Through the *Indian Helper*, Carlisle's bandstand served the same function as the watchtower of Bentham's panopticon, the model prison that Foucault describes as the ultimate tool of disciplinary power and surveillance, at once "visible and unverifiable" (203). The location of observation is highly visible to all inhabitants of the institution, but it is impossible to verify if the observer is present or not. This inability to verify surveillance means inmates must work on the assumption that they are always being watched. Located in a highly visible position on the central lawn of the campus, from which an observer could indeed see students at most of their daily activities, Carlisle's bandstand fits the physical parameters of the panopticon's observation tower. Further, the Man-on-the-Band-stand is not easily identified with a single individual; he is even occasionally described as some sort of "elf" or almost super-natural observer, so his visible physical presence on the bandstand cannot—and need not—be verified.

While the bandstand ably served as the visible manifestation of surveil-lance on campus, the Man-on-the-Band-stand's ambitions stretched far beyond the school's walls. Indeed, as the voice of this figure, simultaneously embodied and disembodied, the *Indian Helper* stood in for the disciplinary power of the Man-on-the-Band-stand and served in turn as a metaphor for the collective voice of authority of Carlisle's educators and administrators. The newspaper became the tangible presence and visible proof of constant monitoring and control. The mobility and reproducibility of this sign was an important part of the production and reproduction of disciplinary power at Carlisle. An article in the *Indian Helper*, for example, ominously predicts: "There may be a flag staff on the Band-stand some day, and the man may buy himself a spy glass. It is not safe to predict that one day his vision may not extend much farther. Already he sees into the homes of the boys and girls who go out upon the farms; and—but let us wait until that 'someday' comes."[20] This as-yet unnamed extension of vision suggests that, at some future point, the Man-on-the-Band-stand will be able to follow the students no matter where they are once they leave the school—either in eastern cities or farms, as Pratt hoped, or back on the reservation, a return that he both discouraged and feared.

The power of the Man-on-the-Band-stand was not based on rhetorical suggestion alone. Coleman reports that "*fear* was a major motivating factor in adaptive responses to the school."[21] Students were frequently punished for infractions of the code of conduct demanded by the school. Although, according to Adams, "Eastern reformers generally abhorred" the most violent corporal punishment, at Carlisle punishments ranged from being locked in the guardhouse for up to a week at a time to dietary restrictions, to occasional beatings.[22] Because students experienced corporal punishment, in addition to the psychological punishment of being publicly cited by "Mr. See-All," they learned to fear the power of the Man-on-the-Band-stand. As Foucault points out, though, punishment is only half of the "punishment/gratification dyad." The *Indian Helper* praised students for exhibiting "civilized" behaviors—in action and in writing—and entertained them with stories that demonstrated the value-system of the schools. The punishment and approval of the Man-on-the-Band-stand proved his ability to watch everything, and students believed in his surveillance. Thus, the Man-on-the-Band-stand and his tangible manifestation, the *Indian Helper*, assured that "the surveillance is permanent in its effects, even if it is discontinuous in its action; that the perfection of power should tend to render its actual exercise unnecessary; that the architectural apparatus should be a machine for creating and sustaining a power relation independent of the person who exercises it; in short, that the inmates should be caught up in a power situation of which they are themselves the bearers" (203). Again, according to Foucault, "He who is subjected to a field of visibility, and who knows it, assumes responsibility for the constraints of power; he makes them play spontaneously on himself; he inscribes in himself the power relation in which he simultaneously plays both roles; he becomes the principle [sic] of his own subjection" (203). The newspaper attempted to convince Indian boarding-school students that they were always watched and would always be watched, that they must always monitor their own evolution.

The need for self-monitoring points to an additional link in Carlisle's metaphorical chain of oppression, described in an *Indian Helper* article titled "Who Is that Man-on-the-Band-stand?" In this piece, the "school poet" responds to a subscriber's concern about the "slight superstitious tendency the Man-on-the-Band-stand's position keeps up in the minds of some of the Indians and some small children." Clearly believing the

Man-on-the-Band-stand is Richard Pratt, the subscriber asks, "How soon can he lay aside old superstition and prove himself the noble man he has long been?"[23] The poet, who signs the poem "E.G.," is most likely school employee E. Grinnell and responds with verse that implicates all students and subscribers in the maintenance of the Man-on-the-Band-stand's power:[24]

Who can this Man-on-the-band-stand be?
Is it Ghost or goblin or shrew?
With an ear that is always ready to hear,
And an eye that is ever on you?

You ask if it's Captain or even Miss B.
With special good spectacles on?
Not these; for you see that reports are still made,
Though these worthy people are gone.

And Ghosts! They don't watch boys and girls now-a-days;
Or live in the white people's land.
I'll tell you the secret you want to find out
About this strange man on the stand:

Just any one, truly, who happens to see
A thing that is worthy of note,
And gossips a little about helpful things,
Gets bits of the "news" that's afloat.

You see it's no secret, but yet, it were well
To have an eye out for the elf.
Have care what you tell, or else you may find,
The Man-on-the-stand is yourself.[25]

The devastating final couplet of the poem narrates the self-sustaining thrust of the school's pedagogy of oppression by linking the students themselves to the disciplinary control of the Man-on-the-Band-stand. By implicating the students in their own oppression, the poet claims to be demystifying or demythologizing the Man-on-the-Band-stand, when she is really contributing to the development and transmission of the school's mythology. The newspaper's claim that it is debunking the superstitions of tribal life as it replaces them with the truth and wisdom of civilization is here transparently false, as we see the educators actively dismantling the validity of tribal culture and replacing it with a "civilized" culture designed to imprison the students within the field of power generated by the Man-on-the-Band-stand. This field of power can easily be extrapolated beyond even the boundaries of the school's administration and seen as the voice of white Americans seeking to cloak their desire both to control Indian resources and to destroy tribal culture with the cover of social evolutionary ideas of progress, designed to protect their own standing as "civilized." Only a thoroughly colonized Indian could fully accept the idea that "the man on the stand is yourself." But this was the goal of the school and its publications—to create an entirely controlled and defined "Indian" identity, replacing students' self-images with replications of the Man-on-the-Band-stand. The *Indian Helper* made examples and representations of assimilation constantly visible, delineating the path a student must take to leave Indianness behind. Through performing the function of constant surveillance, it attempted to ensure that no current or former student strayed from that path.

An article by "representative Indian" Carlos Montezuma in an 1887 issue of the paper further emphasized this chain or field of surveillance in the school. Montezuma's article, "An Apache: To the Students of the Carlisle Indian School," told his life story, in which he detailed his climb from "the most warlike tribe in America" to "the midst of civilization in Chicago."[26] After briefly describing his educational successes, Montezuma concludes by encouraging the students to reach for similar levels of achievement in the civilized world.[27] "Take care!" he wrote, "You are being watched, and time will prove whether you are worthy of being protected and educated."[28] Montezuma's perspective is that Indian children must prove their worth through obedience and amenity toward "progress." He urges the students to appear worthy to their watchers (the Man-on-the-Band-stand confirms that all behavior will be evaluated). Under the cultural replacement theory of identity, this type of surveillance was necessary to chart the students' acquisition of "civilized" characteristics. Once they had attained a critical mass of such characteristics, and subsequently lost the "wildness" of their tribal homes, they, too, could be worthy, could be representative figures to emulate, just like Montezuma. And, like Montezuma (one of the representative Indians who aligned himself most closely with Pratt), the students would go on to monitor and evaluate the next generation of students, enforcing the power of the schools and encouraging obedience through their ability to represent their success.

PAPER INDIANS

It is significant that Montezuma's very language in his article closely mirrors the philosophy and even the style of the Man-on-the-Band-stand, highlighting the tight control exerted over voices allowed into the publication. The Man-on-the-Band-stand wrote nearly every article in the four-page, two-column paper. Those articles that were not written by him were so closely regulated and edited that they only add to the paper's intensely monologic quality. Montezuma was one of the few "representative Indians" who contributed to the *Indian Helper,* probably because the narrative content was so tightly restricted. Instead of opening up the paper to a potential dialogue with Indian people whose experiences may have matched the Man-on-the-Band-stand's expectations and desires to greater or lesser degrees, the Man-on-the-Band-stand sought total control over the newspaper's narrative by inventing Indian voices—"paper Indians" who would speak nothing but the school's mythological narrative and reinforce disciplinary power without question and without the dangers of dialogism.

One example is a serial story that dealt with the touchy issue of "returned students," called "Home Difficulties of a Young Indian Girl." The story appeared in September and October 1887. In the first installment, the reader meets Fanny, a girl who returns to the reservation after completing her education at Carlisle. Fanny is constructed as a sentimental heroine, a girl who has developed the refined sensibilities of "true womanhood" while a student at Carlisle, and these sensibilities are a sign of her evolution.[29] Pleased to see her family again after a five-year absence, Fanny immediately notices the filth and disorder of her family's house. The dirtiness of the log house and the people who live within it are described in great detail: "Meat-bones, old rags, pieces of Indian bread, scraps of greasy bacon and other filthy trash littered the ground floor, while the air in the house was full of tobacco-smoke and other vile odors." Disgusted by the dinner her mother prepares and unable to eat because "she had seen her mother cut the meat with a knife wiped but a moment before on her moccasin," Fanny, though always polite, runs out of the house to the banks of the river and, like a true sentimental heroine, is overcome by emotion: "She threw herself upon the ground, and with face buried in her handkerchief cried as though her heart would break."[30] This heroine's virtue is challenged not by a rakish suitor but by renewed contact with a tribal culture that is portrayed as both promiscuous and diseased. The greatest threat to a young Indian girl, it seems, came from the prospect of "ruining" herself by embracing tribal culture upon her return home.[31] Faced with this peril, the first installment in the three-part serial story ends with the scene of Fanny's despair.

By the second installment, Fanny has regained her courage and her determination and continues her quest to educate her family. While her mother is out gathering wood and traveling to the agency to draw rations, Fanny cleans the house from top to bottom—an activity that is again described in detail, including Fanny's ability to substitute available objects for the cleaning implements she is accustomed to using at Carlisle (a handy housekeeping manual for the returned student). Fanny is crushed when her mother ridicules her first attempts to clean the house and make "white man's bread" for the family. She continually wishes she could go back to Carlisle, but she resigns herself to remaining on the reservation: "I hate this place. I wish I could go back to Carlisle. No, I can't go back to Carlisle. I must stay here. No, I can't stay here. Yes, I will stay here. My poor mother doesn't know any better. I must excuse her."[32] Reassuring herself with her certainty of her mother's ignorance and inferiority and determined to bear with her mother's "queer Indian ways," Fanny determines that, even if she does fail to civilize her family, she will not regress to the point of wearing Indian clothing. With persistence, she finally wins over her father, who shows his approval by "washing and combing before sitting down to eat."[33] Soon the rest of the family follows the father's example, and the mother allows Fanny to keep house as she has been taught at school. Civilization has triumphed over savagery in this Indian home, and through her example, Fanny gains the respect and admiration of her entire community—and even of the white people who work at the agency, who had doubted the ability of schools like Carlisle to civilize the Indians effectively. Fanny is a paragon of virtue, the perfect representative of Carlisle on the reservation. She demonstrates through her every action that she is thoroughly civilized and cultured. Like the "representative Indians," she brings her race up with her.[34] The narrator moralizes; "The temptations are great and successes hard-earned, yet it is POSSIBLE for every

Carlisle Indian girl to do the same kind of good, practical, common-sense work among her people when she goes home."[35]

Fanny's story was surrounded by other articles that discussed similar issues in a less fictional framework.[36] A month before the first installment of the story, Marianna Burgess wrote a letter to the Man-on-the-Band-stand from the Pine Ridge Agency where she was apparently checking up on former students and recruiting new ones. Burgess's letter focuses on the same issues that arise in Fanny's story. Burgess emphasizes the filth of the reservation and comments on food preparation, noting that an old grandmother she encountered "was one of the dirtiest looking objects I ever saw."[37] The elderly woman was mashing chokecherries: "The stuff did not look fit for a dog to eat, but we were told, when it is dried the mush is very good tasted [sic]. Save me from ever eating anything that looked so dirty! The woman's toes were very near the pan of cherries, and every once in a while she would spit close by the heap of food she was preparing. Horrible! Horrible! But that was clean by the side of other things we have seen."[38] As in Fanny's story, the women of the reservation are portrayed as most backward and savage. The educator ridicules their practice of traditional culture and their desire to maintain their way of life. Burgess probably represents the grandmother as being so disgusting in retaliation for the Indian woman's refusal to let Burgess take her granddaughter to Carlisle. Burgess explains, she "got very angry with us for wanting her girl."[39] Burgess takes revenge by transforming her anger and disgust concerning the grandmother who held out against Carlisle's civilizing machine into a fictional tale in which an Indian girl displays the white teacher's own reactions and emotions. Fanny represents the civilized response to savagery— teaching her readers to respond to their parents and siblings not primarily as sons and daughters but as students who have learned to emulate their teachers, who have accepted white culture as their own. Indians who resist assimilation remain voiceless in this newspaper; only "represented Indians"— assimilated and voicing appropriately civilized rhetoric—are given words. They served, like Fanny, as mouthpieces for the reformers' language and ideology.

The same can be said for Zach and Tim, the central characters in another story, almost a Platonic dialogue, called "Two Carlisle Boys at Pine Ridge Talk Over the Sioux Bill." Since Zach and Tim went to Carlisle, "they each have a fair education and naturally fall to talking about things above the ordinary Indian."[40] Their Carlisle-edified conversation leads immediately to a discussion of the Sioux Bill, an act that would allow the sale of eleven million acres of reservation land (for fifty cents an acre) and break the Treaty of 1868 under the guise of allotting land for individual farms. Tim, whose former teacher at Carlisle has thoughtfully provided him with a copy of the bill, has decided to defy the tribal elders and sign it, "for we want the settlers to come and help improve the land."[41]

By the end of the vignette, Tim has persuaded Zach to do the same, convincing him of the wealth that will come with the civilization brought by the settlers and the railroad, and appealing to his desire for power in the tribe (simultaneously a desire for the power to dismantle the tribe). Zach resentfully believes that the old chiefs "would do anything almost, to prevent us young fellows from having a voice in public affairs."[42] Tim commiserates:

> And isn't it too bad. Poor Men! They see their power fast going. When we are educated and get our land in severalty, and once become citizens there will be no more use for chiefs and they are smart enough to see that. Poor Red Cloud, and Sitting Bull and Grass and others have seen their best days as Indians, and they do hate to give up their power, but really, Zach, are you going to be scared out of doing the proper thing?[43]

Reassured that signing the bill is the educated, "progressive" action to take, Zach asserts; "I have believed all along that it was all right, but I was afraid to say so. Now I am *sure* it is all right, and I am going to sign."[44]

Carlisle was deeply implicated outside the press room as well, in gaining the signatures needed for the passage of the Sioux Bill. In 1888, Pratt himself led a special commission (the Pratt Commission), appointed by the secretary of the interior to bring the bill to the Great Sioux Reservation, to gain the signatures of three-fourths of all adult Sioux males, required to ratify the proposal under the procedures established by the Treaty of 1868. According to Raymond Wilson, the Pratt Commission was unable to convince tribal members to sign the bill, which offered "incentives" that were "simply repetitions of older, unfulfilled treaty provisions."[45]

Pratt denounced the Sioux in a scathing report in Washington and attacked the problem of their reticence from a different angle at Carlisle.

Through his representations of "progressive" Sioux boys, "good students" who understood what he indignantly professed was "so clearly in their interest,"[46] Pratt attempted to do with the power of the press what he had failed to do with diplomacy, that is, win the support of an Indian people for a bill that would give away the land they had fought so hard to keep. The week following the publication of Zach and Tim's dialog, the *Helper* published an editorial presenting the same information and advancing the same opinion, this time in the Man-on-the-Band-stand's own voice.[47] Asking the question "Will the Indians Be Cheated If They Sign The Act?" the editorial enumerates the supposed benefits available to each head of family if the act becomes law: two "milch" cows, a pair of oxen, one plow, one wagon, one harrow, one hoe, one axe, one pitchfork, two years' worth of seed to plant five acres and even twenty dollars in cash! The article also celebrates that under the agreement, Sioux schooling will be funded for another twenty years, and the money from the sale of the land—which will not actually be under tribal control, it appears—will all be used (vaguely) "for the Indians." The Man-on-the-Band-stand concludes: "Where is the white man who would think he was cheated if all these things were given him besides a big farm?"[48] The editorial focuses on the "gifts" that individuals would receive, entirely ignoring the cost—in land, in sovereignty—to the tribe as a whole.

Eventually, the Crook Commission (ironically a very apt name, after its leader General George Crook) obtained signatures from "progressive" Indians, which were then fraudulently calculated to appear as if they met the terms of the 1868 treaty.[49] The Sioux Bill became law, due to the mix of "progressive education" and outright thievery that characterized turn-of-the-century Indian policy. The same issue of the *Indian Helper* that urges the Sioux "progressives" to sell their land for a pittance to make it available to voracious white settlers enforces the lesson—that good students support the government's Indian policy, no matter what the cost to the tribes—on both the macro (policy) and micro (school) level. A small news item on the page following the Sioux Bill editorial preaches (without the smallest hint of irony): "Boys, boys, on the girls' play-ground again? Have you not enough territory of your own, without trespassing on the rights of others? Do you want the whole earth?"[50] The close connection between education and land policy—both designed to enrich whites—is clearly visible. By teaching students to value private ownership of land, to stay within "their own territory" as defined by their white disciplinarians, and to view the individually owned family farm as a sign of superior achievement and evolutionary advancement, the school prepared the way for the implementation of laws like the Dawes Act, which claimed altruism while dealing dispossession.

As these examples show, in the *Indian Helper* the educators at Carlisle invented an "Indian" voice that they used in the same way they used the Man-on-the-Band-stand, both personas assumed to disseminate the school's social evolutionary mythology and assimilative ideology. The "dialogue" between Zach and Tim is really just another monologue, designed—as was "Home Difficulties of a Young Indian Girl"—to enforce the editorial, political, educational, and disciplinary control of the Friends of the Indian. The Man-on-the-Band-stand does not allow Indian voices to make the *Indian Helper's* discourse dialogic. Instead, he controls all representations of Indians and educators, of savagery and civilization; and the paper Indians he creates in this journal are the most representative of "representative Indians," speaking only at his whim and desire and working to extend the disciplinary net of the boarding schools across the reservations, in the hope of ultimately controlling Indian response to both cultural and policy issues. The boarding-school system, as founded at Carlisle, used constructed narratives of Indian submission to the school's ideology in order to ensure the continuation of colonial domination and oppression.

STEALING AND SCRIPTING INDIAN IDENTITY

In 1891, Marianna Burgess took the "paper Indian" formula to even greater depths of deceit and misrepresentation, trying to blur further the line between paper Indians and actual Indian people, asserting that they were (or should be) one and the same. Under the pen name of Embe (a native-sounding name she created by phonetically spelling out her initials M.B.), Burgess appropriated the identities of actual Carlisle students—the face of Lucy Tsisnah and the name of Stiya Kowacura, whom she remade as the protagonist and narrative voice of the novel *Stiya: A Carlisle Indian Girl at Home*. This novel—meant to be carried back to the reservation by returned students, and to be read and circulated locally and nationally as a "thrilling" or "pathetic . . . but not overdrawn" representation of the interior and exterior signs of evolution and "right action" of "good" Carlisle students—demonstrates how far the Man-on-the-Band-stand was willing to go to keep Carlisle students—and representations of and by Carlisle students—within his tight control.[51] Robbing the image, voice, and identity of Indian girls, Burgess sought to extend the boarding schools' disciplinary power to the reservations, to enact a pedagogy of oppression that would reproduce the Carlisle curriculum through an "Indian girl's own story." She literally rewrote and re-presented the history and identity of these students, treating the girls as nothing more than bits of type to be rearranged and composed according to the Man-on-the-Band-stand's goals and conceptualizations of Indian identity. She thus utterly denied the possibility of Indian self-representation.

Stiya first appeared in the pages of the *Indian Helper* as a serial story, titled "How an Indian Girl Might Tell Her Own Story If She Had the Chance," that began in the September 20, 1889, issue and continued weekly until its conclusion on December 20, 1889. The story's byline explains that this was a tale "All Founded on Actual Observations of the Man-on-the-Band-stand's Chief Clerk."[52] Like "Home Difficulties," this story focuses on the actions of a female returned student who (in the newspaper version of the story) was called by the common—and therefore "representative"—name Mollie. The first installment begins with a short explanatory note: "The facts as given below are known by the Man-on-the-Band-stand to be true, and in substance, the experience is similar to that of many an Indian girl whom he knows about. In this instance, *if the girl could speak for herself* she might relate as follows."[53] With this introduction, the Man-on-the-Band-stand marks the story as nonfiction, in contrast to both "Home Difficulties" and "Two Carlisle Boys at Pine Ridge," neither of which claim the same degree of veracity.[54] Perhaps one foundation of this truth-claim rests on the revelation of the philosophy behind the use of paper Indians in the Carlisle Press: "truth," as it is defined by Carlisle, is spoken not by actual students but by ventriloquist educators who restrict the chance to speak. "How an Indian Girl Might Tell Her Own Story" is, then, to be given considerable weight, to be used as a type of Pilgrim's Progress for the returned student. (In fact, the final installment of the story begins with a direct allusion to Bunyan's work, claiming that the characters "had many other seemingly insurmountable difficulties to encounter in our progress up the hill of Right.")[55]

The irony of a Pilgrim's Progress for Indians is certainly not lost on Burgess, who consistently used the newspaper to teach Carlisle students their place in a "providential" view of American history, which insisted that progressing as a pilgrim (with all the cultural weight that term carries) was the only way Indians could or should survive.[56] Indeed, this story itself reproduces the ideology of the boarding school with a fervor and a pedantry unmatched even by "Home Difficulties" and "Two Carlisle Boys." Part reductive ethnography and part morality play, "How an Indian Girl Might Tell Her Own Story," or *Stiya,* demonstrates a scenario that returned students might face. But rather than allowing students the opportunity to think through and analyze this scenario and the power issues at play, a technique that Freire claims is essential to a pedagogy of liberation, Burgess shuts down creative response by providing an interpretive monologue, framed as if it were the Indian girl herself thinking through the issues and telling the story in her own first-person narrative. Like Fannie, Mollie/Stiya faces several major challenges to her Carlisle education: the filth of the reservation, the backwardness of her parents, the tribalism of the Pueblo governor who attempts to force her to attend "wicked" tribal dances; and even her own secret longings to be more comfortable, and perhaps more practical, by taking off her tight Victorian dress and returning to the durable, though fashionless, Moqui (Hopi) dresses worn by the women on the reservation. Throughout the text, though, Mollie/Stiya remains staunchly a "good student," who uses the money she earned from outing work to buy furniture and eating utensils in order to create a more civilized domesticity in her adobe home. She subsumes her own desire for comfort in her conviction that she should never regress to wearing Indian dress. She stands firm against both her parents and the governor, even withstanding a public family whipping to avoid participating in "heathenish" kachina dances. Eventually, like Fannie, Mollie/Stiya is able to influence her father, who begins to work shoveling coal for the railroad so that the family can leave the pueblo and move to the town near the railroad station. "I would be glad to go anywhere to get out of this thousand-year-old place—this Pueblo where there are so many who want to go all the time in the old Indian way," Mollie/Stiya gushes in a flood of disgust.[57] Assuring us that "any and every" Carlisle girl can "endure as much and even more than I have and come out of the accursed home slavery," Mollie/Stiya ends her tale with a lengthy description of her possessions and accomplishments, which serve as evidence of her continued evolution and fill her visiting Carlisle teachers with pride.[58]

Reports in the *Indian Helper* indicate that "How an Indian Girl Might Tell Her Own Story" was quite popular in its serialized form. Several November issues of the newspaper proclaim, in the first news item, "Please remember, WE HAVE NO MORE BACK NUMBERS OF THE HELPER CONTAINING THE STORY."[59] The story was read by students and nonstudents alike, and readers from the paper's larger audience responded to it very favorably. One subscriber from South Bethlehem, Pennsylvania, wrote in to the *Red Man:* "The Helper is an interesting little paper. The story of 'How an Indian Girl Might Tell Her Own Story' was particularly interesting, and we were sorry when the end came."[60] Responding, undoubtedly, to reader encouragement, as well as to pressures resulting from Wounded Knee and elevated concern over returned students, Burgess published the story as the novel *Stiya* two years later. An advertisement in the *Indian Helper* describes her motivation for publishing the book: "One of our teachers a few years ago, visited the Pueblos in New Mexico. She climbed their curious ladders, sat down and talked with the returned Carlisle girls in their adobe homes. Her heart was pained by many experiences they gave, and when she returned to the school, out of the abundance of the heart she wrote a story combining in one character the village life of several of our girls."[61] Heavily advertised in all of Carlisle's publications, the novel was touted as an "interesting story . . . for those interested in the future of the educated Indian girl," which would provide both "valuable information" about the importance of education and "an inside view of Pueblo life and their peculiar costumes and dwellings."[62] The book was illustrated with photographs of pueblo scenes and of Carlisle, appealing to a non-Indian audience's interest in "primitivism" while providing, for students, nostalgic images of Carlisle. Copies of the book were sold through the Carlisle papers for fifty cents, with a 20 percent discount offered for orders of ten or more copies. Leslie Silko, whose Grandma A'mooh and Aunt Susie owned copies of the book, states as well that "all Carlisle Indian School graduates who returned to their home reservations received a copy of *Stiya* in an attempt to inoculate them against their 'uncivilized' families and communities."[63]

Burgess claimed to be writing "out of the abundance of the heart," but, Silko's perceptive comment explains, her focus on returned students reflected educator anxieties about how important it was for "Carlisle boys and girls" to stay on the path of "progress." Clearly, Burgess wrote to control both representations of returned students and the students themselves. At the time of the book's publication, in the year following the massacre at Wounded Knee, Carlisle was under fire by opponents who claimed that former Carlisle students "were among the leaders of the hostiles and were engaged in the ghost dance."[64] In addition to spreading an increasingly ridiculous conspiracy theory that blamed the Ghost Dance on an "un-American" popish plot perpetrated by Jesuit troublemakers, Pratt went on a crusade of his own to rescue the reputation of the Carlisle returned student. This reputation had to remain unblemished in order for the school to maintain its insistence on the total transformation of its students, a myth that was crucial to sustaining the reformers' ideological convictions and ensuring the school's continued receipt of government and popular support.[65] The decision to publish Burgess's story in book form was undoubtedly one of the many actions Pratt took to redeem the reputation of the returned students—actions such as the formation of returned students associations on the reservations, which were "social clubs" designed to remind students of the values and the ideology Carlisle had attempted to instill in them.[66]

In fact, Burgess's book came out in print around the same time that Hampton Institute issued an influential study of its returned students, compiled by Cora Folsom, Hampton educator and editor of the "Indian pages" of Hampton's newspaper, the *Southern Workman*. Folsom attempted to prove Hampton's success by ranking former students as "excellent, good, fair, poor, or bad." "Excellent" students were "possessed of unusual ability, or command a wider sphere than most." This group tended to consist of doctors, lawyers, teachers, missionaries, and other professionals. "Good" students were "industrious and temperate, are legally married (if married at all), and are exerting an influence decidedly for civilization of the better kind." "Fair" Indians included the physically or mentally ill, those with very little schooling, and those who were, for various reasons, not quite "good," but who were "worthy of it." The "poor" returnees were "not actively bad" but exerted more of a negative than a positive influence. Finally, the "bad" worked actively against the "progress of civilization." Folsom claimed that approximately 22 percent of Hampton's returned Indian students were excellent, 44 percent were good, 22 percent were fair, 9 percent were poor, and 2 percent were bad.[67]

Following this system, the commissioner of Indian Affairs reported a few years later that, although not every school had as sterling a record as Hampton, overall 23 percent of returned students were failures, while an impressive 74 percent successfully followed "civilized ways of living."[68] While this kind of classification was clearly simplistic and skewed in favor of the schools, the educators still smarted at the need to admit any "backsliding" at all. They frequently found themselves in the awkward position of "defend[ing] students' records while simultaneously acknowledging that relapse did occur."[69] By explaining such relapses in a Senate report with the educators' party line that "[t]he failure of the Indian students upon their return to reservations may be traced practically in every instance to defective moral or intellectual organization and to vicious environment," W. A. Jones, commissioner of Indian Affairs in 1898, framed the problem in a way that exonerated the schools from any responsibility for those students who went "back to the blanket."[70]

As Jones's 1898 statement shows, the returned student problem was not quickly solved. It was a lingering issue that demanded constant attention and damage control on the part of the educators, who insisted on ranking their students according to this biased and simplistic understanding of linear identity change and "progression," and who were embarrassed and angered at the number of students who did not fit comfortably into their "excellent" and "good" categories.[71] Burgess and Pratt would have hoped that the publication of *Stiya* would shore up the boarding schools' position in the extended debate over the ability of returned students to avoid backsliding and to maintain their level of civilization. Through its ethnographic details and its negative portrayal of tribal government, the novel would show critics just the sort of "vicious environments" the students faced on the reservations. As a portable, durable lesson-book featuring an unequivocally "good" student, which could be purchased by a wide audience and kept in the students' reservation homes, it could teach students how to respond "in a civilized manner" to that environment.

These goals could best be achieved by trading on the authenticity of a real Indian girl's identity. While the text of *Stiya* remained essentially the same as the serialized version of the story (the few changes in wording are negligible), Burgess's choices to change the heroine's name and to take the pen name of Embe profoundly change the context in which the story would

be read and understood, heightening levels of surveillance and appropriation, and amounting to misrepresentation and identity theft. The pseudonym
Embe implies that Burgess sought to represent herself as an Indian, writing
from personal experience. Embe poses as a fellow Indian, observing Stiya
and reporting on her actions through a consciousness that has been shaped
by a total acceptance of social evolutionary thought. In the author's preface,
for example, Embe reports that the real-life counterpart of the novel's
traditional tribal leader, described in the book as "the brutal governor,"
was arrested and thrown in jail. She editorializes: "This circumstance gives
those interested in Indian education the hope that a brighter day may now
be dawning, when the home conditions will be so changed that there will
be no more tribal tyranny, but all will be under the protection and enjoy the
privileges of our good Government." By embracing the imprisonment of
traditional leaders and the destruction of tribal sovereignty in favor of the
leadership of "our good Government," Embe is representing herself as an
Indian who has transferred her allegiance from the tribe to the United
States, entirely accepting the philosophy of the school and disavowing any
claim to tribal nationality. This stands in contrast to the newspaper version
of the story, where each installment notes that the tale is written by "the
Man-on-the-Band-stand's Chief Clerk."

Through her pseudonym, Burgess enacts the educators' ideal of Indians
monitoring and publishing the "progress" of other Indians, taking this
much further than Montezuma's vague claims that students are being
watched. Embe, as the "Indian author," judges each character according to
the standards of the school. This outer shell of assumed identity is com-
pounded by her decision to use the name of a real Carlisle student as the
name of her heroine, who seems to be telling her own story in the first
person, to be giving a truly Indian point of view, when in fact her voice
has been manufactured by the white author and educator. At the same
time, the connection between Carlisle and this story and its (re)production
is quite clear. The preface states: "The story of Stiya and her trials is woven
out of the experiences of girls at various times members of the Indian
Industrial School at Carlisle, Pa." Through this statement, the introduction
quietly disclaims the actual Stiya as narrator and asserts the composite
nature of her character, synthesized by an author who has watched them
all, an author intimately connected with Carlisle and yet still claiming to
be of native descent through the fiction of Embe. In other words, the book

Fig. 4. Stiya Kowacura, a Pueblo student at the Carlisle Indian School. Her name was used as the title of Carlisle teacher Marianna Burgess's novel. Cumberland County Historical Society Archives.

wants to have it both ways, to present an authentic Indian voice while still emphasizing Carlisle's control of that voice. The preface reasserts that, even as other returned students will watch and monitor their fellow returnees, Carlisle, too, always keeps watch. Thus, Burgess's double displacement of her own identity ends up consolidating and reinforcing her power, and the power of Carlisle, as the ultimate observer and disciplinary enforcer.

The Carlisle student whose name and voice Burgess stole was Stiya Kowacura, identified in Carlisle records as a member of Acoma Pueblo, and simply as "Pueblo" on a school photograph (see figure 4). She attended Carlisle in the years immediately preceding the publication of the novel, though by 1891 she had returned to the Southwest. She was mentioned in the *Indian Helper* several times during that period. Since she does not have a school file among the Carlisle papers at the National Archives, we know little of the facts of the real-life Stiya's time at school or her life after Carlisle.[72] And her own impressions of her time at Carlisle would probably not have been preserved as part of her school records. What little information is available comes from the pages of the *Indian Helper*, the source least likely to have allowed her to speak for herself. By gathering information from between the lines of the brief news items that mention her, we can learn that, unlike nearly all Carlisle students, Stiya apparently never received a school name. The reason for this is unknown, but it may well be that Stiya was able to keep her name because it appealed aesthetically to teachers such as Burgess, who controlled the renaming of their students.[73] The name Stiya was clearly associated with only one person, as her surname was never mentioned in newspaper articles, and her name was therefore imbued with the weight of authenticity.

There is nothing to indicate that Burgess's words reflect Stiya Kowacura's true feelings or experiences, but obviously Burgess did not feel troubled to provide an accurate representation of the girl's identity. For example, Burgess follows the Carlisle tradition of displaying identity through photographs, in another attempt to authenticate the characters she is inventing, and as the frontis piece of the book, she uses a photograph of a young woman, clearly "Indian," placidly leaning against an ornately carved and upholstered chaise, and dressed in proper "citizen's clothes." The photograph is labeled "Stiya, Carlisle Indian Girl" (see Figure 5). But this photograph is not an image of Stiya Kowacura, despite the caption. The photograph portrays Lucy Tsisnah, an Apache student.[74] Lucy's image was taken and was used to stand in for Burgess's acquiescent Carlisle apologist. Burgess uses both Lucy and Stiya as symbols, divesting them of the meaning the girls found in their own lives. To Burgess, they are simply figures to be manipulated, to be rewritten and marshaled as evidence of identity transformation. She turns them into "representative" images, their names used to lend authenticity to allegorical figures. Their real lives—from their names to their faces to their tribal identifications—are effaced as Burgess writes over their own stories with her narrative of assimilation and supplants their repertoires of identity with the monologic identity of "Carlisle Indian Girl."

Just as she felt free to appropriate and rename Lucy Tsisnah's image, Burgess obviously felt she could claim and own Stiya Kowacura's means of self-expression. It is fascinating to note that almost every time the Man-on-the-Band-stand mentions Stiya Kowacura, he makes reference to her voice. In an 1888 issue of the *Helper*, for instance, the Man-on-the-Band-stand reports that Stiya gave a recitation, but it was hard to hear her speak.[75] Though Stiya possesses a voice, she cannot seem to make the Man-on-the-Band-stand hear it. An 1889 issue states, "Mary Natwawa, Martha Napawat, Grace Red Eagle, Stiya, and Melissa Green had a lively discussion about

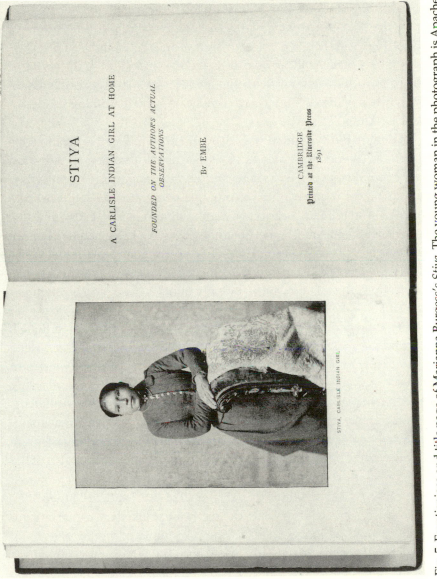

STIYA

A CARLISLE INDIAN GIRL AT HOME

FOUNDED ON THE AUTHOR'S ACTUAL OBSERVATIONS

By EMBE

CAMBRIDGE
Printed at the Riverside Press
1891

STIYA, CARLISLE INDIAN GIRL

Fig. 5. Frontispiece and title page of Marianna Burgess's *Stiya*. The young woman in the photograph is Apache student Lucy Tsisnah.

the Red White and Blue, and after a vigorous waving of flags sang a stanza or two of the song. Little girls must remember that we have a big hall now and little voices must ring out to fill it!"[76] Once again, Stiya's voice does not proclaim the propaganda of civilization loudly or convincingly enough to satisfy the Man-on-the-Band-stand. In her novel, Burgess fills in the real Stiya's quiet with her own voice, overpowering the thoughts and experiences of the student with her own ideas and scenarios. Carlisle, incapable of hearing Stiya, then stole her voice and made it proclaim the school's assimilative message through Burgess's complicated and disturbing process of characterization.

Yet Burgess did even more than steal Stiya's voice. She stole her thoughts as well, as she demonstrates through her use of first-person narration throughout the novel. Stiya's constant internal monologue begins when she gets off the train near her pueblo, five years after she left it to go to Carlisle.[77] Though her "heart gave a great thump of joy" every time she thought about returning home, her arrival does not bring her the pleasure she expected. She narrates not only her verbal comments but also her internal thoughts about her disappointment with her parents and her home. For example, she relates: "I also took my father's hand, and through my tears smiled as best I could; but he never shall know how I suffered with mortification and regret that he was such an Indian."[78] Though Stiya's father may never know how he failed to measure up to her school-generated standards, her readership has access to this very private assessment. In this way, *Stiya* stages the fulfillment of the most important of the boarding schools' fantasies about their impact on Indian life—that Indian students express complete adherence to the schools' mythology as an internal monologue, a monologue supposedly meant to be heard only by Stiya though exhibited in the pages of the book. Even the most intimate thoughts of the truly transformed student would reflect her transformation and progress. If educators could plant these thoughts in all of their students' heads, they would succeed in "civilizing" their charges to the point where Indian or tribal identity would no longer exist, having been replaced by the absolutely internalized supremacist culture of the schools. This is the power of Burgess's narrative strategies.

While significant lessons are imparted in "dialogues" Stiya enters into with her parents, the governor of the pueblo, and a friend from Carlisle (dialogues that are constructed along the lines of Tim's and Zach's exchange in "Two

Carlisle Boys at Pine Ridge"), much of the exegesis of such lessons takes place inside Stiya's head. Such thoughts, because internal, should be absolutely private and fall outside the sphere of the educators' surveillance. But Burgess's novel claims that even a student's unvoiced thoughts are accessible to the disciplinary power of the press and simultaneously implants an appropriately civilized internal monologue into the head of a character who bears the name of a Carlisle student.

The change in title between the serialized story and the book version speaks volumes—any uncertainty about knowing the inner workings of an Indian girl's mind is removed. This is not how she might tell her story if she could. This is, simply, Stiya—completely known, completely open to scrutiny, inside and out. Through this narrative structure, Burgess tells her readership exactly what to think as she suggests to them that their very thoughts can and will be read like a book to ensure that those thoughts are consistent with "going forward."

The first lesson Stiya teaches current and returned students is that they must remember the realignment of their loyalties that they were taught at school. Their parents should be respected to the extent that Christian doctrine requires. But, as Stiya immediately notices, her parents have not progressed and must be understood as inferior and backward, worthy of less esteem and admiration than the "school-parents" who deserve the students' undying loyalty and obedience. When she first sees her parents, Stiya comments:

> Was I as glad to see them as I thought I would be? I must confess that instead I was shocked and surprised at the sight that met my eyes. "*My* father? *My* mother?" cried I desperately within. "No, never!" I thought, and I actually turned my back upon them. . . . "My mother?" I cried, this time aloud. I could not help it, and at the same time I rushed frantically into the arms of my *school*-mother, who had taken me home, and I remembered then as I never did before how kind she had always been to us. I threw my arms around her neck and cried bitterly, and begged of her to let me get on the train again. (2–3)

When Stiya begs her school mother not to force her to go with "that woman," the school mother tenderly tells her to "make the best of these people" and to go to her mother. Stiya shakes hands with her mother, "for I knew nothing else than to obey my school mother" (4). The lesson this scene provides to returned students is clear: "Savage" parents should not have any substantive authority over their "civilized" children if the children are to resist backsliding, even if this seems to reject the teachings of the Bible. But school parents should always be quickly obeyed and trusted to provide guidance. As Stiya's friend and fellow returned student, Annie, comments "in distress," "'Our people don't know what is really good for us, do they?'" (54). Stiya hammers home the lesson by replying, "'It is best to obey our fathers and mothers, but, Annie, I think we know so much more than they do now that if we are kind to them we ought at the same time to do what we know is right, even if it is contrary to what they wish. Don't you think so?'" (55). This edifying conversation merely reinforces both Annie's and Stiya's internal convictions and undercuts any claim to authority that the "backwards" and "ignorant" parents might have to enforce tribal beliefs and customs on their children. These scenes also enact the white author's fantasies about her own superiority—both racial and maternal—and place the author-as-school-mother in the gratifying position of being chosen above the parents of a child who has been kept from home and family for a significant percentage of her short life. Aside from the ways in which Burgess is perhaps betraying the secret longings and fantasies of her own psyche, her novel's opening reflects the Friends of the Indians' fondest beliefs about themselves and their role in Indian life. Utterly paternalistic in their politics and creeds, they saw themselves as able, literally, to take the place of their students' parents and families, replacing family values and interests with their own personal and political goals and ambitions.

Stiya not only believes in the ideas of the Friends of the Indian but also supports the continued indoctrination of Indian students into their oppressive mythology. Faced with the possibility that knowing "civilized ways" might only serve to make reservation life untenable, Stiya tosses and turns in her bed, "thinking one minute that schools were a good thing for the Indians, and the next moment thinking they were not." (19). It is no surprise that she concludes:

Yes, they are of use, especially those far away from our homes. . . . I never in the world would have learned to be disgusted at this way of living, had I not been taken clear away from it, where I could not see it, nor learn anything about it for years. . . . We *must* learn to feel disgust for these things. If we have no disgust for them we will never try to make them better. We MUST be disgusted, I say, and I *am* thoroughly disgusted this moment at the way the Indians live, if *this* is the way they live. I know, however, that some live in great deal worse houses than this. (19–20)

The only positive aspect of Pueblo culture, to Stiya, is that it is somewhat less disgusting than the culture of other tribes. Stiya admits that Pueblo culture is filthy, primitive, and lewd, and the only cultural practice not described with disgust in the text is the manufacture of pottery, an achievement that ranked high on Lewis Henry Morgan's social evolutionary scale and that was viewed as a picturesque, and commercially and popularly palatable activity.[79] Such quaintness holds no lasting attraction for Stiya, though. The depth of her conviction that the boarding-school system should be maintained—complete with its policy of keeping children isolated from homes and families for years—is evident. Stiya is filled with exaltation at her own transformation and displays all of the signs of one who inscribes herself within the disciplinary system. Her thinking will keep her under the control of the school's pedagogy of oppression even while back on the reservation, and her reflections intimate that she will attempt to bring others under that control, which is just what Embe hopes her character will teach other native girls to do.

This line of thought explains Burgess's continued focus on the school's alumnae in her fictions. Burgess notes in a published journal entry in 1903 that "white tormentors" like to "hurl" questions at educators about Indian girls going back to the blanket, since educators and critics alike firmly believed that for the assimilative process to succeed, the culturally conservative women must be won over and kept with the program.[80] Commissioner of Indian Affairs Thomas J. Morgan explained in an 1890 *Indian Helper* that Indian girls need a boarding-school education even more than boys because, "They make the home and feed the children. Why are white children so happy? It is because the white women are educated. If we educate the Indian women to make happy homes, to train their children to industry and thrift, we redeem the Indian race through them."[81] Indian girls, therefore, must be taught how to reproduce the schools' ideology in conjunction with their own physical reproduction. In their role as mothers, they should act as extensions of the school, providing the same surveillance over their children that their teachers exercised over them, and replacing tribal tradition and familial affection with disciplinary control over their community's evolution.

One element of the boarding school mythology that *Stiya* reproduces with devotion is a nostalgic representation of Carlisle. The heroine frequently looks back upon and reevaluates her years at the school and finds herself "desperately homesick for Carlisle," realizing events that had previously seemed traumatic and negative had really been in her best interest all along. The best example of Stiya's nostalgia comes as she braves twenty lashes during the public whipping she and her family are forced to undergo because she refuses to participate in the Pueblo ceremonials. As she is beaten, Stiya comforts herself with memories of her precious time at school:

> In the midst of the fearful agony and excitement, thoughts of dear old Carlisle came to me,—my duties in the school-room, in the dining-hall, in the laundry, in the cooking-class, in the sewing-room, in the quarters,—the whole beautiful picture of sweet content on the faces of the boys and girls, as they went their daily rounds, loomed up before me and gave me courage. I even remembered how at times I had been a little tired, and thought the work and studies harder than they ought to be, and how then for a few moments I would wish for home and friends, for father and mother, and for the bright New Mexico sun. But I never dreamed that when I did come home I would experience such a trial as this. . . . "This is what a Carlisle school-girl must endure, is it, if she wishes to follow the RIGHT?" said I to myself. . . . "Strike me again; hit harder, you cruel man!" . . . I could have endured twice the pain. I was RIGHT. (86–97)

Along with her certitude that defying tribal leadership and shunning traditional religious ceremonies are the ways to advance, Stiya looks back on her time at Carlisle with a fondness she does not direct toward her childhood or her family. Although the historical record shows that fear played a major role in boarding-school life, Stiya remembers only pleasure. In this novel, fear, physical danger, and torment come at the hands of the tribe, and Stiya's sunny memories of her school days stand in stark contrast to all representations of tribal life found in the book. By providing this nostalgic view of Carlisle, she urges students to skew their memories of the institution, to remember comfort and contentment rather than labor, isolation, discipline, and punishment. She teaches that Carlisle is a paradise that all returned students should try to maintain and regain, in whatever ways they can.

The most important way that Stiya keeps her memory of "dear old Carlisle" alive is through her use of old issues of the *Indian Helper*. In the novel, as in real life, the newspapers served as the visible sign of the discipline and surveillance of the schools, as a stand-in for the Man-on-the-Band-stand himself, both on and off Carlisle's campus. Stiya first deploys her old newspapers practically as an agent of civilization by using them as a makeshift tablecloth for her newly purchased table. The meal she prepares for her parents moves her father, who says, "'This is nice. . . . We will never eat from the floor again, will we?'" (97). He decides that the family will move out of the pueblo because he "want[s] to live in a place where the people think more about school than foolish things" (98). Her father does not even have to read the newspapers to be swayed by them to abandon his place in the pueblo. Their mere presence exerts a civilizing influence upon him. Stiya does read her *Helper*s, though. After completing her nightly tasks, she takes her self-bound set of newspapers from her trunk and reflects, "At school, every week when done reading the little paper I put it in my trunk. 'I *thought* I would be glad to have you in my home,' said I, talking to them as though they were a person. 'And now I *am* glad.' I really believed I kissed the papers, I was so pleased to have them at that lonely hour of the night. I sat down by the fire, and for an hour lost myself reading over what we had done at Carlisle in years gone by" (108). Here, nostalgia shades into surveillance, as her memories of Carlisle activities serve to remind her of how she should act at home. The newspapers, which she treats as though they were a person, receive her affection and demand from her proper signs and professions of continued progression. Stiya welcomes them into her home as sentient beings and reminds Carlisle students that they, too, should be saving their newspapers for their return to the reservation, when they will need the newspapers' comfort, entertainment, and guidance. In this scene, the Man-on-the-Band-stand arrives on the reservation and is embraced by the returned student who "loses herself" in his presence and celebrates her place within the school's disciplinary web.

As if the Man-on-the-Band-stand's presence was not enough to convince Stiya and her readers that their actions were still being monitored and evaluated when they left Carlisle, Burgess ends her novel with unequivocal proof of the school's continued surveillance. Once Stiya has achieved her new home, full of furniture and inhabited by parents whom she has incited to progress, her diligence is rewarded with a visit from two of her Carlisle teachers. Stiya states with pride:

> My teachers praised the Carlisle pictures and others which adorned the wall, and spoke well of the appearance of our best room. . . . When they saw my cousin's little girls wearing nicely made dresses and aprons, and the little boys in good fitting suits, all made by me on my new sewing machine; when they ate the bread and cake and pie I baked, and the meat and eggs and potatoes and cabbage and other good things I prepared and set before them on a table, spread with a clean tablecloth (a real one), and had napkins, too, they seemed so delighted that I felt more than repaid for the hard times I had passed through. (114–15)

Stiya is tested—both by the trials she is forced to undergo at the hands of the "tribal tyranny" and by the scrutiny of her teachers—and she passes the test. Burgess's narrator tells her readers exactly what will please visiting teachers, as she also reminds them that their progress will be monitored; that even the reservation does not fall outside the gaze of the Man-on-the-Band-stand and his clerks. Since, as Foucault states, examinations are a "space of domination," fortifying hegemony, Stiya's story indicates that reservation life will be turned into a space of domination in which returned students will be kept within the confines of the school's pedagogy of oppression.[82] The conclusion of the novel strongly suggests that future punishment or praise await returned students, who can count on being continually examined and evaluated by their teachers. By serving simultaneously as conduct manual and instrument of surveillance, *Stiya* strongly reinforces the message of the Carlisle Press as it extends its reach across Indian Country. "Carlisle is stamped on [the] very faces [of its students]," a white trader tells Stiya, and through her narrative she shows her readers how Carlisle should imprint itself on their minds, hearts, and identities in addition to their bodies (45).

No record remains of Stiya Kowacura's response to Burgess's novelistic representation of her life and thoughts. But we do know how two Laguna Pueblo women— Maria Anaya Marmon and Susie Marmon—responded to the book, which they, as returned students, received shortly after its

publication. Marianna Burgess knew Maria and Susie—Leslie Silko's
Grandma A'mooh and Aunt Susie—personally. During a trip west in 1903,
Burgess stopped at Laguna and reported that she saw "Mrs. Robert Marmon
[Grandma A'mooh] and several of her children at their door waving hands
of welcome. She is the same gentle sweet Maria she ever carried herself when
a girl at Carlisle." Burgess's traveling companions, "curious to see an educated Indian lady with baby in arms[,] rushed in and soon filled the house to
overflowing." Impressed with the lace curtains and with one daughter's
performance at the piano, the travelers were "delighted with the people, with
their comfortable residence and handsome, refined, and educated children."
Burgess was particularly pleased with Walter Marmon, Aunt Susie's husband, who has a "fine team and farm wagon" and "a thousand head of cattle
and other stock." Grandma A'mooh and her family encountered—and
passed—the same test as Stiya, and Burgess represented "gentle, sweet,
Maria" as another Stiya both to her fellow-travelers and to the readers of the
Red Man and Helper, in which she published her travel journal.[83]

Grandma A'mooh was polite enough to greet her former teacher and
to welcome her into her home, but she was no Stiya. In fact, her reaction
to the book was certainly not what Burgess would have wished. Leslie
Silko recounts the story of Grandma A'mooh's and Aunt Susie's responses,
and since it is the only contemporary Native evaluation of *Stiya* that I have
found, I will quote her at length:

> Those who had graduated some years before were quite curious
> about the book. Aunt Susie would have been one of the first to finish
> reading *Stiya* because she loved to read. Grandma A'mooh began
> reading the book but, as she read, she became increasingly incensed
> at the libelous portrayal of Pueblo life and people. . . . About this
> time, Aunt Susie came over. Aunt Susie loved discussions and she
> was anxious to find out what Grandma thought about the book. But
> Grandma A'mooh was in no mood for discussion; she told Aunt
> Susie the only place for this book was in the fire, and she lifted the
> lid on her cookstove to drop in the book. Aunt Susie was a scholar
> and a storyteller; she believed the *Stiya* book was important evidence
> of the lies and the racism and bad faith of the U.S. government with
> the Pueblo people. Grandma A'mooh didn't care about preserving
> historical evidence of racist, anti-Indian propaganda; a book's lies

should be burned just as witchcraft paraphernalia is destroyed. Arguments and face-to-face confrontations between mother-in-law and daughter-in-law were avoided if possible, but that day they argued over a book. Aunt Susie could not persuade my great-grandmother that the book should be spared for future Pueblo historians. So finally Aunt Susie said, "Well, if you are going to burn the book, then give it to me." According to Pueblo etiquette, it would have been unthinkable for my great-grandmother to refuse her daughter-in-law's request for the book, especially since my great-grandmother was about to destroy it. So Grandma A'mooh gave Aunt Susie her copy of the *Stiya* book, and our side of the family didn't have a copy of the notorious book.[84]

As Silko tells the story, the lessons Grandma A'mooh and Aunt Susie learn from the book are not the lessons Burgess wished to teach. Instead of viewing Stiya's subservience as a model for their own continued evolution, these two returned students see the book as the equivalent of witchcraft and as proof of government mistreatment. It is significant that, throughout their confrontation over the book, they respond to it and to one another as participants in Laguna culture. Grandma A'mooh's initial decision to burn the book like witchcraft paraphernalia is motivated by her belief in and adherence to the norms of Laguna culture, and so is her eventual decision to give the book to her daughter-in-law. Aunt Susie's concern is to save the book for Pueblo historians of the future, as she is convinced of the vitality and continuance of tribal culture and sovereignty.

Their encounter itself, preserved in story form by Leslie Silko, has become part of their family and tribe's oral tradition, which testifies to the survival of Laguna identity as a response to a novel devoted to teaching them how to eradicate that identity. This is where the Foucauldian model of unresistable domination breaks down, since we can see in Aunt Susie's and Grandma A'mooh's responses that the space of the reservation seems not to be a space of domination. Instead, returned students have the freedom to bring together elements of white culture with values and practices from their tribal cultures.[85] *Stiya*, which claimed to speak as and for Pueblo women who had attended Carlisle, really speaks for Marianna Burgess, herself the voice of the Man-on-the-Band-stand, and describes the Pueblo life and student response that she wanted to see, rather than the complexity that was really there.

INSCRIBING THE REPRESENTED INDIAN

If attempts, like the publication of *Stiya*, to extend the school's surveillance to the reservation were not entirely successful, the power dynamics were very different for current students, who lacked the dialogizing space of the reservation and the safety and support of family and tribe. The lessons provided by Stiya and her paper counterparts were not lost on Carlisle students. *Stiya* showed them how good students were supposed to represent themselves in print, and current students knew that their written words were invariably scrutinized. With the exception of occasional writing by Montezuma, writing by Indian people in the *Indian Helper* is the student voice—closely controlled, and very aware of being watched and judged. Nowhere is this more evident than in the excerpts from students' lessons that were reprinted in the papers. While the Carlisle Press tended to reprint essays or speeches by more advanced students, the Indian Department of the Hampton Institute's newspaper, the *Southern Workman*, occasionally printed work by students in the early stages of their education, who were engaged in learning the most basic lessons the schools attempted to teach. One example from *Southern Workman*'s "Indian Department"—the department edited by Elaine Goodale, the white teacher who would later become the wife of representative Indian Charles Eastman—provides a sense of how classroom lessons and the lessons of the newspaper reinforced one another.

The article, called "Our World," claims that "nearly every card in the Second Division was marked 'Excellent' in Geography last month." Samples of this "excellent" work, reprinted in the section of the article called "Work and Fun in the Geography Class," show what students were taught about themselves and about their place among the other races on the social evolutionary continuum. One student wrote, in the examination: "They are five races, which are the white and yellow, and black and red and brown. The yellow race likes to eat rat, and the black race likes to eat man, and the white race likes to eat frog, and the red race likes to eat buffalo." Another explained: "The Caucasian is away ahead of all of the other races—he thought more than any other race, he thought that somebody must made the earth, and if the white people did not find that out, nobody would never know it—it is God who made the world." A third student proclaimed: "The white people they are civilized; they have everything, and go to school, too. They learn how to read and write so they can read newspaper. The yellow people they half civilized, some of them know to read and write, and some know how to take care of themself. The red people they big savages; they don't know anything."[86] These lessons in self-hatred highlight several important components of the boarding schools' mythology, such as imposed Christianity, the importance of literacy (including the primacy of newspapers), the social evolutionary stages of the races (based on a deeply entrenched belief in white supremacy), and the implied need for Indian people to eradicate their cultures in order to become as white as possible.

Excellent examinations—validating the "truth" of Black cannibalism and Indian savagery and stupidity—were reprinted as lessons to all students. Foucault, who analyzes the examination as the "ritual" or "ceremony" of discipline, points out that examinations expose the superimposition of power relations and knowledge relations within the disciplinary system. Through the examination process, educators have the ability to scrutinize students, forcing them to reproduce the "knowledge relations" deemed "truth" by the schools, then punishing them or rewarding them for their ability to write themselves into the disciplinary web. Since constant visibility and scrutiny maintain the subjection of the oppressed individual, the examination holds its subjects "in a mechanism of objectification," becoming a "space of domination" in which "disciplinary power manifests its potency."[87] These reprinted examinations, then, are a doubly oppressive ceremony in which students are objectified, observed, and evaluated through the exam itself and again in the printed article, which is distributed in order to aid in the objectification of the rest of the student body, implicitly asking them to evaluate themselves and each other in comparison to the reprinted excellent examination narratives. Examinations thus served as agents of normalization by asserting "correct" knowledge and thought patterns. At Hampton, as at Carlisle, this "knowledge" was political—and blatantly anti-Indian—and was used to promote social evolutionary thought among the students, teaching them that normality and the values of "civilization" are one and the same. By publicizing and reproducing these lessons, by rewarding students who provided the answers the educators required, the boarding-school newspapers reinforced the mythology presented in the classroom and taught students that "excellent" narratives should be given voice in print, while "poor" narratives would be silenced. Publication as a reward for progressive, "right" thinking served as the gratification portion of the punishment/gratification dyad of the school's disciplinary machinery.

Further evidence that the students knew what would get them punished and what would get them praised (and maybe even published), can be seen in printed excerpts from the letters students were required to write to their families each month. An 1888 issue of the *Indian Helper* contained excerpts from four such student letters. It is striking that none of these letters expresses homesickness or sadness at the students' distance from their families and friends. Instead, each excerpt has a tone of distinct superiority toward those back home, and at least two of the four directly parrot Pratt's views on literacy in English. The first student wrote:

> I was very much pleased to receive your letter. But you wrote in Indian language so I couldn't quite understand, because I never learn how to read in that way, never will. I laughed at some of the Carlisle boys those who went away from us here, after they got home, . . . forgetting what they learned at Carlisle school and trying to learn to read in Sioux language. . . . They will go backward. We Indian boys and girls here at the east learn nothing but the English language only. We hope we will go forward day after day. I hope your next letter will be written in English.[88]

Mirroring the reformers' dislike for literacy in a tribal language, the student uses the language of social evolution to establish his or her superiority for learning "nothing but the English language only."[89] As a good student (and, therefore, an ally of civilization like Fanny, Zach, Tim, and Stiya), the writer urges the family to write in English, to move forward, and to be comprehensible to the now-English-speaking student, who hopes never to be literate in the language of his or her birth. Another letter more bluntly states: "We know that you big Indian people can not write a letter as well as we can because you never went to school like we. But you could get someone to write for you and you can do the talking for yourself."[90] Ironically, it is the Indian student—so condescending toward the "big Indian people"—who can write in English, but who cannot speak for him or herself. The letters mirror the Man-on-the-Band-stand's views so closely that the voice we hear in these letters is his, the same voice that ventriloquized the speeches of the paper Indians. The English lesson such letters provided to the *Helper*'s student readers did not concern itself merely with grammar or epistolary conventions. In fact, their consistently non- or substandard usage was perhaps intended to serve as a continuing reminder of supposed Indian inferiority, even as they argued for English literacy. Instead, the letters provided a broader lesson on how to respond to the Carlisle education and how to use the English language to represent the school's ideology in print to those back home.

This lesson was certainly internalized by the students. It is useful to note that they were well aware school officials would read their letters, looking for markers of assimilation. Indian-school teacher Marguerite Bigler Stoltz explained that home "letters were corrected and re-written [in class] before they were sent out. That was how I got much campus news. Some were written only for my benefit."[91] Since students and parents did not see each other for years at a time "probably what [the student] wrote meant little to either one of them."[92] Some students wrote, then, to their disciplinarians, with an understanding that their letters needed to affirm their teachers—their *school* parents, whom they "knew nothing else but to obey" (*Stiya*, 4)—whether or not the letters communicated their thoughts to their biological parents. While some genuine student acceptance of part or all of the school's ideology cannot and should not be denied or disregarded, endorsements in print of Carlisle's version of progress are as likely to reveal students' understanding of their own situation of oppression and their ability to survive through manipulation of the system as they are to reveal colonized minds.

Historian Brenda Child's study of unpublished student and parent letters in *Boarding School Seasons* underscores this point, as she distinguishes between material that would be published in the newspapers and letters that students actually directed home, emphasizing the degree of control exercised by the newspapers over the ideology proclaimed in their content. Child explains: "Newspapers reflected the culture of boarding schools; even articles authored by American Indians were destined for a public audience and must therefore be approached with a measure of skepticism. Again, unpublished sources such as the boarding school letters introduce a less censored opportunity to study Indian motivations, thoughts, and experiences."[93] The boarding-school newspapers, carefully edited to project and to teach a certain kind of Indian identity, did not acknowledge the complexity and dialogism that Child's important findings suggest. What these documents do illustrate, though, is the degree to which the schools attempted to define what it meant to write "Indian," establishing the centrality of writing and narrative production to the struggle over Indian identity that took place in the schools.

The issue of English literacy, so central to the reformers' vision of Indian assimilation, was the frequent target of The Man-on-the-Band-stand's editorializing. A year after the commissioner of Indian affairs decreed that English must be used in Indian schools and forbade the use of Indian languages in education, Pratt sponsored a "debate" on the issue and offered to print the winning student paper in the November 18, 1887, issue of the *Indian Helper*. "The Prize Paper," as it was proudly introduced, was written by representative Indian Dennison Wheelock, then a student at Carlisle. Wheelock titled his paper, "Is It Right for the Government to Stop the Teaching of Indian Languages in Reservation Schools?" Predictably, Wheelock's answer to that question expounds Pratt's own views on the matter:

> I think the Indian language is one that few person who wish to live as human beings can use.[94] It is a language that is of no use in the world, and should not be kept any longer. You can't express a wise idea with the Indian language in a way that would be wise and you can't make a law with it, and you can never make a speech as well and as good, as you would with the English language. Why? because the Indians never made laws, never saw so many things to talk about as the white men see, and do not do much thinking for the future, and talk mostly by signs, and thus they have, only a few words in their language. . . .The Indian language . . . is also the cord that pulls down the race, who have been bound by the same cord to ignorance and barbarism for centuries.[95]

Wheelock's essay presents many of the racist notions about the supposed lawlessness, inarticulateness, and naïveté of Indians current at the turn of the century. It is almost unbelievable that anyone who had learned to speak an Indian language could claim that Indians "talk mostly by signs" and have "few words in their language." Wheelock demonstrates that, for the Friends of the Indian, the power of the press as described by Marianna Burgess in "Song of the Printer" obtained only to the "civilized" languages. Tribal languages themselves are "the fetters of the oppress'd" which "pulls down the race," but which the printed English words "shall break."[96] While Wheelock is demonstrating his ability to use English, to literally write the word "Indian," he shows no evidence here that he has learned to actually write "Indian," as his essay mimics the words of his teachers, giving the impression that his brain had indeed been wiped clean of tribal knowledge and reimprinted with the ideology of the educators—an impression that a study of his mature work, especially his musical compositions, does not bear out, I might add.[97] In this newspaper, however, such blind following of the creed of the educators was celebrated, and Wheelock, knowing what was required, provided it and was rewarded. Students learned to parrot the views of the teachers in order to be successful, in order to survive, even if those views denied the students' own experiences and caused them to appear to support the obliteration of their own cultural heritage. A note following Wheelock's essay indicates that not all of the students agreed with him. Yet no essays representing the opposing view were ever printed in the *Indian Helper*, although the note indicates that papers on both sides of the issue would be printed in the *Morning Star*, a Carlisle newspaper that was geared toward a broader audience. Even the "opposing view" found in the *Morning Star* did not amount to a validation of the legitimacy of tribal languages as valuable vehicles of expression and culture. Instead, Kish Hawkins, a Cheyenne student, argued that missionaries should use tribal languages to convert older Indian people on the reservation. The tribal languages should only be used as a point of entry in the missionaries' civilizing work, though, since

> What you need to do towards the civilization of the young Indians is that you must first go for the old Indians and destroy the Indian in them and let them have the reservations divided among them and have their freedom in every way—to be taught the word of God through their "heart language" by missionaries and others and to have the young Indians be taught the Indian at the same time with the English. . . . Christianity alone will destroy the Indian in the old Indians.[98]

Neither of these positions posits any sort of resistance to the social evolutionary goals of the schools. Neither offers an argument for tribal cultural survival. Hawkins wrote, in fact, "I would rather see you take all the Indians in the United States and take them to the ocean and drown them, than to let them be in the reservations for the next ten years, and be as Indians." This type of "opposition" can hardly be called dialogical, since each of the essayists represents simply a difference of opinion within the assimilationist camp—slight variations still well within the party line. Clearly, the only voices the Carlisle Press allowed into print were those that denied the efficacy of Indian language, which referred as much to attempts to articulate Indian views as to the tribal languages themselves.[99]

Student writing in the *Indian Helper*, then, was printed to reward students who displayed signs of "progression" and assimilation in their writing. These students used the paper Indians as literary models for their own use of the English language. As their work shows, they learned a painful rhetoric of anti-Indian racism and oppression even as they learned their English grammar and vocabulary. By tying these lessons together and by linking them to the school's disciplinary surveillance through the Man-on-the-Band-stand, the Carlisle Press devised a system that attempted to dominate students' actions, thoughts, and self-representations all at once. Student writing was used to supplement the photographic images of transformation that the school deployed as propaganda to prove to the government and to the students and their families and tribes that the Indian boarding schools eradicated tribal culture in the drive for assimilation. To control Indian self-representations was to control Indian identity, with the end goal of redefining Indianness in a manner that would destroy tribal sovereignty.

COMPLICATING THE MAN-ON-THE-BAND-STAND

While the disciplinary power of the Carlisle Press was an undeniably powerful and effective weapon in the struggle for control over Indian identity at the turn of the century, its monologue did not remain unchallenged; and the replacement model of identity change on which it based this monologue is inadequate to explain the complicated manner in which Indian boarding-school students learned to write "Indian"—to use the representational tools they gained at school to represent themselves as individuals, as tribal members, as Indians, as artists. Maria Anaya Marmon's and Susie Marmon's reaction to *Stiya* supplies evidence of complex student responses that reveal major fissures and gaps in the schools' supposedly monolithic disciplinary power.

A discussion of the Man-on-the-Band-stand would not be complete without a brief examination of the mature work of Dennison Wheelock, the Carlisle student turned faculty member who claimed for himself a place on the bandstand that both complicates and dialogizes that sign of oppression and control. Wheelock's musical compositions strongly suggest that Carlisle's disciplinary web was not as tightly woven as the Man-on-the-Band-stand had hoped, that there was room to subvert and to open up the Foucauldian structures of oppression to make room for resistance and play. Wheelock—whose essay "Is It Right for the Government to Stop the Teaching of Indian Languages in Reservation Schools?" might have been written by one of the Man-on-the-Band-stand's paper Indians—served as the director of Carlisle's marching band, beginning in 1892, after his graduation from the school, which he had attended for between five and seven years.[100] Although his early schoolboy essay suggests the total acquiescence to Carlisle's ideology displayed by the paper Indians, which would indicate that he had progressed up the social evolutionary ladder in a linear movement that left tribal or Indian identity completely behind, his mature work, and especially his musical compositions, provide an argument in favor of students' creative abilities to develop their own repertoires of identity, complicating the all-or-nothing linear view of assimilation and testifying to the ultimate inadequacy of the Carlisle Press's rhetorical panopticon to enforce this type of zero-sum identity change among its students.

Wheelock's marching band was intended to serve as yet another lesson in civilization for the students, replacing tribal musical repertoires with the regimented, often patriotic, music of turn-of-the-century brass bands. The military-style uniforms and precise marching formations would enforce the disciplinary techniques of drilling, in which all students participated. Furthermore, by performing as a type of pep band during school events and activities, the band would increase student enthusiasm for and identification with the institutions and philosophies of "dear old Carlisle." Perhaps most important, for the educators, the band was supposed to act as a visual and audible measure of the success of the school's assimilative purposes, proving audibly what the Carlisle Press worked to prove in print. In the words of one New York newspaper reporter who covered the group's national tour in 1900: "An interesting proof of the plane of development to which the American Indian is capable of being elevated is afforded by the Carlisle Indian Band. Little of the primitive influence of the monotonous beat of the tom-tom or the clash of the rattle, which are the main stays of the instrumental recitals that accompany Indian religious rites or merry-making, can be detected in the performance of the musicians."[101] Because such civilized music was clearly more advanced—as well as more melodious—than the tribal "monotonous beat," the forms and sounds of brass band music should replace the less-advanced "primitive" forms and repertoires among the progressive Indians.

Almost all Indian boarding schools had brass bands, most of which played music by white composers that had been chosen for the students' edification.[102] In addition to the works of Wagner and Strauss, Indian brass bands performed arrangements such as Voelker's "Warrior's Dream," or a piece called "The Lewis and Clark March," all composed by non-Indians that represented "Indian themes" from a non-Indian perspective—the musical equivalent of paper Indians.[103] Carlisle's Indian band, under Wheelock's direction, began to complicate this formula by including Wheelock's original compositions in its repertoire. Though the scores for his work are not currently available, the titles of his arrangements and press comments that describe them indicate that Wheelock used his musical compositions to express complicated fusions and repertoires of identity.[104] One of his works, a piece called "From Savagery to Civilization," which one critic described as "illustrative of the development of the race," appears to celebrate Indian "advancement" in exactly the terms used by social evolutionary thought, the language of the Man-on-the-Band-stand. However, another piece, known variously as "Festival and Dance of the Red Man" and "Aboriginal Suite," was described as "in some passages, very Indian in character, especially in the 'Dance.'"[105] The title of this composition indicates Wheelock's attempt to represent Indian identity as still present, even if deeply embedded in a non-Indian musical form. Wheelock dialogizes brass band music by injecting rhythms—and perhaps even forms—from tribal musical repertoires into one of Carlisle's signs of transformation, making it something other than either a sign of civilization or a sign of savagery.

Wheelock's artistry allowed him to create space for his own self-expression on the bandstand. Today, the actual bandstand still stands in the middle of the campus of the Carlisle Indian School, which is now used as the U.S. Army's War College, but it bears the name not of Pratt or of Burgess, or of some elfish Man-on-the-Band-stand, but of Dennison Wheelock (identified even on the historical marker as a member of the Oneida Nation), who, through his musical negotiations, displayed the complex constructions of identity that most Carlisle students developed, resisting the surveillance and discipline the school exerted in the classroom and in print as part of its pedagogy of oppression. Wheelock's place on the bandstand is certainly not unequivocally defiant. But he demonstrates that students were able to break through the web constructed by the Man-on-the-Band-stand's disciplinary power and were able to assert their own creativity to develop and maintain complex identities, which included tribal and Pan-Indian identities.

This assertion did not take place within the pages of the *Indian Helper*, the locus of the Man-on-the-Band-stand's power. The *Helper* and the publications like *Stiya* that sprang from its pages remained a weapon that produced tightly controlled representations of Indian students. While stories featuring paper Indians as well as some Indian student writing can be found on its pages, there is no Indian voice in the newspaper—only various versions of the Man-on-the-Band-stand's voice, enforcing his overwhelmingly monologic ideology of evolution and assimilation. These represented Indians taught Indian students what "educated Indians" were supposed to sound like and how they were supposed to act. As the title of the newspaper suggests, the publication was intended to help Indians by providing examples and representations of assimilated Indians, marking the road that led away from Indianness and toward civilization. There were no real identity choices along this path, according to the educators. A student who learned these lessons well, who was "successful," was expected to ventriloquize the views articulated in the paper and mimic these representations in his or her own writing.

The boarding schools' pedagogy of oppression focused on representation for a reason. The educators hoped to "fashion the world" through their words, to reshape America—and especially Indian Country—with the products of their presses. They counted on the mobility and reproducibility that print technology afforded them to spread their proassimilation message across the continent targeting land-claim issues like the Sioux Bill and working to undermine tribal governance and authority.

These relatively small newspapers have had a huge impact on how Indian people have been—and continue to be—represented. Though we may think that contestation over representations of Indian boarding-school students is a thing of the past, a recently published children's book from Scholastic—*My Heart Is On the Ground: The Diary of Nannie Little Rose, a Sioux Girl* (1999)— seeks to represent Indian children at Carlisle much the way Burgess did in *Stiya*. Ann Rinaldi, the non-Indian author, poses as a

Lakota girl who writes a diary of her experiences at school. Rinaldi's name does not appear on the book's cover, making it seem as if Nannie is the author. Like Burgess, Rinaldi stole the names of actual students (in her case from tombstones at the Carlisle Indian cemetery). In her author's note, she explains her process:

> [At Carlisle] I found the Indian burial ground, with dozens of white headstones bearing the names of the Native American children from all tribes who had died while at the school. The names, with the tribes inscribed underneath, were so lyrical that they leapt out at me and took on instant personalities. . . . [T]heir personalities came through to me with such force and inspiration, I had to use them. I am sure that in whatever Happy Hunting Ground they now reside, they will forgive this artistic license, and even smile upon it.[106]

Rinaldi stole situations from the autobiographies of former boarding-school students including Zitkala-Ša, Francis La Flesche, and Asa Daklugie as well, changing the presentation and context of those memories (most of which relate moments of resistance) to provide fake evidence of acquiescence in the values of the boarding schools through the narration of "good student" Nannie.[107] In her children's book, the legacy of the Carlisle Press remains.[108] Whether the voice she manufactures for her protagonist, Nannie, comes from her own anti-Indian politics or from research that relied too heavily upon the Man-on-the-Band-stand's representations of life at Carlisle is uncertain. What is clear is that conflict over the representation of the Indian boarding-school experience remains. The *Indian Helper* produced an image of "good students" so monolithic that it still must be fought today.

Despite Rinaldi's claims that the former Carlisle students would smile upon her rewriting of their experiences from their Happy Hunting Grounds, contemporary Indian people are angrily still contesting these representations today. According to Leslie Silko:

> It is because of books like *Stiya* that Native American communities concern themselves with the origins and authorship of so-called Indian novels and Indian poetry. Books have been the focus of the struggle for the control of the Americas from the start. The great libraries of the Americas were destroyed in 1540 because the Spaniards feared the political and spiritual power of books authored by the indigenous people. As Vine Deloria has pointed out, non-Indians are

still more comfortable with Indian books written by non-Indians than they are with books by Indian authors.[109]

If the Indian boarding schools had been successful, we would not have American Indian literature as we know it today. Writing by people of American Indian descent would portray only the disgust for the "backwardness" of "savage" tribal culture that Stiya was so grateful Carlisle had taught her. It would be a "literature" expressly designed to conform to white scrutiny, to make white people proud of Indian ability to overcome the "limitations" of their race, to prove themselves as white as possible. It would not—as Paula Gunn Allen writes in an essay that seeks to define American Indian literature—provide any sort of "Indian consciousness."[110] It would testify only to the absence of such consciousness, of the inability of native people to write "Indian." Such a literature of absence would long ago, no doubt, have ceased to exist at all. The culture-killing narratives contained in the *Indian Helper* and other products of the Carlisle Press demonstrate the poisonous lengths to which the boarding schools would go in order to control Indian self-representation and, through this control, to consolidate power to define Indian tribes out of existence. As Critical Race Theorists and particularly Lumbee legal scholar Robert Williams emphasize, the colonization of the Americas by Europeans is part of a continuing narrative tradition, and "this still-vital narrative tradition of tribalism's incompatibility with the supposed superior values of the dominant society is . . . reflected throughout modern federal Indian law and discursive practice."[111] Williams does not connect this narrative tradition solely to Indian boarding schools, but their discursive practices clearly fall in line with the narrative tradition he describes. As Williams's work demonstrates, the stakes in controlling narratives of Indianness have always been very high and are linked to both historical and contemporary legal struggles and claims for sovereignty. Despite an overwhelming imbalance of power, Indian people did not and have not given up the representational struggle for articulations of tribal sovereignty and individual freedom. Dismantling the narratives of oppression created by the boarding-school press, learning to write "Indian" to counter the destructive words of the schools' paper Indians, has been—and continues to be—an important focus of American Indian literature.

CHAPTER 3

Francis La Flesche and Zitkala-Ša Write the Middle Ground and the Educators Respond

B y the turn of the century, increasing numbers of Indians who were taught literacy in English at boarding schools began to make careers for themselves as writers and scholars, a fact that undoubtedly pleased boarding-school educators even as it gave rise to anxiety over the way these writers might represent the school experience and both tribal and Indian identity as they moved beyond the control of the educational institutions. Two of the most prominent of this group of Indian writers were Francis La Flesche and Zitkala-Ša, whose achievements were compiled by Jessie Cook when she named them among the "representative Indians." Of La Flesche, she wrote:

> There is Mr. Francis La Flesche, an Omaha, for years a resident of Washington, DC, in the Government employ, whose life reads like a romance; he was made a Fellow of the American Association for the Advancement of Science, for his valuable and original scientific work, while he has rendered efficient service to the Royal Museum of Berlin, Germany, and is an active member of societies engaged in researches among the aborigines of our country; and he still finds time in his busy life to write a book which promises to let us into the secrets of Indian boy life as no other book has done or could do.[1]

Cook's praise for Zitkala-Ša is briefer but no less adulatory: "Miss Zitkala-Ša, a Yankton Sioux, is a young girl numbered among the contributors to the 'Atlantic Monthly,' and gifted with unusual musical genius."[2] In the early months of 1900, as Cook mentions in her contemporaneous article, both La Flesche and Zitkala-Ša published important autobiographical works dealing with their experiences at school. *The Middle Five: Indian Schoolboys of the Omaha Tribe* was La Flesche's book-length rendition of his experiences as a schoolboy in an on-reservation Presbyterian boarding school in the mid-1860s, while Zitkala-Ša's work in the *Atlantic Monthly* in 1900 consisted of three autobiographical essays that covered her early childhood on the reservation, her experiences as a student at a Quaker off-reservation boarding school, and her brief stint as a teacher at Carlisle.

Pratt, like other educators, wanted to highlight the contribution he felt the schools had made to the success of these two representative Indians, so he used La Flesche's and Zitkala-Ša's published autobiographical accounts to promote his system in a series of articles published in Carlisle's news-papers, the *Red Man* and the *Red Man and Helper* (both of them intended for a wide readership). Since Pratt obviously saw the schools as responsible for the writers' accomplishments and saw the writers themselves as "good"— even "excellent"—students, he would have expected his philosophy to be expressed in their writings, thus a pro-school, anti-tribal endorsement of assimilation. In effect, Pratt and his cohorts wanted to use La Flesche and Zitkala-Ša and their achievements as a type of "after" picture of total assimilation. These highly educated and politically savvy Indian leaders, however, were no longer young schoolchildren to be contained by the rhetoric of a Man-on-the-Band-stand. There is a distinct tension between Pratt's desire to view these people as "his" Indians, and their own desires to be articulate spokespersons for their own people, holding true to their own experiences. While many of the representative Indians, like Montezuma, were usually in agreement with Pratt and could therefore be used as repre-sented Indians, others, like La Flesche and Zitkala-Ša, vocally disagreed with Pratt on significant issues. They represented their educations in a manner that contradicted the reformers' beliefs about how identity worked, and about the degree to which the schools "killed" the Indian within their students. La Flesche chronicles the development of repertoires of identity among the students at the boarding school he attended, providing an implicit argument against any zero-sum view of identity. Zitkala-Ša, in contrast, exhibits her own developed repertoire of identities, utilizing her identity as an Indian writer to criticize the schools and redefine the nature of the successful student. The tension between these writers and the institution that taught them literacy builds and then erupts on the pages of Carlisle's newspapers in 1900, as Indian self-representation flies in the face of the establishment's propagandistic urges.

THE ASSIMILATIONIST APPROPRIATION
OF LA FLESCHE'S TEXT

Francis La Flesche was born on the newly created Omaha Reservation in Nebraska in 1857, the son of Chief Joseph Iron Eye La Flesche, the Franco-Ponca Omaha leader, and his full-blood Omaha second wife, Tainne or Elizabeth.[3] Joseph La Flesche supported assimilative policies but also led a fairly traditional private life during his son's early childhood, and Francis grew up within a household that followed the Omaha practice of polygyny and participated in ceremonials and tribal buffalo hunts. Francis took part in three hunts, serving as the runner on the tribe's last hunt of the nearly depleted buffalo population.[4] La Flesche's childhood took place during a time of significant change for the tribe. As La Flesche and Alice Fletcher wrote in their study "The Omaha Tribe": "Nothing belonging to the past now seemed stable to the Omaha; only the familiar landscape remained to remind them that they were still in the land of their fathers."[5]

Life on the new reservation required innovation for survival. Once Joseph and his first wife, Mary, converted to Christianity, and Joseph resigned from his position as one of the tribal chiefs to become the leader of the small band of progressives in 1866, the La Flesche family realigned its relationship to the rest of the tribe. Francis's mother—a second wife who had borne three children with Joseph—was removed from her newly christianized husband's household. According to Joan Mark—the biographer of Francis's close collaborator, Alice Fletcher—La Flesche felt pulled between his father and his mother, becoming "doubly marginalized" within the community, which derided his father's "imitation white man" settlement, and within his family, which reluctantly thrust his mother aside as an embarrassment to their newly adopted religion. Mark explains that La Flesche worked through these identity issues in his career by combining his life in Washington, D.C., and his work as a cultural mediator (his father's interests) with his dedication to tribal traditions (his mother's interests). Beginning with his work as a translator and an "informant" for linguist James Owen Dorsey, who worked on a manuscript on the Omaha for the Bureau of Ethnology from 1878 to 1880, and continuing through his collaboration with Fletcher and in his own fieldwork and study, La Flesche spent his life gathering information on tribal languages, ceremonies, and music, constructing a complex relationship to this ethnographic data.[6]

By the last years of the century, La Flesche began to contemplate a literary career in addition to his anthropological endeavors. His first and most significant literary production was his memoir of his school days, *The Middle Five*. Although he was encouraged by Alice Fletcher and other acquaintances, in June 1899 La Flesche's manuscript was rejected by Doubleday and McClure because they were dissatisfied with the type of Indian identity it portrayed. Editor H. W. Lanier wrote to the author: "It does not seem to us that the school life should necessarily be excluded, but certainly the burden should be thrown upon the other *wilder* existence."[7] La Flesche resisted the publisher's urgings that he rewrite his manuscript to "really show the outside world what the life of the Indians actually was and is."[8] But while the publishing world may have thought that La Flesche's story did not portray the true Indian, the Friends of the Indian, equally reductive about the identity issues in the text, were convinced that a book about supposedly "whitemanized" Indians at school would, in Cook's words, "let us into the secrets of Indian boy life as no other book has done or could do."[9] In fact, La Flesche's text was finally published at least in part because of the influence of his mentor and companion, Alice Fletcher, who personally sent the manuscript to its eventual publisher, Small, Maynard and Company.[10] Fletcher, who had played a significant role in writing and passing the Dawes Act, and who was responsible for implementing allotment on La Flesche's Omaha Reservation, strongly favored the assimilationist policies of the schools and the supposedly accompanying transformation of identity that she saw as inevitable. It is likely that she read *The Middle Five* as a positive portrayal of assimilation and loss of Indianness, and that her sympathy with this goal was one reason for her involvement in the text's publication.[11]

Richard Pratt clearly assessed the book this way and valued the manuscript for the very reason Doubleday had rejected it. In the months before La Flesche's *Middle Five* was published, Pratt had attempted to use Zitkala-Ša's successful publication of three autobiographical essays in the *Atlantic Monthly* as proof of the efficacy of the boarding-school education, but her extremely negative portrayal of her own experience as both a student at a Quaker-run Indian school and a teacher at Carlisle deeply embarrassed him. Since La Flesche's memoir, however, was not overtly anti–boarding school, it therefore must be pro–boarding school according to the assimilationists' all-or-nothing formula. While critics claimed that Zitkala-Ša's essays should not be accepted as a true picture of boarding-school life, Pratt, like Cook, thought that La Flesche, the "romantic Indian" turned respected scientist, could provide insight into the process of successful transformation. Pratt told La Flesche that he was moved to tears by his reading of the book, and "he encouraged La Flesche to write a sequel about a lone boy off the reservation, which he thought would be particularly instructional for boys."[12] In an unsigned review of *The Middle Five* in the August 21 issue of the *Red Man and Helper*, the reviewer notes; "There is scarcely a hint of the wild life in this little book; not even the Indian names are used; so that the novelty seekers and those who turn to it hoping for something of aboriginal strangeness are likely to be disappointed."[13] According to the review, La Flesche has eschewed representations of tribal life and culture both to discourage such "novelty seekers" and to impress upon his audience the supposedly obvious "realities" of contemporary Indian life. The reviewer goes on to describe the cover illustration in detail. It was drawn by the Winnebago artist and representative Indian Angel de Cora: a "homesick little newcomer in beads and buckskin is being comforted in the most winning fashion by an older boy in the school uniform" (see Figure 6).[14] The cover illustration, mirroring the "before" and "after" photographs used as propaganda to promote the schools, reveals that this is a story of assimilation, of cultural evolution, to the eyes of the reviewer. The sad boy in the buckskin will become the capable child in the school uniform—and will go on to encourage other young children to leave their tribal lives behind, as La Flesche himself seems to be in the process of doing in the text.

The reviewer also makes a suggestion to the reader: "These sketches should by all means be read by all readers of Zitkala-Ša's reminiscences of her school days in the *Atlantic Monthly*, as their sane and cheerful spirit form a wholesome antidote to the morbid introspection and exaggerated bitterness of those remarkable essays."[15] Yet a careful reading of *The Middle Five* would likely have unsettled Pratt as well, since the book denies the complete assimilation of boarding school students. Pratt celebrated the

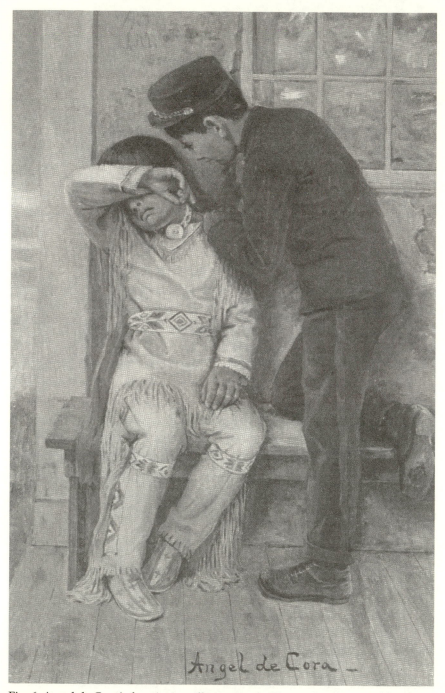

Fig. 6. Angel de Cora's frontispiece illustration for Francis La Flesche's *The Middle Five*. Michigan State University Special Collections.

book, however, and promoted it to his readership because this "before" and "after" way of viewing the world, this linear understanding of cultural change and identity formation, allowed them to see it only as an "after" image of assimilation and "sane and cheerful spirit."

Pratt's blindness to—or manipulation of—La Flesche's complicated representation of boarding-school life is evident in the decontextualized excerpt from the book that accompanies its review in the *Red Man and Helper*, which describes "a pitiful scene—there, sitting on the green grass was a crippled old woman."[16] This grandmother has come to the mission school with her young grandson and leaves him there, explaining: "These White-chests [missionaries] are kind; they will clothe and feed you. I can no longer take care of you, so I must give you to them. See these boys, what nice caps and coats they have! You will have these things, too, and you will have plenty to eat."[17] Begging the missionaries to treat her grandson kindly, she hobbles away. Stopped here and taken out of context, this excerpt allegorizes Pratt's philosophy of education—the old, withered, traditional Indians can no longer care for their young, so they must turn them over to the kind educators, who will provide a better life for them. The "miserable, naked boy" (132) will be clothed in the school uniform and furnished with symbols of the Western culture he will acquire, which is clearly better than what his grandmother can give him. As in the stories and letters in the *Indian Helper*, the grandmother or mother, the repository of traditional culture, is better left behind if the child is to progress and "move forward" toward civilized society. La Flesche appears to be representing this moment of separation as poignant, but necessary, just as Marianna Burgess and other Carlisle recruiters felt it should be.

This is not the point, however, of La Flesche's full text. After portraying the sentimental and heart-wrenching scene of the grandmother entrusting her grandson to the missionaries, La Flesche goes on to describe how Joe, as the boy became known, accidentally hit the teacher, Gray-beard, with a clod of dirt misfired from a slingshot made of rags. When Joe shies away from Gray-beard's attempt to strike his hand with a piece of board:

> Gray-beard dealt blow after blow on the visibly swelling hand. The man seemed to lose self-control, gritting his teeth and breathing heavily, while the child writhed in pain, turned blue, and lost his breath. It was a horrible sight. The scene in the school-room when

the naked little boy was first brought there by the old woman rose
before me; I heard the words of the grandmother as she gave the boy
to Gray-beard, "I beg that he be kindly treated; that is all I ask." (138)

La Flesche attempts to comfort the boy and to deal with the feelings he has
developed toward Gray-beard. "The vengeful way in which he fell upon
that innocent boy created in my heart a hatred that was hard to conquer,"
he wrote, "I tried to reconcile the act of Gray-beard with the teachings of the
Missionaries, but I could not do so from any point of view" (138). Rather
than an allegory of the inevitability of boarding schools as the progressive
choice for Indian children, the full incident portrays the hypocrisy of the
educators who promise protection but deliver violence. The poignancy of
the scene of the old grandmother becomes clear only when read in the
context of the later abuse of the child she entrusted to the school. Although
it requires a willful misreading of this incident to view it as pro–boarding
school, Pratt attempted to frame La Flesche's response to the boarding-
chool experience the way his photographer framed the photographs of
students—both showing only what fit the ideological mold. Pratt appropriated and distorted La Flesche's autobiography, encouraging people to
read it as a narrative of assimilation.

CREATING MULTIVALENT IDENTITIES
IN *THE MIDDLE FIVE*

Despite Pratt's use of *The Middle Five* as pro-Carlisle propaganda, La
Flesche's autobiography actually deals with a boarding-school situation
that was dissimilar to the Carlisle experience in several important ways.
La Flesche attended the Presbyterian Indian Mission School located at the
Omaha Agency headquarters, about eighty miles north of the city of
Omaha.[18] The school was, therefore, very close to the students' families,
and the student body shared the Omaha tribal affiliation and a common
tribal language. These factors allowed students more contact with their
shared tribal culture than they would have had at Carlisle and made it
easier for La Flesche to develop complex relational identities and to portray
those identities in his memoir. Perhaps because of his proximity to his
family and other members of his tribe, La Flesche does not seem to be
trapped in the rhetoric of social evolutionism.[19] Instead, he feels free to
define himself and his fellow students situationally and to describe the

various identities that made up a student's repertoire. In the Omaha settlement, for example, La Flesche was the son of "the principal chief of the tribe and leader of the village of the 'make-believe white-men'" (11)—the progressive village. Even within the structure of the tribe, then, La Flesche and his fellow students possessed a repertoire of identities since Omaha tribal identity is itself complex and multileveled. Tribal members belong to one of two main divisions, the Sky people or the Earth people, and each of these divisions contains five ceremonially based villages, each of which is further divided into several smaller groups and subdivisions.[20] Each member of the tribe would thus have several important affiliations and would possess a number of roles and identities within these different groups. "Post-contact" identities as "traditional" or "progressive" only added to the complexities of Omaha repertoires of identity. La Flesche thus carried with him to the school an appreciation for rich and layered identities. Among the schoolchildren, he struggled to gain an identity as a member of "the Middle Five" gang, even as he was to his teacher, Gray-beard, "an exceptionally bright scholar" (13). La Flesche recognizes that identity is relational when he writes about the different ways of determining social status among the Omaha community, and among the schoolchildren:

> Before schools of any kind were known among the Omahas, Indian parents warned their boys and girls against a free association with the children of parents who did not bear a good character. . . . At the school we were all thrown together and left to form our own associates. The sons of chiefs and of prominent men went with the sons of the common people, regardless of social standing and character. The only distinction made was against cowardice; the boy who could not fight found it difficult to maintain the respect of his mates, and to get a place among the different 'gangs' or groups of associates the boys had established among themselves. (10–11)

No student was entitled to a place in the school's social structure on the basis of his or her parents' position in the larger Omaha society. In La Flesche's world, status and identity at school were determined by the rules developed by the schoolboys whereas status and identity at home were determined by tribal norms and customs. The boys could identify themselves differently based on the context in which they sought to represent themselves. Significantly, they chose to identify themselves at school primarily according to gang membership, which was ultimately decided by the students themselves, rather than by grade levels, which was how the teachers chose to identify them. They moved back and forth among the identities in their repertoire as they moved from school to home and back again. Attending the mission school provided the impetus for forming new identity options, but tribal identity was not supplanted by school-based identity in a linear process of transformation.[21] Instead, the boys adopted, discarded, and altered identities based on situations and contexts.

Michael Coleman, who examined over one hundred boarding-school student memoirs for his study *American Indian Children at School*, determined that "La Flesche was especially alive to patterns of pupil behavior, and provided the clearest example of a student subculture developing independently of school-sanctioned activities."[22] The formation of a student subculture itself belies the simple model of acculturation. The student culture portrayed in *The Middle Five* blends elements of Omaha culture with distinctive innovations on the part of the students, as well as with accommodation to the boarding-school system. What is created comes closer to matching Malcolm McFee's concept of the "150% Indian"—one who has become well versed in both Indian and white cultures—than it comes to reflecting a linear, assimilative process at work.[23]

The majority of *The Middle Five* consists of descriptions of a student life and culture that the school administrators were not even aware existed. For example, La Flesche had a sweetheart at school, "pretty little black-eyed Rosalie," but "the teachers never knew that there were lovers among the pupils and that little romances were going on right under their eyes" (49). To the extent that these activities went on under the eyes of the school's administrators but without their knowledge, the students were able to escape the control of the rigid educational system. They were able to create options for themselves that lay outside of the assimilationist rhetoric and practice of the educators. This type of escape was not unique to La Flesche's school and situation, despite the institutions' claims to "See All," exemplified by Carlisle's Man-on-the-Band-stand.[24]

Manifestations of this secret student culture highlighted systems of meaning that the students created in response to their school experience. One such manifestation was the use of cake as currency—"the one slice of brown ginger-cake we were each given for Sunday noon lunch was the only delicacy we tasted. This cake became a currency among the boys, and all contracts for cakes were faithfully kept" (71). This currency has meaning and value only within the boarding school. Ginger cake was not inherently valuable to either European American society or Omaha society, so by valuing ginger cake as capital, the students are acting outside of the linear path of assimilation. Cake currency was neither an old savage value nor a new civilized value, and hence, it was invisible to educators who sought to monitor only the progress of "evolution." This creative use of ginger cake demonstrates that the students were not the passive learners Freire describes in his explanation of the banking model of the pedagogy of oppression, meekly accepting what was put before them and dropping their previous beliefs and practices by the wayside. Instead, they were active forces, using the school as a "middle ground"—a space in between cultures where they could develop a whole new system of meaning, or even several concurrent systems of meaning, along with new situational identities that they added to their repertoires.[25]

Perhaps the most important aspect of the student culture, to La Flesche, was the gangs. The title of the book, after all, refers to the gang that he joined, and his status as a member of the Middle Five was the most significant identity option he had while a student. The gangs provided students with both a social and a ceremonial structure, and, according to Coleman, they contained elements of tribal social organization: "Like tribal societies, each of these new groupings, often age-graded, had its own roles, rules, and ritual."[26] La Flesche vividly portrays the ritual life of the gangs in his anecdote about the Middle Five and the Big Seven sharing a secret. The first time the members of the Middle Five are allowed to stay up as late as the older boys in the Big Seven, the leader of the older gang approaches them and speaks to them "in the Omaha language, fearlessly breaking one of the rules of the school" (113). Aleck, the leader (named after Alexander the Great), invites the Middle Five to join with the Big Seven in a special ritual known as "Obeying the Command." As Aleck calls on two of the boys in the Middle Five, the first, George, answers "present" as if he were answering the roll, and the boys laugh at him. Edwin, on the other hand, answers the Word of Command with "'Ah-ho!' . . . giving the response and imitating the voice of a grown-up and serious warrior" (114). The mixture of English and Omaha illustrates a fearlessly syncretic student cultural activity. Aleck instructs the two younger boys to sneak out of the school after Gray-beard has gone to bed. They are to go to the Omaha village and enter a specific house, where they are to speak to the woman they find inside and say, "we are the commanded and the bearers of the Word of Command. Of you we demand a bag of pemmican. Give willingly, and you shall go beyond the four hills of life without stumbling; there shall be no weariness in the pathway of life to hinder your feet, and your grandchildren shall be many and their succession endless!" (114–15). The formal diction used in this speech signals the ceremonial and therefore resistant nature of the activity, the syntax and style intended to connect the endeavor even more closely to Omaha culture.[27]

When George and Edwin obtain the pemmican, it becomes clear that Obeying the Command is associated with Omaha rites, for the man whose wife gives them the pemmican jokes with them; "'Did those old White-chests [missionaries] teach you all that? . . . If they did, they have been stealing the rituals of some of our priests'" (117). The boys finish the ceremony by feasting on the pemmican and telling stories in an empty schoolroom. (118). Certainly, this ritual has its basis in Omaha custom, but the boys have adapted it to the boarding-school situation. Lowering boys from the upstairs window just above the teacher's bedroom becomes part of the ritual and the added danger of speaking the Omaha language in a place where it was forbidden becomes part of the process as well. In the context of boarding-school life, the use of the Omaha language, the feasting, and the storytelling take on a different meaning than they would have had back in the village.[28] These acts become more than just a childhood game. They are acts of defiance, demonstrating Coleman's claim that "All cases of syncretic blending of traditions should be seen as cultural resistance to school demands for total rejection of the tribal past and total acceptance of the Christian civilization."[29]

Through a developed and often syncretic student culture, La Flesche and his peers found ways to break through the boarding school's disciplinary web and express resistance to the educational process, as La Flesche's autobiography illustrates. He recounts that "there were times when the pupils became very tired of their books, and longed to take a run over the prairies or through the woods. When this longing came upon them, they sought for ways and means by which to have the school closed, and secure a holiday" (67). The children loosened the connections between the segments of the stovepipe, so it collapsed as they marched in from recess, "filling the room with smoke, and covering the floor with soot," thus canceling class

(67); or they put tempting corn outside the hog pen, right next to a weak spot in the fence, and were called out of class to help recapture the hogs once they broke loose: "All the afternoon we chased the pigs, and had a glorious time," he recalls, and when they entered the dining room "flushed with our exciting chase, . . . the superintendent, looking at us with a kindly smile, thanked us for the good service we had rendered that afternoon!" (68). Covert acts such as these not only disrupted the classroom but also put the students in the position of knowing what their teachers did not. By making their teachers look foolish, they asserted their own power. It was a small quantity of power in comparison to the power the missionaries had to regulate almost every aspect of their lives, but any assertion of strength or acquisition of power by students in the boarding-school situation disrupted the schools' web of disciplinary power and reworked the schools' social evolutionary model.

The students also offered more overt forms of resistance to the control of the educators. Such moments are linked, in La Flesche's text, to representations of flexible identity repertoires. In an interesting incident involving white perceptions of what students should be and how they should respond to their educations, La Flesche recounts that a group of visitors came to the school, and asked, "Have your people music, and do they sing?" (100). The men requested to hear an Indian song, and though the students knew they were not allowed to speak their language or practice the Omaha culture at school:

> suddenly a loud clear voice close to me broke into a Victory song; before a bar was sung another voice took up the song from the beginning, as is the custom among the Indians, then the whole school fell in, and we made the room ring. We understood the song, and knew the emotion of which it was the expression. We felt, as we sang, the patriotic thrill of a victorious people who had vanquished their enemies. (100)

Students with English names like Abraham Lincoln and William T. Sherman, who could recite by rote lessons on Columbus's "discovery" of America (99), were also able to seize control of the classroom, if only for a moment, and fill the air with a meaningful song of protest. The white visitors were clearly disconcerted by the rendition of the Victory Song and shook their heads and muttered "That's savage, that's savage!" (100). While the students felt the thrill of patriotism and victory, the visitors responded with the uneasy feeling that perhaps giving the students the names of white American heroes, dressing them in uniforms, and teaching them English may not have killed off all that is "savage" in them. The students were comfortable with the multivalent identities revealed in their performance, displaying equal prowess at lessons taught in the school and by their tribe, while the visitors showed signs of distress and confusion. La Flesche posits students' survival on their own terms, because he can envision inventive student resistance and cultural creation in the face of a system that intended cultural genocide.

While these examples of student resistance are significant, it is important to distinguish between resistance and rejection and to recognize that La Flesche does not come nearly as close to rejecting the entire system of education as Zitkala-Ša does. Indian students and their parents often found good reasons to obtain an education in the boarding schools. Coleman claims:

> These Indian adults pushed upon their children the education of the Christian civilization for salvation in the present life—individual and tribal salvation. Indeed the new skills could even be used to preserve the wisdom of the past. Indians such as Joseph La Flesche, [and] Geronimo . . . exhibited an adaptive, modern "tribal patriotism"; they accepted certain elements of white civilization in order *to defend* tribal identity, rather than to be assimilated into American society. (Original emphasis)[30]

In fact, Joseph Iron Eye La Flesche, Francis's father, requested that the Presbyterian Church establish the mission school that Francis attended.[31] Coleman's analysis emphasizes that assimilation was not the goal of most Indians who encouraged their children to attend the schools. Instead, tribal communities that agreed to white education for their children expected that the children would come away with a knowledge of the white world without losing their sense of themselves as tribal members. This expectation corresponds to one of McFee's "types" of 150 percent Indians—the Interpreters. According to McFee: "The Interpreters can talk to and better understand both sides. Yet they are Indian-oriented. They live with and want to be accepted by the Indian group and to maintain their Indian identity."[32] Not all boarding-school students became Interpreters, but the very existence of such an identity option, which does not fit on the linear path of assimilation upon which the reformers based their understanding of Indian education, proves the inability of social evolutionary theory to account for Indian response to the schools.

The final pages of *The Middle Five* describe the death of Brush, La Flesche's best friend and the leader of the Middle Five. As he lays dying, Brush puts his arm around La Flesche and whispers in the Omaha language: "Tell the boys I want them to learn; I know you will, but the other boys don't care. I want them to learn, and to think. You'll tell them, won't you?" (151). La Flesche sadly leaves his friend, who sees his dead grandfather calling him to his side, and the book ends with only four of the Middle Five remaining. Brush's deathbed wish for his friends may appear to be an endorsement of the educational system, but he speaks in the Omaha language and sees in his dying moments, not visions of angels and saints, but his grandfather calling to him. The ambiguous message Brush leaves behind suggests that he desires his friends to become educated without losing their connection and ability to return to Omaha culture.

Brush's message was one that resonated in Francis La Flesche's own life, and in the lives of all of the La Flesche children. Speaking specifically of the La Flesche family, Wilbert Ahern comments: "These returned students neither cut ties with their community nor became apologists for either the Office of Indian Affairs or White neighbors at the expense of the tribe. They brought to their community a strong sense of mission, one that emphasized a selective retention of the old ways along with accommodation as a group to the surrounding population."[33] While La Flesche's claim at the beginning of *The Middle Five* that "the school uniform did not change those who wore it" (xv) is not entirely true, it most certainly did not automatically change the schoolchildren in the way that the proprietors of Indian schools hoped. The La Flesches did not leave the schools acculturated in the way Pratt and other educators assumed they must be, even though, by viewing Francis La Flesche and his contemporaries through the lens of social evolutionary theory, educators claimed that he was, indeed, the embodiment of an "after" photograph.

La Flesche left the mission school when it closed in 1869, and without additional formal Euro-American education, became an interpreter, a mediator, and an anthropologist, working both with Alice Fletcher and on his own to produce important ethnographies of the Omaha and the Osage.

Much of what La Flesche accomplished in his professional life appeared to be "salvage ethnography" (attempting to record the remnants of tribal life before it disappeared forever), which would seem to indicate his acceptance of social evolutionary theory. Clearly, others sought to put this spin on his work. W. H. Holmes, chief of the Bureau of American Ethnology, ended his introduction to La Flesche's and Fletcher's work *The Omaha Tribe* with the claim that the study traced "the gradual but inevitable molding of the weaker race to conform to the conditions imposed by the new order of things."[34] Indeed, the changes La Flesche had seen among the Omaha and the Osage within his own lifetime were profound and significant. But even a quick comparison between La Flesche's anthropological work and that of his contemporaries (including Fletcher's, which he aided) reveals that La Flesche's ethnography emphasizes syncretism and continuity despite the specter of loss. In his work with the Osage elder Saucy Calf, for example, La Flesche turns the hegemonic anthropological relationship between scientist and informant, outsider and insider, on its head. Rather than viewing Saucy Calf simply as the repository of vanishing knowledge who must give up that information in the interest of scientific study and general knowledge, La Flesche treats him with respect and affection, sharing stories and information with him. Speaking to one another in their mutually intelligible tribal languages, La Flesche and Saucy Calf began their collaboration by comparing Omaha and Osage tattooing and corn rites.[35] In a reversal of the power relations in the anthropologist/informant model, Saucy Calf initially chose La Flesche to write down Osage ceremonial information for the use of future generations. Calling his informant "father," La Flesche melded his interests as an anthropologist with his and Saucy Calf's concerns about maintaining tribal knowledge for tribal use.[36] La Flesche was, for example, especially interested in keeping songs and prayers within their ceremonial context rather than mining them for publication and decontextualizing them, which might prevent their future use.[37]

Most important, La Flesche's study of the Osage religion brought him into contact with a number of peyotists, and he became an advocate of the Native American Church.[38] Among the Osage, tribal religious ceremonies were being abandoned, but not for Christianity, as a linear understanding of assimilation would dictate. Instead, their practice waned with the ascendancy of the Native American Church, which blends aspects of traditional tribal religions with ancient southwestern and Mexican peyote ceremonies and elements of Christianity into a creative pan-tribal faith that grew in popularity after 1890 and continues to thrive today.[39] Hertzberg notes that the Native American Church "had a solid core of leaders from the Eastern boarding schools and Haskell," who saw their involvement in the Church as an important part of their repertoires of identity, allowing them to update tribal religions to maintain their practice in the changing world.[40] It is no surprise that Pratt and the Friends of the Indian were no friends of this innovative religious movement. La Flesche's support of the peyotists made him unpopular with Pratt, who attacked him, saying that he was a victim of the ideas of the hated Indian Bureau: "He is not lifting up his race."[41] For Pratt, the once-praised La Flesche had ceased to be a representative Indian.[42]

La Flesche's support of the syncretic Native American Church is consistent with his understanding of the constructed nature of culture and identity. La Flesche found nothing unusual or uncomfortable in the creation of new identity options, especially syncretic recombinations of identities already available to American Indians at the turn of the century. Unfortunately, La Flesche's position was difficult to understand for people who believed in inevitable Indian assimilation, and they kept trying to retouch the image he presented them with, to simplify him, reduce him to either "before" or "after"—as can be seen, literally, in the photograph that accompanied La Flesche's obituary. While most published photographs of La Flesche show him dressed in formal citizen's clothes (a conservative suit and tie) (see Figure 7), "his obituary was accompanied by a photograph of a bare-chested La Flesche clad only in a buffalo robe. The original photograph had been retouched to remove the shirt and tie he was actually wearing under the robe"[43] (see Figures 8 and 9). Even at the moment of his death, people could not accept that La Flesche could possess a large repertoire of different identities, that he could be something other than a pristinely traditional Indian or a thoroughly assimilated make-believe white man. People who choose to read La Flesche's life, and his autobiography, as a narrative of assimilation must retouch the picture he provides to make it work with their theories. In his writing, La Flesche sought to undermine the preconceptions of his readers and to represent the complex, multivalent identities that he used to navigate through the personal and professional terrain of his life, including

Fig. 7. Francis La Flesche in "citizen's clothes." National Anthropological Archives, Smithsonian Institution, negative no. 4805.

Fig. 8. La Flesche wearing a buffalo robe over a suit. National Anthropological Archives, Smithsonian Institution, negative no. 3939b1.

Fig. 9. The photo that ran with La Flesche's obituary. Note how evidence of the suit he wore beneath the robe has been airbrushed out. National Anthropological Archives, Smithsonian Institution.

his time at school. *The Middle Five* captures the process of syncretic cultural creation that took place in the boarding schools.

ZITKALA-ŠA'S INDISPUTABLE IMPRESSIONS

Zitkala-Ša focused on the genocidal potential of the boarding schools more than did La Flesche, whose work has been called a "gentle reproach for the harms caused by forced acculturation" by a contemporary scholar.[44] Her writing about boarding schools provides the best example of the tension between the reformers' concept of the representative Indian, and the self-representing Indian. Zitkala-Ša was very conscious of the politics of self-representation and quite comfortable with representing herself differently in different situations. While La Flesche chose situational identities from a repertoire that included Omaha tribal member, interpreter, anthropologist, and writer, Zitkala-Ša's repertoire included orator, musician, poet, storyteller, political activist, Dakota, half-blood, Indian, pagan, and Catholic (see Figure 10).[45] The best evidence of her agency in choosing among the identities in her repertoire is her self-naming.

Although her family gave her an English name, Gertrude Simmons, she named herself Zitkala-Ša—a Lakota name that translates as Red Bird— because of a disagreement with her sister-in-law about her education: "[M]y brother's wife—angry with me because I insisted upon getting an education—said I had deserted home and I might give up my brother's name 'Simmons' too. Well, you can guess how queer I felt—away from my own people—homeless—penniless—and without even a name! Then I chose to make a name for myself—and I guess I have made Zitkala-Ša known."[46] That she chooses a Lakota name for herself actually because of an accusation of her distance from that culture underscores the complex relationship between representative codes and identities in Zitkala-Ša's life. This complexity is first evident in her decision to take a Lakota name even though she was probably brought up speaking the different (but closely related) Nakota language. As Jane Hafen has remarked, "Bonnin's [Zitkala-Ša's] life traverses the breadth of Sioux language and society" from her Nakota speech to her Lakota name to the native-language texts she wrote in Dakota.[47]

Continuing to use the name Gertrude Simmons (later Gertrude Simmons Bonnin) in her personal life and as a reformer and political activist, she used her self-given Lakota name as a literary nom de plume, claiming in "School Days of an Indian Girl" that it was her "Indian nature" that was her muse and her voice, "the moaning wind which stirs [her sad memories of school life] for their present record."[48] Even after her supposed indoctrination into Western culture through her schooling, she maintains an identity in her repertoire that she associates with her Indianness, and she uses the literacy in English that she gained in the schools to present this Sioux identity to the world. It is important to recognize that she meticulously constructed her identity as Zitkala-Ša, emphasizing or excluding elements of her heritage, biography, languages, politics, and available literary forms to suit the needs of this situational self. For example, as Zitkala-Ša she never mentions that her father was white, choosing instead to stress her Dakota roots, a strategy that both illustrates that her identity is situational and complicated and, as Susan Bernardin explains, "forecloses any attribution of her achievements to her 'white blood.'"[49] Through her choice to give herself a Lakota name after her years as a student and to claim her authorial success as a result of her Sioux heritage, she reverses the educators' process of providing the "savage" students with "civilized" English names,

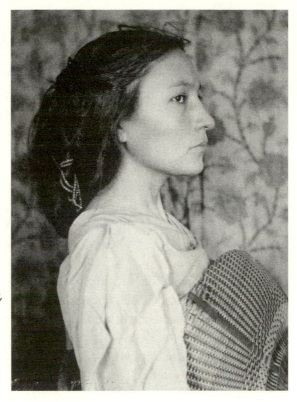

Fig. 10. Gertrude Käsebier, *Zitkala-Ša*. Photographic History Collection, National Museum of American History, Smithsonian Institution, negative no. 83-904.

emphasizing that for her, education is not a linear process of assimilation. Zitkala-Ša deploys her carefully constructed identity as a highly literate Indian woman in order to dismantle the image of the "represented" or "paper" Indian in which Pratt and the Carlisle Press were so deeply invested.

Yet, according to the criteria established by Hampton, Zitkala-Ša was an "excellent" student at White's Manual Institute, a Quaker school in Wabash, Indiana, and at Earlham College, where she won awards for oratory, before teaching at Carlisle from 1898 to 1899. After leaving her position at Carlisle, Zitkala-Ša published a series of autobiographical essays in the *Atlantic Monthly* in 1900 and several short stories in *Harper's* in 1901.[50] David Adams calls her essays a "devastating attack" on the ideologies behind the boarding school education; likewise Michael Coleman characterizes her as "unusually bitter" about her experiences both as student and as teacher at off-reservation Indian schools.[51] Nevertheless, a series of articles published in the *Red Man* and the *Red Man and Helper* chronicle Pratt's desire to use Zitkala-Ša's literary achievements as proof of the potency of his own assimilative methods, even as his newspaper also reflects his anger and embarrassment at the strongly anti–boarding school content of her essays.

Zitkala-Ša's first autobiographical essay, "Impressions of an Indian Childhood," published in the January 1900 issue of the *Atlantic*, follows her life until she leaves her reservation to attend White's Manual Institute and lays the foundation for her argument against the schools. As her reminiscences make clear, Zitkala-Ša was not uneducated when she was taken to the boarding school. Rather, she was a young woman who was in the process of being educated in the culture of her tribe.[52] By insisting on the presence of Dakota culture, and by presenting an alternative mode of education, Zitkala-Ša negates Pratt's assertion that Indian students arrive at the schools like a blank book, ready and willing to be imprinted with the text of civilization.

It is significant that this respected, respectful learning of Dakota culture does not take place in a pristine, pre-contact Indian past. Zitkala-Ša's world has always been one of accommodation to white encroachment, as she makes clear in the first sentence of "Impressions of an Indian Childhood," in which she tells of the weather-stained canvas "wigwam" in which she and her mother lived. Their tipi is no longer made from buffalo hide but from canvas (a small detail illuminating an entirely changed lifeway), and the word used to describe this structure, "wigwam," is an Algonquin term that is perhaps the more familiar word to an eastern white audience—an act of linguistic accommodation. Furthermore, Zitkala-Ša's overarching childhood impression is of her mother's sadness and anger at white colonial expansion. When Zitkala-Ša tells her mother that she looks forward to the day she will be grown-up enough to fetch water from the spring, her mother replies: "'If the paleface does not take away from us the river we drink.'"[53] Thus the stories of Zitkala-Ša's childhood are not only Iktomi legends, the trickster tales she listens to with delight, but also stories of removal and abuse—of the death of her sister and her uncle during a forced march, when the community was "driven like a herd of buffalo" by the "heartless paleface" who "has stolen our lands and driven us hither" (10–11). As these details communicate, Zitkala-Ša never lived the "before" picture, so crucial to the schools' construction of themselves as institutions of transformation. She was already used to living with multiple cultural influences, even within her very Dakota-identified childhood in which her Dakota community neither died out under the "light of civilization" nor assimilated into white society. Instead, it found alternative strategies—sometimes accommodating, sometimes rejecting—to deal with an oppressive, colonial white presence.

Zitkala-Ša's traditional education becomes even more meaningful within the context of her community's dispossession. Although her Yankton band has lost so much, they maintain their culture and transmit it to the young despite some accommodation to white presence. Zitkala-Ša's mother, Táte I Yóhin Win, played an essential role in educating her daughter in Dakota culture. We see from the first section of "Impressions," titled "My Mother," that like La Flesche (and also Burgess and Pratt), Zitkala-Ša associates women with the preservation of culture and the dissemination of power. Paula Gunn Allen explains: "Women's traditions are largely about continuity," about "all that goes into the maintenance of life over the long term"; and, specifically in Plains cultures, "power was and is gained, accrued, mediated, and dispensed only through the grace and beneficence of female influence."[54] Zitkala-Ša's portrait of the woman who was her own source of cultural knowledge and continuity differs drastically from the Indian women portrayed in the pages of the *Indian Helper*. Here, instead of a filthy, spitting, disgusting creature is a multifaceted, accomplished woman—a teacher, an artist—who instructs her daughter in beadwork and gives lessons in Dakota values such as hospitality, all the while nursing the wounds caused by removal and the loss of family and friends.

Zitkala-Ša reports that she and her young friends "delighted in impersonating our own mothers. We talked of things we had heard them say in their conversations. We imitated their various manners, even to the inflection of their voices" (21–22). Observation, active participation, and creative play were important elements in Zitkala-Ša's Dakota education, and these are present in the two most significant scenes of education in the essay. In the first, "The Beadwork," Zitkala-Ša describes her mother as an artist, "spreading upon a mat beside her bunches of beads, just as an artist arranges the paints upon his palette" (18). Zitkala-Ša does not merely watch her mother "with a proud, beaming face" (18), she also participates in the beading. Sitting beside her mother with a small bit of buckskin, she began her "practical observation lessons in the art of beadwork" (19). Táte I Yóhin Win set certain standards for her daughter's training—she must design her own patterns, and she must finish whatever she starts. In addition, she saw the role of teacher as simultaneously the role of protector; because porcupine quills have sharp poisonous points, as a child Zitkala-Ša was not permitted to do any quill work alone. Within these guidelines, Táte I Yóhin Win gave her daughter freedom to be creative, while constantly checking on her work. "The quietness of her oversight made me feel strongly responsible and dependent upon my own judgment. She treated me as a dignified individual as long as I was on my good behavior; and how humiliated I was when some boldness of mine drew forth a rebuke from her!" (20). This method of education encourages children to watch the adults and to emulate them, while allowing the children to make their own creative decisions within a protected, respectful environment.

Such respect for children also appears in the second significant scene of education, "The Coffee-Making." While her mother is outside of their home, an old grandfather comes to the tipi and waits for her mother to return. "At once I began to play the part of a generous hostess," Zitkala-Ša relates. Although the fire had died out, and the coffee pot contained only grounds, the young child made "coffee" the best she knew how—by dumping warm river water on top of the grounds and setting the pot on the cold ashes for what seemed to be the right amount of time. She served "a cup of worse than muddy warm water" to the elder, along with a small piece of bread. Táte I Yóhin Win walked in to find the old man eating this "light luncheon," and he told her: "'My granddaughter made coffee on a heap of dead ashes, and served me the moment I came.' They both laughed . . . but neither said anything to embarrass me. They treated my best judgment, poor as it was, with the utmost respect. It was not till long years afterward that I learned how ridiculous a thing I had done" (29). Once again, Zitkala-Ša is made to feel like a significant participant in her own culture, and even her mistakes are not cause for rebuke.

Although she was obviously very Dakota-identified during her childhood, Zitkala-Ša does depict her awareness of a budding repertoire of identities—of her own self-difference—in this essay. Her recognition of self-difference is playful as well, coming as she recognizes a relationship between herself and her shadow, and chases it across the prairie:

On one occasion, I forgot the cloud shadow in a strange notion to catch up with my own shadow. . . . I began to run; and away flew my shadow, always just a step beyond me. Faster and faster I ran, setting my teeth and clenching my fists, determined to overtake my own fleeting shadow. But ever swifter it glided before me. . . . My shadow slipped away, and moved as often as I did. Then [my friends and I] gave up trying to catch my shadow. (23)

Zitkala-Ša recognizes herself as an individual, substantial enough to cast a fully formed, Zitkala-Ša-shaped shadow. But she also describes her recognition of her own multiplicity and her realization that she has several linked identities, which cannot be contained but which do not contradict one another as boarding-school educators seemed to think individual and tribal identities conflicted.

THE "UTTERLY UNTHANKFUL" ZITKALA-ŠA

A complex child—possessing a unique subjectivity as well as a strong Dakota identity— Zitkala-Ša turns away from her freedom when she is tempted by the missionaries' offer of knowledge and of "big red apples," both of which are available at a boarding school in the East. Zitkala-Ša clearly represents the missionaries' efforts to convince her to attend their school as a rewriting of the Eden myth, in which she casts the missionaries in the role of Satan.[55] Although her life on the reservation is not edenically pristine nor unequivocally joyful, Zitkala-Ša makes it clear that her decision to leave for school is a fall, which reverses the reformers' understanding of the direction of improvement and evolution. By specifically invoking a story that supports degenerationist ideology—a belief that humanity is not evolving, but devolving in the post-Edenic world—Zitkala-Ša refutes the assumption that going from the reservation to boarding school, from the West to the East, was the equivalent of progressing from savagery toward civilization.[56]

Nevertheless, it appears that Pratt, at least, was able to overlook the last scenes in "Impressions of an Indian Childhood" and view the essay instead as a leave-taking from and a nostalgic tribute to a dying way of life. Again, because the essay stops short of Zitkala-Ša's arrival at the boarding school and it is, therefore, not overtly anti-school, an assimilationist could use it (as with *The Middle Five*) as a text whose publication signifies the literary achievement of the author, and hence the success of the schools. The *Red*

Man mentions this essay only briefly, stating: "In the January number of the *Atlantic Monthly*, Zitkala-Ša (Miss Gertrude Simmons) dwelt with much simplicity upon the picturesque 'Memories of an Indian Childhood.'"[57]

The same article, found in the February 1900 issue, reprints several episodes from "School Days of an Indian Girl," Zitkala-Ša's second auto-biographical essay. The unsigned article introduces the episodes—"The Cutting of My Long Hair" and "Iron Routine"—with a brief commentary that praises her skill as a writer, while decrying her presentation of the boarding-school experience:

> She has a striking gift of characterization. Her satire is keen. She excels in giving what seem to be the genuine records of the mind of a child, uncolored by later knowledge and experience. We regret that she did not once call to mind the happier side of those long school days, or even hint at the friends who did so much to break down for her the barriers of language and custom, and to lead her from poverty and insignificance into the comparatively full and rich existence that she enjoys today.[58]

Instead of lauding the schools and presenting the educators as "friends" who led her to success and "significance" through their instruction, these two episodes, along with the rest of the essay, explicitly present Zitkala-Ša's critique of the schools as civilizing machines that oppressed their students.

In "The Cutting of My Long Hair," Zitkala-Ša takes on the moment of physical transformation that promotional photographs of the students sought to capture. She proves that the students' altered appearances did not indicate a corresponding inner transformation. On her first morning at the school, she is led into the dining room by a "paleface woman," feeling very uncomfortable because her blanket had been "stripped from [her] shoulders" (52). She immediately notices the "stiff shoes and closely clinging dresses" of the other girls. "I looked hard at the Indian girls, who seemed not to care that they were even more immodestly dressed than I, in their tightly fitting clothes," she recalled (52–53). The uniforms, which to the reformers indicated discipline and conformity to civilized standards, meant the exact opposite—immodesty and indecorum—to the young Zitkala-Ša.

When she hears from her friend, who understands a little English, that their hair is to be cut, she responds with outrage, rather than with the static submission to the inevitability of progress that "before" and "after" photos claimed to capture. Short hair meant something very different among the Dakota than it did at the school: "Our mothers had taught us that only unskilled warriors who were captured had their hair shingled by the enemy. Among our people, short hair was worn by mourners, and shingled hair by cowards!" Vowing "'I will not submit! I will struggle first!'" Zitkala-Ša attempts to avoid her haircut by hiding under a bed (54). Though she is found, she cries and shakes her head in protest while her braids are cut. This type of vocal, reasoned protest to the physical indignities that the schools inflicted on the incoming students threatened the picture of progressive transfiguration that Pratt and the reformers sought to promote through their propagandistic before and after images. In this episode, Zitkala-Ša forces those monologic signs of assimilation into a dialogue, by reading them from a perspective that validates Dakota culture and portrays herself as a young Dakota warrior in captivity.

"The Cutting of My Long Hair" deeply challenges the reformers' representations of their successes, and the contents of "Iron Routine" are potentially even more menacing to the reformers' desire to maintain congressional funding and public support. Zitkala-Ša describes how the schools dehumanize their students by treating them as merely names on a checklist, or bodies to place in line at the sound of a bell for roll call. Pratt censors the version of this essay that he reprints in his paper—without any indication, such as ellipses, in the text—and leaves out a damning incident in which a "dear schoolmate" of Zitkala-Ša's lies on her deathbed, attended by a white woman whom Zitkala-Ša censures for her "cruel neglect of our physical ills" (67). She makes it clear that the dying girl who "talked disconnectedly of Jesus the Christ" was a fatality of a system that treated its students like animals, making them "suffer in silence rather than appeal to the ears of one whose open eyes could not see [their] pain" (66). She depicts the nurse as "a well-meaning, ignorant woman who was inculcating in our hearts her superstitious ideas" about Christianity while giving "a row of variously ailing Indian children" the same ineffective medicine (67). This version of life in the boarding schools was too much of a threat for Pratt to reprint, even in an article that called Zitkala-Ša to task for her writing.

While the death of the classmate is perhaps the most sensational challenge to the system in this essay, it is not the only moment in the text when Zitkala-Ša questions the ideology of the reformers. While the Friends of the Indian viewed teaching the students English as a necessary step toward civilization, Zitkala-Ša associates learning English with self-protection and rebellion. Students who did not understand the instructions or rules given to them in English often faced harsh punishment, as Zitkala-Ša and her friends Thowin and Judéwin discover when they play in the snow against a matron's orders. Judéwin, who speaks very limited English, instructs the others to respond to whatever words of punishment were directed at them with "no." Unfortunately, the matron asks Thowin, "Are you going to obey my word the next time?" (58). The girl unwittingly replies with the only English word she knows, "no," and is whipped for her apparent impudence. "During the first two or three seasons" Zitkala-Ša explains, "misunderstandings as ridiculous as this one of the snow episode frequently took place, bringing unjustifiable frights and punishments into our little lives" (58). Not speaking English could be terrifying and dangerous for the young students; learning the language was essential for self-preservation.

Learning English did not automatically alter Zitkala-Ša's way of thinking, or make her more amenable to the schools' assimilating project. Instead, "As soon as I comprehended a part of what was said and done, a mischievous spirit of revenge possessed me" (59). Learning to speak, and later to write, in English provided the means for her to wage a linguistic rebellion against the boarding-school ideology. Her first recorded act of resistance, which calls to mind La Flesche's tales of student manipulation of the system, is explicitly linked to her newfound competency in English. When she was punished for breaking a rule "which seemed to me very needlessly binding," she is put on kitchen duty and ordered to mash turnips. Taking the words of her disciplinarian literally—"The order was 'Mash these turnips,' and mash them I would!"—she attacks the turnips with such violence that she crushes the bowl that holds them, and they fall out the bottom when a matron attempts to bring them to the table (60). She is mildly sorry for ruining the jar, but she is ecstatic about her success at turning the lessons—and the words—of the educators back on themselves. She concludes: "As I sat eating my dinner, and saw that no turnips were served, I whooped in my heart for having once asserted the rebellion within me" (61).

These episodes, along with her tale of using a slate pencil to cut a picture of the devil out of the school's bible—an act Ruth Spack describes as using a "sign of a literate culture . . . to perform the ultimate act of revision, . . .

obliterat[ing] a threatening Christianity"—shook Pratt and his cohorts to their core.[59] The *Red Man* insisted:

> We do not for a moment believe that "Zitkala-Ša" desires to injure the cause of her own people, whose title to the blessings of enlightenment and civilization has so lately found a general recognition, but we do feel that the home-sick pathos—nay, more, the underlying bitterness of her story will cause readers unfamiliar with Indian schools to form entirely the wrong conclusions. Her pictures are not, perhaps, untrue in themselves, but, taken by themselves, they are sadly misleading.[60]

The newspaper reprinted Zitkala-Ša's words precisely to put its own spin on this bold Indian self-representation, to discipline her for refusing to write as a paper Indian. Zitkala-Ša was using her "striking gifts" to pen a representation of the boarding schools that Pratt could not directly control as he could manipulate the pictures of boarding-school life (both photographic and verbal) that he himself created. Therefore he continually tried to contain Zitkala-Ša's work within his carefully constructed web of representation.

Pratt's rebuke, relatively soft and temperate, did not seem to have the desired effect on Zitkala-Ša. The April issue of the *Red Man* printed an excerpt of her letter of response: "To stir up views and earnest comparison of theories was one of the ways in which I hoped [my essay] would work a benefit to my people. No one can dispute my own impressions and bitterness!"[61] An earnest dialogue and comparison of theories did not, however, interest Pratt, especially when an Indian, someone who should have been forever grateful for the blessings of enlightenment and civilization provided by the schools, suggested the comparison. This type of articulate challenge by a successful boarding-school alumna clearly vexed Pratt. Unable to reconcile Zitkala-Ša's self-representation with his ideological beliefs about the inevitable replacement of savage identity traits with civilized ones through the process of education, he continued to try to use her publications to his advantage and continued to be stung by her denunciations of his system.

The June 1900 issue of the newspaper illustrates Pratt's dilemma. This issue contains a reprint of Cook's article lauding Zitkala-Ša's status as a representative Indian, but Pratt also reprints an article from the *Word Carrier,* the newspaper published by the Dakota Mission School at the Santee Agency, which insists that her autobiographical essays are mere fictions, and "her portraits are either so exaggerated as to be untrue or are pure inventions."[62] The *Word Carrier* accuses Zitkala-Ša of manipulating her readers with her fabrications, insisting that "It will relieve the tension to remember that this is simply dramatic fiction."[63]

The *Word Carrier* tries to use Zitkala-Ša's talent as a writer against her, warning us she is so adept at writing a good piece of fiction that we may be unwittingly convinced that removal, or white squatters on reservations, or unhappy students in the boarding schools are actually real! The reformers clearly felt the danger of the unchecked voice of this Indian woman, who represents the story of her life with a passion and an emotion that will move her audience. This is the danger of the "half-civilized" Indian that the Board of Indian Commissioners feared in 1880—an Indian who can use the tools of the white world against it. Such a voice would have to be discredited, its perception of reality challenged. Some contemporary critics have suggested that Zitkala-Ša may have "fictionalized her own life" to a certain extent, "blur[ring] the distinction between fact and fiction."[64] While Zitkala-Ša is undoubtedly offering a representation of her life (and is, therefore, shaping and molding her experiences to fit both literary conventions and her political agenda), she insists that no one should dispute her own interpretation and portrayal of her life. She is claiming the right to represent herself and, in the process, to proclaim her own truth.

The *Word Carrier* article goes on to attack Zitkala-Ša personally, perhaps encompassing Pratt's feelings for her, and claims: "She is utterly unthankful for all that has been done for her by the pale faces, which in her case is considerable. It would be doing injustice to the Indian race whose blood she partly shares to accept the picture she has drawn of herself as the true picture of all Indian girls. They average far better."[65] This unthankful, ungrateful Indian should not be considered representative of all Indian girls, the article proclaims, just a few pages after Cook's essay praises Zitkala-Ša as an "unusual genius." Her thankless representations of herself and her teachers do not portray a true picture, because they contradict the image the schools wished to depict. Simultaneously exemplary and substandard, Zitkala-Ša's literary talent makes her an excellent example of what Pratt feels off-reservation schooling can achieve, but the voice that comes along with such a talent torments and embarrasses Pratt and other Friends of the Indian.

It is not surprising, although Zitkala-Ša's first two autobiographical essays are mentioned by name in the pages of the *Red Man,* that no direct mention is ever made of the final essay, "An Indian Teacher among Indians," which talks about her time as a teacher at Carlisle. (The *Word Carrier* article does mention scenes from that essay, but without naming it.) In this third essay, Zitkala-Ša directly challenges the role of the Indian boarding schools in the "improvement of the race." When she is sent back to her reservation to recruit new students and to recover her health after an illness (Pratt disrespectfully tells her, "I am going to turn you loose to pasture"), she spends some time with her mother, who is living in a ramshackle cabin (85). Challenging the schools' representation of reservation Indians as dirty and indifferent, she writes her own dialogue with her mother, who explains that she is unable to keep her house in good condition because she is poor. Táte I Yóhin Win has become too old to do her beadwork, and on the reservation Dawee, Zitkala-Ša's boarding-school educated brother, "has not been able to make use of the education the Eastern school has given him" (90–91). Socioeconomics and the disruptive school curriculum, not social evolutionary status, keep Táte I Yóhin Win from living in a clean dry house.

This encounter with her mother serves to sharpen Zitkala-Ša's critique of the schools and their assimilative project. Realizing the price she has paid for her white education and continuing to learn from Táte I Yóhin Win, her Dakota educator, Zitkala-Ša is able to analyze the boarding schools systemically. She recognizes that "white teachers in Indian schools had a larger missionary creed than I had suspected. It was one which included self-preservation quite as much as Indian education" (95). After accusing the educators of hoodwinking the federal government by showing inspectors sample student work that was made especially for the inspection and that was not representative of the educational standards of the school, she makes a blatant attack on the social evolutionist reformers, using their own vocabulary against them: "At this stage of my own evolution, I was ready to curse men of small capacity for being the dwarfs their God had made them" (96). Although she uses social evolutionary terminology, her evolution was not transformative progression resulting from the curriculum of the schools but, instead, a growing awareness of the evil consequences of the educators' ideology, brought on by a combination of her physical illness and her mother's teachings about "encroaching frontier settlers" (96). As if these criticisms were not cutting enough, she ends the essay with a devastating blow to Pratt's philosophy, which recalls La Flesche's anecdote about the visitors who asked the children to sing:

> Examining the neatly figured pages, and gazing upon the Indian girls and boys bending over their books, the white visitors walked out of the schoolhouse well satisfied: they were educating the children of the red man! . . . In this fashion many have passed idly through the Indian Schools during the last decade afterward to boast of their charity to the North American Indian. But few there are who have paused to question whether real life or long-lasting death lies beneath this semblance of civilization. (98–99)

The outward signs of assimilation are nothing but a "semblance of civilization" to Zitkala-Ša, representing what she believes is a program of cultural genocide. She unquestionably felt she could not do any good for Native people as a teacher at Carlisle, and the effort to work there, to become successful according to the standards of the educators, made her ill. She wrote:

> Like a slender tree, I had been uprooted from my mother, nature and God. I was shorn of my branches, which had waved in sympathy and love for home and friends. The natural coat of bark which had protected my oversensitive nature was scraped off to the very quick. Now a cold bare pole I seemed to be, planted in a strange earth. Still, I seemed to hope a day would come when my mute aching head, reared upward to the sky, would flash a zig-zag lightning across the heavens. With this dream of vent for a long-pent consciousness, I walked again amid the crowds. At last, one weary day in the schoolroom, a new idea presented itself to me. It was a new way of solving the problem of my inner self. I liked it. Thus I resigned my position as a teacher; and now I am in an Eastern city, following in the long course of study I have set for myself. (97–98)

The new way of "solving the problem of [her] inner self," the tension she felt between the various identities in her repertoire (and especially between the identities of educator and Indian), was, it appears from what we know of her biography, to move to Boston and develop her artistic self-representations—publishing essays and stories and studying the violin. Although she felt that she had lost her voice and the freedom to express her true self from the moment she first left home with the missionaries, she made use of the English language to regain a voice for herself as "Zitkala-Ša," creating the identity by which she is best known today.[66]

Almost unbelievably, given the scathing criticisms of Carlisle that appeared in "An Indian Teacher," the *Red Man and Helper* tried one last time to claim her as a representative Indian. The July 13 issue of *Red Man and Helper* celebrates an "Indian Year in literature and art," mentioning that *Harper's* magazine will publish several articles and stories by and about Indians, including Zitkala-Ša's short story, "The Soft-Hearted Sioux." The newspaper quotes the editor of *Harper's*, who praises Zitkala-Ša, saying that her "culture stands as a suggestive possibility in the progress of her race."[67] This story was, however, one of Zitkala-Ša's most pointedly anti-boarding-school works. It tells of a young man—formerly a promising young warrior and hunter—who returns home to his parents after years away at a mission school, where he was taught to "hunt for the soft heart of Christ" rather than for game (112). Zitkala-Ša writes the story from the point of view of the returned student. He has been indoctrinated into the ideology of the school and has, in fact, returned as a missionary—a representative of the school whose task is to convert the rest of his people—but his tribe's medicine man, whom he views as a "cunning magician," calls him a "traitor to his people" (117). The medicine man and the rest of the village move away and leave him behind with his elderly mother and his ailing father, saying: "With his prayers let him drive away the enemy! With his soft heart, let him keep off starvation!" (118). Because the student's years away at school had interrupted his tribal education, he had never learned to become a hunter or a warrior; therefore he cannot meet the physical needs of his family, and his ailing father dies from starvation. The returned, "civilized" Indian ends up poaching cattle from a white-owned ranch. He kills a white man and is sentenced to death, his life and his family's life ruined by his far too successful boarding-school education. This, Zitkala-Ša says, is what a truly "successful" student would be, a detriment to himself and his entire community, a crazed murderer, a useless son, a traitor to his people—the exact opposite of Fanny, Pratt's insipid version of the returned student. Zitkala-Ša's vision of the representative Indian— the student who truly absorbs and adopts the assimilative, social evolutionary ideology of the schools, who thinks of his or her own people as savage and uneducated heathens—is far different from Cook's. In her fiction,

Zitkala-Ša represents the representative Indian as culturally and spiritually dead, killed by the civilizing machine of the schools.

This time, Pratt places his indictment of Zitkala-Ša on the front page of the paper, under a headline, "'The Soft-Hearted Sioux'—Morally Bad." Again, what is published is a reprint from the vitriolic *Word Carrier*, prefaced by a comment from Pratt's editorial voice, angrily writing:

> All that Zitkalasa [*sic*] has in the way of literary ability and culture she owes to the good people, who, from time to time have taken her into their homes and hearts and given her aid. Yet not a word of gratitude or allusion to such kindness on the part of her friends has ever escaped her in any line of anything she has written for the public. By this course she injures herself and harms the educational work in progress for the race from which she sprang. In a list of educated Indians we have in mind, some of whom have reached higher altitudes in literary and professional lines than Zitkalasa, we know of no other case of such pronounced morbidness (1).

Zitkala-Ša is an educated Indian whose voice, now that she has found it, can no longer be controlled. It is a voice that demands its freedom to criticize the educational system itself, a freedom that Pratt's publication and his system of beliefs does not willingly allow. Through her own representations, Zitkala-Ša utterly rewrites the concept of the representative Indian, overturning its assumptions and exhibiting a repertoire of identities that disrupted and negated the reformers' zero-sum concept of identity. Pratt and the other reformers were confounded by trying to read such a woman, and their solution was to describe her as morbid and perverse. The last sentence in the *Word Carrier*'s condemnation of her story reads: "The story is written in an easy, engaging style, and has a certain dramatic power, but is morally bad" (1). Zitkala-Ša was an aberration according to their theories and was, therefore, immoral.

Zitkala-Ša, for her part, responded to the *Word Carrier*'s attack by turning the language the educators used to attack her directly against them in her essay "Why I Am a Pagan." She recounts that "a missionary paper [was] brought to my notice a few days ago, in which a 'Christian' pugilist commented upon a recent article of mine, grossly perverting the spirit of my pen."[68] This emphasis—from both sides—on perversion, morbidity, and immorality points to the deep ideological schism that divided Zitkala-Ša from the Friends of the Indian, and the conflict indicates what was at stake in the construction and representation of Indian identity at the turn of the century. In a nation where white people insisted Indians would eventually die out either physically or culturally, literate Indians who spoke as Indians to a wide audience were deviants from the evolutionary path. Because of their work—the stands they took against the utter obliteration of tribal life, culture, and religion—both Zitkala-Ša and Francis La Flesche were denounced and their representative status was questioned. Once they began to express their interest in and support of syncretic traditions or showed how they had managed to maintain Indian, Sioux, or Omaha identities in their repertoires, they were denounced. Their choice, according to the reformers, was either to be censored and forced to reproduce the party line in their writing, or to be censured and accused of working against the best interests of all Indians.

Why did a few essays and a memoir provoke such heated and intense responses on the part of Pratt and the boarding-school press? Because "narratives are not only structures of meaning, but structures of power as well," as Edward Bruner reminds us. "Stories construct an Indian self; narrative structures are constitutive as well as interpretive."[69] Indian identity became a contested sign in the struggle over representation—a struggle with very high stakes. The Friends of the Indian hoped to use the narrative of social evolutionism to predict and to create a future in which Indians would be entirely assimilated into white European American culture, leaving the land and resources they possessed available to whites and constantly affirming the superiority of white culture and civilization. This narrative would consolidate and enforce the power of European Americans.

La Flesche and Zitkala-Ša, among others, countered this narrative with their own story, which emphasized cultural continuity, creativity, and resistance to assimilation. Perhaps most significant to us, at the beginning of the twenty-first century, this Indian counternarrative used English as a language of Pan–Indian solidarity and created a pan-tribal Indian identity option that has become increasingly important in providing Indian people (including those who maintain strong tribal affiliations and identifications) with a voice in political and social issues. The schools did keep people from assuming certain roles within tribal life, as Zitkala-Ša shows in "The Soft-Hearted Sioux," but students like the La Flesches were also often able to bring back skills to their tribes that aided in their fight for cultural and political survival. One significant example is the case of the newspapers. Though boarding-school papers like the *Indian Helper* did not allow students to have editorial input, students were essential to their production. Since the *Indian Helper* alone had a circulation of around nine thousand, the apprentice printers were trained to publish a good-sized newspaper.[70] As apprentices, the printer boys learned every mechanical aspect of the trade, and many of them took their knowledge back to their communities and later played prominent roles in printing and producing tribal newspapers that voiced the concerns of the tribes rather than the concerns of the reformers.[71]

Additionally, Pan–Indian activists at the turn of the century learned to value newspapers as a tool of reform, with Native journalists using existing media outlets and also creating their own media vehicles to work toward their reform goals. They established periodicals like the *American Indian Magazine*, the publication of the Society of American Indians that Zitkala-Ša edited for several years, which would allow America to hear another side to the story of Indian survival. La Flesche's and Zitkala-Ša's texts display complicated repertoires of identity and show that, through their creativity and their flexible understanding of identity, boarding-school students represented themselves as much more than paper Indians or Cook's representative Indians, icons of cultural assimilation. Instead, they fashioned a creative space for self-articulation and for complex, syncretic identity formation out of a restrictive, potentially genocidal institution.

CHAPTER 4

REPERTOIRES OF REPRESENTATION IN BOARDING-SCHOOL-ERA AUTOBIOGRAPHY

B oarding-school educators and other assimilationists who ascribed to social evolutionary thought firmly believed that literacy in English was the "fair test of civilization," and its achievement by Indian students would reveal their loss of Indianness and attainment of American-ness.[1] Their theory further asserted that as the students acquired the representational tools of Western "civilization," their creative expression would be as completely transformed as their identities. This metamorphosis, then, would take place on the level of literary or representational form as well as on the level of content. Pratt's incredulity and anger at Zitkala-Ša's representations of her educational experiences and the control exerted by the Carlisle educators over student writing demonstrate just how much the educators had invested in Indian self-representations. While the educators sought to regulate literary production in English among those Indian people associated with the schools, in order to ensure that they portrayed themselves as appropriately "civilized" (such as Pratt encouraging La Flesche to write a story about a lone boy living off the reservation), the larger American public continued to clamor for "authentic" stories of "savage" Indian life. Editor H. W. Lanier told La Flesche that a book about his "wild life" would be a "great big thing" that "would make a stir" and "could hardly fail of [commercial] success."[2] While Pratt believed that the book he had proposed for La Flesche would demonstrate that author's assimilation and trans-formation, the editors at Doubleday and McClure hoped that his "wild" book would present the "authentic" Indianness of his past, though in a form that could be easily understood and digested by an American public conversant with Western literary conventions (in other words, the type of "authentic" story that could only be written by an "assimilated Indian"). So while American Indian autobiographers were often encouraged to write about their presumably past Indian identities, their very success as published authors evidenced their apparent assimilation into the ranks of American society.

Within this context, two Sioux writers associated with the Indian boarding schools published important autobiographical works. Zitkala-Ša's three autobiographical essays, first published in the *Atlantic Monthly* in 1900, along with a fourth autobiographical piece, short stories, and a political tract, all were collected as *American Indian Stories* in 1921. Charles Alexander Eastman (a Santee Dakota) was educated at the Santee Normal School (publisher of the *Word Carrier*) as well as at Beloit, Knox, and Dartmouth colleges and the Boston University Medical School before he worked as an agency physician at Pine Ridge during the Massacre at Wounded Knee, as outing agent and recruiter for Carlisle, and as Indian Secretary for the YMCA. Among his eleven books, Eastman produced two autobiographical volumes—*Indian Boyhood* (1902) and *From the Deep Woods to Civilization* (1916)—written with at least some collaboration with his white wife, Elaine Goodale Eastman, who briefly served as editor of the "Indian Department" of Hampton Institute's the *Southern Workman* and Carlisle's the *Red Man*.[3] Both Eastman and Zitkala-Ša presented more than one version of their life stories, and through their situational representations of their complex identities, they challenge not only turn-of-the-century understandings of identity construction and its expression in literature but also our contemporary sense of the relationship between identity, form, and authenticity in American Indian autobiography.

Until recently, publishers and literary critics have viewed American Indian autobiography as an oxymoron—first, because, if literate, an Indian was said to be assimilated, and therefore no longer capable of writing as an authentic Indian; second, because the concept of autobiography was viewed as a European phenomenon, and the urge to engage in life-writing was itself viewed as a sign of an obliterated—or at least irreparably compromised—Indian sensibility.[4] These closely overlapping modes of reasoning have led contemporary literary critics to examine American Indian autobiographical texts for markers of authenticity and to suspect the "authentic Indianness" in anyone using a "Western" form.[5] Thus, while most social scientific thought from Franz Boas onward has completely discredited social evolutionism, some of its most basic tenets still lurk in contemporary literary criticism of American Indian autobiography.[6] Even the field's best critics have tended to expect that the form alone can tell them all they need to know about the ideological and cultural positioning of the author. They have used the autobiographical writing to "fix" the author with an identity—the more "Westernized" the form, the more assimilated the author; the more "Indian" the form, the more traditional, conservative and Indian the author. Critics have applied this essentialist and reified understanding of the relationship between identity and form to both early and contemporary American Indian autobiography; but this critical praxis is especially problematic when used to evaluate autobiographies written in the boarding-school era, because it reproduces the scientifically unviable and politically reprehensible doctrines of the assimilationists. Eastman's and Zitkala-Ša's autobiographies prove that a linear theory of identity is too confining and reductive to apply to their work. They lived and wrote on geographical and ethnic borderlands, and on borderlands of identity. Their autobiographies demand a theory that takes these complexities into account by decoupling the supposed essential links between identity and literary form.

Paul Kroskrity's model of the repertoire of identity provides a very useful framework through which to understand the identity issues facing the boarding-school students. Most important, Kroskrity's theory highlights individuals' agency to select from and switch among identities to meet their needs and desires. "[T]he model naturally focuses attention on the *when, how* and *why* of switches within the repertoire of identity" (emphasis in the original).[7] Kroskrity's research among the trilingual Arizona Tewa further recognizes the multivocality of the expressive tools used to represent an identity. The English language, for example, could have a variety of associations for a given person—the language of bureaucracy, literacy, oppression, citizenship, Pan-Indian solidarity, and so on. At times, a person might speak English in order to express an identity as an American citizen. In other contexts, the use of English may express a pan-tribal Indian identity. Since a given expressive code will have a range of associations, each code must be interpreted as part of a communicative context for its meaning to be determined.[8] In this model, writing or speaking in English does not automatically mark a Native speaker or a text as assimilated or affiliated with Western hegemony.

Kroskrity's conception of "expressive code" can be extended to encompass literary form as well as language choice, since Eastman and Zitkala-Ša, bilingual and schooled in both Dakota/Nakota and European American literary traditions (like many boarding-school-era autobiographers), are choosing not only a language but also a particular set of formal conventions that aid them in expressing a situational identity. Their formal choices must be interpreted within the context of their communicative goals in order to understand their active role in shaping the textual representations of their identities, which are not fixed but, instead, mobile within a repertoire of choices.

Bringing this model to bear on Eastman's *Indian Boyhood* and Zitkala-Ša's "Impressions of an Indian Childhood" and "School Days of an Indian Girl" (read in dialogue with the authors' other autobiographical texts and self-representations) allows us to shift the focus from the preoccupation with authenticity that has too often accompanied studies of American Indian autobiography. Having explored the proliferation of student identities, we now examine each author's formal expression of only one identity from his or her repertoire, asking not if these autobiographies exhibit a self that is Indian or Westernized, but how and why Eastman and Zitkala-Ša present these particular versions of their lives. We see them choosing from among a repertoire of identities and a repertoire of autobiographical forms. His agency in choosing the form to write in illuminates the way that Eastman employs what critics have identified as traditional, preliterate forms of life-telling to create a self that is communal and representative—not to reflect an authentic, unassimilated Indianness, but to show that any Indian is as capable of success in the white world as he has been, which he sees as a post–Wounded Knee strategy of survival. Zitkala-Ša, on the other hand, employs more Western modes of life-telling, drawing on tropes of sentimentality to create a self that is individuated and autonomous. This formal choice does not function to reflect an essentially assimilated sensibility, but rather, to focus her own anger and resistance and to call the forces of the pro-assimilation movement into question.

AUTOBIOGRAPHICAL TRADITIONS

Brief overviews of both American Indian and European American or Western traditions of autobiography and their associated forms help explain the established, essentialized, and overgeneralized categories that have set "white" and "Indian" as absolute opposites, encouraging the compartmentalization of autobiographers and the forms they write in. Critics have used various patterns and understandings to make sense of the differences between American Indian and European American autobiographical form. These categories point toward the ways that critics seek to reify authors such as Eastman and Zitkala-Ša by evaluating them according to essentialized criteria.

Autobiography is the presentation of a self, or a life, through verbal art. This definition presupposes an understanding of a self or a life that can be presented, or represented in a telling. Hertha Wong argues that the Indian concept of the self differs strikingly from that of European Americans, and this difference is reflected in different methods of telling about the self. Warning that one must be careful not to overgeneralize and collapse diverse Native cultures into an undifferentiated mass, Wong claims:

> a native American concept of the self differs from a Western (or Euro-American) idea of self in that it is more inclusive. Generally, native people tend to see themselves first as family, clan, and tribal *members*, and second as discrete individuals. . . . There is the tendency to see identity in a spiritual context, to place one's self in relation to the cosmos. . . . Often, the sense of a relational self is connected intimately to a specific landscape. . . . In many cases, this identity is also dynamic; that is, it is in process, not fixed. (Emphasis in original)[9]

In contrast, the European American concept of self stresses individuality and a fixed, unified identity where relationality merits only secondary consideration. Arnold Krupat summarizes: Indian "conceptions of the self may be viewed as 'synecdochic,' i.e., based on part-to-whole relations, rather than 'metonymic,' i.e. as in the part-to-part relations that most frequently dominate Euramerican autobiography."[10] Krupat's collapsing of "conceptions of self" into "autobiography" in his comparison illustrates the near-ubiquitous critical assumption that differing senses of self require different forms of life-telling to represent them—an assumption certainly not limited to those who study American Indian autobiography.

Krupat explains; "the autobiographical project, as we usually understand it, is marked by ego-centric individualism, historicism, and writing.
These are all present in European and Euramerican culture after the
revolutionary last quarter of the eighteenth century."[11] Arguably, the
European American understanding of secular autobiography can be traced
back to Benjamin Franklin's *Autobiography*, written between 1771 and 1789,
which stresses the individual's improvement from a "lower" state of being
to a "higher"—for example, the rise from childhood to adulthood, from
rags to riches, from obscurity to fame—and offers evidence of a written
tradition of representing this type of linear, progressive self. Franklin is also
an innovator of "psychological autobiography," looking to his childhood to
explain the person he becomes. This sense of becoming, of childhood as a
formative stage, places an emphasis on turning points and moments of
epiphany (like Wordsworth's spots of time) as the structuring forces in a life's
linear trajectory. The protagonist of the Western autobiography is therefore
understood as unified, individual, and (importantly) autonomous.[12]

In *American Indian Autobiography*, David Brumble points toward genres
of life-telling that existed in pre-contact America—genres that significantly
differ from standard European American autobiography. Brumble's contribution is important because it contradicts earlier critical assumptions that
Native literatures had no way to tell life histories before the coming of
Europeans.[13] Brumble locates precedents for autobiography in traditional
oral Native literature, identifying six "fairly distinct kinds of pre-literate
autobiographical narratives"—coup tales, tales of warfare and hunting,
self-examinations, self-vindications, educational narratives and tales of the
acquisition of powers.[14] To these six, Hertha Wong adds vision-stories and
naming practices, as well as a range of pictographic autobiographical
forms. For the most part, such autobiographical narratives are brief and
episodic, focusing more on action than analysis and seldom depicting an
entire life.[15] In fact, Brumble claims that "in general, the more tightly unified
the published autobiography of a non-literate Indian, the more likely we
are to be seeing the sensibility of the Anglo editor at work"—here clearly
linking the form with the identification and positioning of the author.[16]
Both Brumble and Wong extend this reasoning beyond the transcribed oral
narratives of non-literate Indians and apply it to the work of literate,
English-speaking Indians as well. As Brumble warns the critic of Indian
autobiography: "To confine ourselves to written autobiography—if I may

be allowed a useful redundancy—would encourage us in a false sense of just how the literate Indian autobiographers came to write as they did."[17] Their status as "Indian autobiographers" depends, at least in part, on their ability to reveal an "Indian" self through "Indian" forms. The assumption that Brumble makes, then, is that shared autobiographical forms point to a shared "Indianness," though in order to reach such an opinion he must, as Greg Sarris explains, invent "'an Indian' . . . [by identifying] anything non-recognizable or unfamiliar . . . as authentic, as Indian as opposed to Euro-American."[18] Working with an "Indian–European American" dichotomy, these critical assumptions flatten repertoires of identity and representation into the dualistic worldview of the Friends of the Indian.

Like the Friends of the Indian, scholars have too often assumed that American Indian writers are automatically and essentially transformed by contact with the English language and have too often insisted that Indian authors are held in bondage by literary form rather than actively choosing from a repertoire of options within a particular context to represent a chosen version of the self. Generalizing from his reading of Charles Eastman's *From the Deep Woods to Civilization,* David Murray contends: "It is tempting to see this situation [what he calls Eastman's 'linguistic' impasse] as paradigmatic of a certain historical stage in Indian writing, in which the enabling means of expression, and of the creation of a self, are also deeply implicated in the destruction of any self rooted in a traditional past."[19] Murray gives in to this temptation, claiming that "Eastman was able to write about an Indian past only once it had been placed under erasure by situating it within a Romantic framework."[20] In other words, using the English language, and a Western literary form, necessarily indicates the obliteration of any traditional identity. In fact, for Murray as for the Friends of the Indian, it is the process of writing itself—part of a "historical stage" or level of "progression"—that kills the Indian to make the "man" that is the product of Western autobiographical form. Murray mourns that the savage-civilized opposition "is just not usable to describe what has happened" to Eastman, and, in fact, "can oversimplify a complex process into a series of crude oppositions," and he insists that in Eastman's work, which is at the mercy of this language, "Indians inevitably are presented as 'other.'"[21]

The passive voice deletes Eastman's agency and subjects him to the (supposedly) inexorably transforming properties of the English language.

At its core, this belief—reflected also in contemporary anthropological assertions that "the only truly authentic voices that document the American Indian past come to us in native languages accessible solely through translation"[22]—is as reductive as the savage-civilized opposition Murray decries. It more accurately reflects the theories of boarding-school educators and policy makers than the reality of English-language education in the schools, a process Spack labels "translingualism" in order to describe "the creativity of writers and intellectuals who cross-culturally appropriate, recreate, and critique a language."[23]

No doubt, contemporary scholars of American Indian literature do not view themselves as ideologically similar to the Friends of the Indian, and most would find such an affiliation repugnant. Indeed, much of the work of the scholars cited here celebrates the continuance of American Indian literature. Through their groundbreaking studies in the field these scholars have kept Indian autobiography visible within the academy and have enabled further interpretation and theorizing of these important texts. But by presupposing an inflexible relationship between identity and form, even seminal theorists of American Indian autobiography can be trapped into approaching the texts with strictly defined ideas about what type of self can be associated with Native autobiography, and what type of self (or self-representation) excludes a "Native consciousness."

Sarris criticizes literary scholars for their tendency to ignore the agency of Indian "informants" in collaborative autobiography (but he does not extend his critique to their treatment of self-authored texts such as those discussed here):

> What these scholars do not seem to see is that while purportedly defending Indians and enlightening others about them, they replicate in practice that which characterizes not only certain non-Indian editors' manner of dealing with Indians but also that of an entire European and Euro-American populace of which these editors and scholars are a part. The Indians are absent or they are strategically removed from the territory, made safe, intelligible on the colonizer's terms.[24]

In *Keeping Slug Woman Alive*, Sarris offers a method of reading that counteracts this critical "removal" by seeking to understand the motivations and innovations of both parties in a collaborative text. Scholars of American

Indian autobiography must develop a critical praxis that also tries to make present the agency of authors in autobiographies authored solely by Native writers. Critics must decouple form and identity when studying American Indian autobiography, acknowledging that turn-of-the-century Native writers did not always have equal access to and freedom to choose from any and every possible literary form. Power relations at the turn of the century certainly did set limits on the texts Native writers could publish conventionally since their work needed to be comprehensible to the marketplace, engaging with, if not agreeing with, mainstream paradigms (and eastern publishing houses recognized little market in, say, Dakota-language texts). But these authors still worked dynamically with a cross-cultural repertoire of literary forms. Eastman and Zitkala-Ša make use of several of the forms or codes associated above with Western or Indian autobiography; but by hybridizing them, by demonstrating a flexible understanding of the situational nature of identity, and by actively choosing forms to represent situational selves with specific political and communicative goals, these boarding-school-era Indian autobiographers upset critical expectations and resist removal from the literary terrain.

CHARLES ALEXANDER EASTMAN'S *INDIAN BOYHOOD*

Charles Alexander Eastman's repertoire of identity was extremely complex, and in fact impossible to enumerate fully. After receiving a Dakota education from the time of his birth in 1858 until he moved to the Christian Dakota settlement at Flandreau, South Dakota, with his father in 1872 (the period of his life covered in *Indian Boyhood*, his first autobiographical volume), Eastman spent the next eighteen years as a student in a variety of European American educational institutions. He was affiliated with Carlisle and Hampton through his own work and through that of his wife, who held a number of teaching and administrative positions in the federal Indian schools. Associated with many aspects of Indian education and considered by many to be "the most famous Indian of his day," Eastman was highly visible to both Indian and non-Indian people in a number of roles—from Dakota hunter and warrior-in-training to doctor, camp counselor, Indian Bureau employee, husband in a mixed-race marriage, and author.[25] Even at any single moment in his life, Eastman inhabited more than one identity. The purpose here is not to catalog these identities but rather, to

Fig. 11. Charles Alexander Eastman in "citizen's clothes." National Anthropological Archives, Smithsonian Institution, negative no. 3463.

show that Eastman in fact possessed a full repertoire of identities, and then to examine closely the manner in which—and the purpose for which—he articulates one of those identities in *Indian Boyhood*.

Eastman's Perilous Repertoire of Identity

At times, as with La Flesche or Zitkala-Ša, the possession of a repertoire of identities could be subversive or empowering, while in other circumstances this multiplicity was at best uncomfortable, at worst dangerous. Such is the case with the multiplicity of identity options Eastman exhibited in his first job as a medical doctor. He was a government physician on the Pine Ridge Reservation in the winter of 1890. At Pine Ridge—and inevitably at Wounded Knee—Eastman was both a Dakota Indian man experienced at witnessing government violence toward his people, and a government employee, pledged to uphold the institutions that sanctioned and engaged in the massacre of Indian people.

Fig. 12. Eastman in Dakota regalia. National Anthropological Archives, Smithsonian Institution, negative no. 3462a.

Eastman arrived on the Pine Ridge Reservation in November 1890, and though he did not feel out of the ordinary, his multiple identities were highly visible. "In 1890 a 'white doctor' who was also an Indian was something of a novelty, and I was afterward informed that there were many and diverse speculations abroad as to my success or failure in this new rôle, but at the time I was unconscious of an audience," he wrote in *From the Deep Woods*.[26] Pine Ridge in 1890 was a difficult place to hold both "white doctor" and "Indian" identities at once. The Ghost Dance was at the peak of its influence on this desolate Lakota reservation, where food shortages and the government's refusal to fulfill treaty obligations had encouraged hungry, angry, disillusioned people to take up a new religion that promised relief.[27] Eastman immediately experienced the poverty and neglect of the reservation and the agency. His ramshackle office came nowhere near the sanitary conditions a white doctor would expect, and "everything was covered with a quarter of an inch or so of fine Dakota dust." Eastman's response indicates the affinity he felt with the people of Pine Ridge: "This did not disconcert me, however, as I myself was originally Dakota dust!" (77). Strongly feeling his cultural and linguistic connection to the Lakota, Eastman's assignment to the reservation was a homecoming with a twist. He had returned feeling like a tribal member, but he held a position of governmental authority at a time and in a place where "government" and "Indian" identities were highly polarized. Throughout his first weeks at Pine Ridge Agency, Eastman constantly crossed between identities that for others were drawn like lines in the sand. He made a point of "examining each patient and questioning him in plain Sioux—no interpreter needed!" (81)—clearly a contrast to his white predecessor who merely doled out medication through a window opening cut into the wall of the physician's quarters (78). Eastman also made an allegiance that was unthinkable for any other Sioux man at Pine Ridge at the time—he became engaged to marry Elaine Goodale, the white superintendent of Indian Schools in the Dakotas and Nebraska. Eastman recognized how his matrimonial decisions were refracted by the tensions at the agency. "For me, at that critical time, there was an inward struggle as well as the threat of outward conflict," he wrote. "And I could not but recall what my 'white mother' had said jokingly one day, referring to my pleasant friendships with many charming Boston girls, 'I know one Sioux who has not been conquered, and I shall not rest till I hear of his capture!'" (105). Acceding to the "conquering" of his heart by a white assimilationist educator on the very eve of the invasive military action that would later be heralded as the "closing of the frontier," Eastman announced his engagement to Goodale on Christmas Day, four days before the massacre.

The manifold loyalties that these actions and affiliations imply placed Eastman in a conspicuous and dangerous position in the days surrounding the massacre. He recounts an incident in which only a passionate speech from the Lakota leader American Horse kept a crowd of "wild Indians" from killing the Indian police. According to Eastman: "It is likely that

[American Horse] saved us all from massacre, for the murder of the police, who represented the authority of the Government, would surely have been followed by a general massacre. It is a fact that those Indians who upheld the agent were in quite as much danger from their wilder brethren as were the whites, indeed it was said that the feeling against them was even stronger" (95). Placed in peril because of his affiliation with the government, Eastman was similarly held in suspicion by government officials for his ties to the Lakota community. Although he tried to convince the agent not to send for the troops who would eventually perpetrate the massacre, "the agent had telegraphed to Fort Robinson for troops before he made a pretense of consulting us Indians [who worked for the government], and they were already on their way to Pine Ridge" (98). In the days following the massacre, Eastman found himself in particular demand by the wounded, the "tortured Indians [who] would scarcely allow a man in uniform to touch them," even though "the army surgeons were more than ready to help once their own men had been cared for" (110). Eastman led an uneasy search and rescue party made up of "a hundred civilians, ten or fifteen of whom were white men," hoping to find survivors at the scene of the massacre (111). As the extent of the brutality became clear, the white members of the search party feared for their lives, and Eastman was placed in the position of reassuring them. When all members of the search party feared that small groups of warriors might attack them as they brought the few survivors back to the agency, it was Eastman who was chosen to ride alone to the agency to gather an army unit to escort the caravan. This image—Eastman alone and in danger as he rode on the line between identities—starkly portrays the imminent danger he faced from real-life implications of what might seem like merely theoretical issues concerning identity and representational options (113–14). His own statement about his emotions at that time is muted, glancing over the surface of his turmoil: "All this was a severe ordeal for one who had so lately put all his faith in the Christian love and lofty ideals of the white man. Yet I passed no hasty judgment, and was thankful that I might be of some service and relieve even a small part of the suffering" (114).

Clearly, then, along with his heartsickness at the army's brutality, Charles Eastman experienced pain because of his multiple identity choices, and yet felt unwilling to discard entirely one of his identities to immerse himself fully in another. He would neither deny his Dakota or Indian identities nor dissociate himself from Western medicine and its accompanying role and position. However, in his first autobiographical book, *Indian Boyhood* (in contrast to his self-representation in *From the Deep Woods*), Eastman attempted to achieve rhetorically what he did not accomplish in actuality. Through the use of tribal autobiographical genres, Eastman presents the myth of a unified, progressive self—a representative, relational self that could serve as a model for the linear progression of all Indian people. The danger Eastman felt at Wounded Knee stretched into the decades following that tragic event and left lingering effects on something so apparently removed as autobiographical form. Wounded Knee was a "severe ordeal" that not only forever changed Eastman himself but also deeply marked his choice of self-representational strategies and contributed to his production of what Malea Powell calls a "rhetoric of survivance," a use of language directed to enable a simultaneous and complex combination of survival and resistance—in fact, for Eastman, survival *as* resistance.[28] The specific manifestation of the self in *Indian Boyhood*, shows how Eastman actively put autobiographical form to work to represent *one* identity from his repertoire—for bounded political ends in the post–Wounded Knee world where, having borne witness to violent attempts to exterminate Native people, Eastman sought alternative strategies for resistance and survival.

A "Representative" Indian Boyhood

In *Indian Boyhood,* Eastman uses coup tales, naming stories, hunting and war stories, and educational stories (genres identified by Brumble and Wong as "Indian" forms of life-telling) to represent a self that is diffused and relational.[29] Rather than simply presenting his own life story, Eastman gathers together traditional stories and songs as well as ethnographic data and binds this information to stories of his own life, capturing what he describes as the last moments of his people's tribal existence. The loosely chronological volume is episodic and does not possess the tightness of structure that Brumble attributes to the hand of the white editor, despite the editorial input of Elaine Goodale Eastman.[30] Accordingly, one might argue that *Indian Boyhood* is itself a reflection of Eastman's Indianness. Such a line of thinking has led some critics to read the book's preface as an "aberration," Brumble reports.[31] This preface begins: "The North American Indian was the highest type of pagan and uncivilized man. He possessed not only a superb physique but a remarkable mind. But the Indian no longer exists as a natural and free man. Those remnants which now dwell upon the reservations present only a sort of tableau—a fictitious copy of the past." Clearly, this is not the beginning of a book written by a man who identifies as an Indian without qualification. While the "remnants" remain on the reservations, Eastman represents himself as the best of this "highest type of uncivilized man," elevated to the level of the civilized due to his education, his religion, and his very desire to leave the reservation behind, to recognize that the lifestyle he is about to discuss belongs in the past. Eastman's goals are clear—"these fragmentary recollections of [his] thrilling wild life" are set down not only as a reminder of the fact that they are in the past, but also as an indicator of how far he has come, and how any Indian who does not want to be part of a static, lifeless tableau can achieve success in a world in which tribal life is increasingly constrained by U.S. hegemony.[32]

Although the blunt power of that hegemony was made brutally visible to Eastman at Wounded Knee, he chooses to focus on a much earlier period of his life in *Indian Boyhood*. And yet Eastman's early years—which he describes as idyllic, and which, critics have pointed out, are represented as largely isolated from white contact—are framed in *Indian Boyhood* by another violent encounter—the Sioux Uprising of 1862. When Eastman was only a four-year-old boy, a small number of Santee Dakota people in Minnesota, starving because of the loss of tribal land and delayed annuity payments, engaged in violent resistance, a struggle that was called, at the time, "the Sioux Massacre," a label intended to refer to the killing of white settlers by the Dakota. More than three hundred settlers were killed in the Dakota attempt to reclaim their land, but the U.S. government diverted a large fighting force from the Civil War to hunt down and punish the Sioux people, indiscriminately displacing, killing, or imprisoning thousands of Santees, Yanktonais, Hunkpapas, and other Sioux bands, most of whom had played no role in the uprising, actions that suggest this conflict could be viewed as a massacre of Sioux people—punished and killed without regard to their particular band or national identity—as well.[33] The Dakota Uprising had a huge impact on Eastman's life. The Dakota were pushed almost entirely out of Minnesota, and the Wahpeton band's exodus into Manitoba was "a journey still vividly remembered by all our family."[34] Eastman's father, Many Lightnings, was imprisoned, sentenced to death, and it was assumed executed, in the wake of the uprising.

Eastman's isolated childhood, in which he was brought up and educated in Dakota ways by his grandmother Uncheedah and his uncle Mysterious Medicine, was the result not of pristine, pre-contact "authenticity" but of violent colonial conflict, a conflict expressed only quickly and quietly at the beginning of *Indian Boyhood*. The majority of the book relates the young boy's peaceful immersion in Dakota culture until the time that Many Lightnings returned to the Wahpeton, revealing to his shocked relatives that he had escaped death, converted to Christianity, taken the name Jacob Eastman, and moved to a settlement of Christian Dakota at Flandreau.

The title of *Indian Boyhood* points to Eastman's concern with his status as a representative Indian. "Indian"—as opposed to "Santee Dakota," or "Sioux," or even "native"—was a marked term at the turn of the century, indicative not only of publishing conventions but also of the growing Pan-Indian movement. The term itself, and the collective identity it refers to, were not indigenous, of course. Hertzberg notes: "On the whole, it was a somewhat fragile identity, lacking in the rich and deeply-rooted associations of tribal identity. The tribe represented the way of life of the people; *Indian* was a way of differentiating aborigine from European."[35] In this sense, Eastman's was not an Indian boyhood at all, but a Santee Dakota boyhood. His choice of the term "Indian" in the title is indicative of the social forces (of which he was a shaper) that were moving Native people toward a collective identity. Viewing himself as a spokesperson for Indians, Eastman was active in the Society of American Indians, the most prominent of the Pan-Indian societies that sprang up in the first years of the twentieth century. A champion of the Dawes Act, he actively worked to encourage an Indian identity, which would allow one to belong to and have pride in "the race" while potentially viewing tribally oriented and reservation life as part of the past.[36]

Yet, Eastman's autobiography is "synecdochic," as much about his tribe as it is about him, for despite the pan-tribal flavor of the title, the contents include ethnographic information that is distinctly Dakota. One example of the detailed ethnography he provides is his description of a ritual known as the Maiden's Feast. Eastman unfolds a drama in which he is not, himself, involved, describing the Dakota social event where the virginity of unmarried girls and women is proclaimed and affirmed by the community. Eastman's description of the event is strikingly similar to an episode in Ella Cara Deloria's novelistic ethnography, *Waterlily*.[37] In both accounts, the girls approach a red-painted rock and arrows stuck upright into the ground and swear an oath of purity. As they gather around the rock and arrows, their claims to virginity may be challenged by any man who knew them to be "unworthy" (Eastman, 183). Both accounts portray the tense moment in which a man challenges a young woman. In Deloria's account, this accusation is true and the woman is disgraced—not so much for having lost her virginity as for having presented herself as something she was not.[38] In Eastman's version, however, the accusation is false, the resentful challenge of a spurned lover, and the woman's honor is upheld.

Both Deloria and Eastman are rather self-consciously animating tribal customs in these accounts. That is one of the purposes of *Waterlily*—to present ethnographic information about the Dakota through a fiction that would bring the scholarship alive. Eastman, too, wants us to be able to experience the culture of his tribe vividly. While he clearly feels a sense of pride in the actions of his people, Eastman also turns this tale to his larger purposes. He ends his anecdote by emphasizing; "Each maid, as she departed once more, took her oath to remain pure until she should meet her husband" (187). His goal is to display the affinity of the Dakota for the Christian virtue of chastity. By including this tale, Eastman hopes to show again the way that tribal life, though seemingly passing, can provide the values necessary to allow Native young people to become good civilized Christians. In fact, they already practice Christian morals, but unknowingly. It is important to remember that Eastman is not involved in this scenario in any way. He does not even describe himself as a witness to the event, and for these reasons it may seem to be an odd incident to include in an autobiographical work. Though this moment is not directly related to his own, individual life, however, it exemplifies the morality of his tribe, proving that the representative Indian—male or female—is but one step away from being a member of "civilized" society, since Native people already possess one important element of civilization—an (unnamed) Christian ethos.

From the first pages of his autobiography, Eastman's concept of the communal or representative status of the self becomes apparent in the way he moves between first- and third-person narration of his life. The following description of his treatment by his grandmother is but one example of this shifting: "[My grandmother] made all my scanty garments and my tiny moccasins with a great deal of taste. It was said by all that I could not have had more attention had my mother been living. Uncheedah (grandmother) was a great singer. Sometimes, when Hakadah [Eastman's boyhood name] wakened too early in the morning, she would sing to him" (7). "I" becomes "he" in the course of just two sentences, shifting the perspective from a first-person insider's account to a third-person observer's report.

Hertha Wong states that "there seems to be no pattern" to Eastman's pronoun shifts, perceptively associating this behavior with his "double vision," which allows him to be "part anthropological observer . . . and part Santee Sioux participant."[39] In addition to portraying a double vision, these shifts act as a distancing device that serves other objectives beyond anthropological observation. So emotionally and intellectually distant from his childhood identity that he refers to himself in the third person, Eastman uses the distance to create picturesque scenes. The child-Eastman is, in fact, set in a series of tableaux resembling the preface's vision of reservation Indians. An example of the picturesque quality of such scenes is Eastman's description of his first offering to "The Great Mystery." "It was [his grandmother's] custom to see to this when each of her children attained the age of eight summers," Eastman relates. "They had all been celebrated as hunters and warriors among their tribe . . . because she had brought them early to the notice of the 'Great Mystery'" (102). His grandmother requests that he sacrifice his dog, Ohitika, his close companion, and urges: "Come, . . . let us go to the place [of sacrifice]. When the last words were uttered, Hakadah did not seem to hear them. He was simply unable to speak. To a civilized eye, he would have appeared at that moment like a little copper statue. . . . He swallowed two or three big mouthfuls of heart-ache and the little warrior was master of the situation" (107). As immovable as a statue, the young boy is iconic—a static representation of inert tribalism to the "civilized eye" of his audience. And by placing the scene in the third person, Eastman places himself among the "civilized" audience who can turn a discriminating eye on composed images of tribal life. Notably, Eastman does not mention the fact that after killing his dog in sacrifice, he swallowed not only two or three big mouthfuls of heartache, but also two or three big mouthfuls of dog, since the ritual would have included the consumption of the offering. This omission demonstrates his desire to construct a tableau only displaying those Dakota customs that could be integrated easily with white sensibilities and stereotypes of a certain type of "noble savage" stoicism.[40] Unlike Frances La Flesche, whose goal in *The Middle Five* was to show the development of an entire repertoire of identities, Eastman carefully composes the particular version of "Indian" identity that he chooses to display.

Viewing himself through the "civilized eye" he has since obtained, Eastman the literate author distances himself from the "little warrior" he was and portrays the events of his childhood as clearly representative. Hakadah/Eastman is giving his first meaningful offering to the Great Mystery as his relatives have done before him, and as any boy who would be successful will do. Since his childhood experiences are only what any child in his tribe would have gone through, his subsequent success can and should be replicated by any member of his tribe who can achieve a civilized (i.e., off-reservation) environment. Anyone can be a "savage" little Indian boy if he is living in the deep woods, Eastman seems to be saying, but, by the same token, anyone, especially any Indian, can become a "civilized," contributing member of hegemonic American society if only he or she is taken from the tribal setting, sent to schools in the East, recognized as a citizen, and taught how to live as whites live.

Eastman allegorizes his potential for dramatic change in the story of his naming rituals. Wong notes that nineteenth-century Plains Indian names can be considered to be "serial but non-linear 'autobiographical acts.' . . . In Plains Indian traditions the proper name might reflect accomplishments of the past, aspirations for the future, or connections to family, to clan or to the spiritual world in the present."[41] Charles Eastman's names can be read as serial but nonlinear connections to his family and to his tribe, and in that sense as acts of traditional native autobiography. At his birth Eastman was given the name Hakadah, meaning "the pitiful last," because he was "so unfortunate as to be the youngest of five children who, soon after [he] was born, were left motherless" (4). Hakadah was called by the humiliating name until he "should earn a more dignified and appropriate name" (4). The moment of redesignation came when Eastman was four years old, when he was named Ohiyesa, or "winner" to commemorate his band's victory in a lacrosse game (38–39). At the moment the name is conferred, a tribal medicine man tells the boy: "'Be brave, be patient and thou shalt always win! Thy name is Ohiyesa'" (45). The name, therefore, represents both his band's victory within a traditional context (the lacrosse game) and Ohiyesa's potential for future success. While he later changed his name to Charles Eastman, he continued to use Ohiyesa as a comment on his identity in white society, identifying himself as Charles Alexander

Eastman (Ohiyesa) on the title pages of his books, juxtaposing the English and Dakota languages as he claimed authorship.

Eastman's Dakota names reveal his connection to his tribe in at least two ways. They not only tie him to concrete moments of familial and communal significance but also serve as allegorical markers for the transformational potential of the people. Eastman saw himself as the pitiful last of his immediate family, and of his tribe's whole way of life. Born at what he considered to be the end of tribal existence, Eastman believed that the "pitiful" remainders of a once proud, though uncivilized, people could transform themselves into "winners" in the white world, and he kept his name to remind himself of his own transformation as well as his belief in the ability of other Indians to become winners in America. Telling the story of his namings, and showing how Ohiyesa was not only an individual moniker but also a community achievement, helps him to reflect his representative status.

While he cherished his Dakota name, Eastman found it necessary to use an English name to participate as an adult in hegemonic American society. Eastman valued the "life of the forest" for young boys; he was very active in the Boy Scouts movement and "described Indian life as the prototype for the Boy Scouts and the Campfire Girls."[42] But the form of *Indian Boyhood* makes it clear that Eastman wanted to equate life as an adult with life lived in white society in 1902. Brumble notes that Eastman's autobiography reflected the anthropological discourse of social evolutionist beliefs in the progression and evolution of the races (ideas that were at the height of their influence when Eastman was writing *Indian Boyhood*), whereas David Carlson emphasizes that Eastman's text is filtered through the legal discourse of allotment, which specified that individual ownership of land was one way that Indian people would grow "out of boyish 'savagery' into a more 'mature,' civilized form of identity."[43] Through these related lenses, Eastman portrayed his tribe as childish and naïve: "Such was the Indian's wild life. . . . They are children of Nature, and occasionally she whips them with the lashes of experience, yet they are forgetful and careless" (17).

Indeed, the "lashes of experience"—the Sioux Uprising and the Wounded Knee Massacre—that serve to mark Eastman's fall from innocence to experience suggest the pain and uncertainty he associated with the future of Indian nations. His autobiography links Indianness with boyhood, professing a belief that the "child-races" could mature with the guidance of the "adult" white race.[44] For Eastman, the movement "from the deep woods to civilization" was inevitable—because it was the safe path of survival—for Indians at the turn of the century. The end of *Indian Boyhood* reflects this inevitability. Eastman is reunited with his father Many Lightnings or Jacob Eastman who, although presumed dead, has escaped execution and has chosen to live according to the customs of the whites. Jacob Eastman's return is shocking, but his determination that his son Ohiyesa will move to Flandreau with him is not. The boy simply leaves his tribe and the rest of his family, with scarcely a backward glance.

It is instructive to compare the ending of *Indian Boyhood* with the beginning of *From the Deep Woods to Civilization*, both of which describe Eastman's moment of leave-taking. In *Indian Boyhood*, the transition takes only four pages of text, beginning with the discovery that Eastman's father was in fact not killed by the American soldiers, as the family had thought, and ending with Eastman joining his father in his new, "assimilated" community:

> In a few days we started for the States. I felt as if I were dead and traveling to the Spirit Land; for now all my old ideas were to give place to new ones, and my life was to be entirely different from that of the past. . . . Later in the fall we reached the civilized settlement at Flandreau, South Dakota, where my father and some others dwelt among the whites. Here my wild life came to an end, and my school days began. (288–89)

With these words, and with the start of his Western education, the book ends. Aside from a briefly startling encounter with a train, which Eastman quickly associates with the "fire-boat walks-on-mountains" of which he has already heard, there is little sense of discomfort, fear, or sadness (289). Although he speaks of his journey as a death, it is not necessarily negative since it is as much a rebirth as a loss. The shift is immediate and, for the most part, as painless and natural as social evolutionists claimed it could be. And yet here, as in his description of the Maiden's Feast, Eastman also wants to emphasize that elements of civilization are already known to the Dakota, to suggest that his movement from tribal life to civilization is immediate and abrupt, and yet somehow already comfortable and familiar. In contrast, at the beginning of *From the Deep Woods* Eastman tells this story again, but this time he informs us that his grandmother accompanied him and his father, making the transition less abrupt, and he reports that before he leaves his tribe he hears a voice within him warning him that his father's life among the whites is "A false life! a treacherous life!"[45] This voice is not heard in *Indian Boyhood*. Indeed, it cannot be heard if we are to accept without question the move into white society.

The supplemental voice of *From the Deep Woods* confirms that *Indian Boyhood* was not the only way Eastman's childhood could be told. Although it follows a chronological pattern of development and includes more "self-reflection" than in *Indian Boyhood*, Eastman's second volume of autobiography does not use these generic markers of Western autobiography to represent the same, "progressive" self that he portrayed in *Indian Boyhood*. Writing in 1916, at a safer distance from the dangers posed by Wounded Knee to those who crossed the borders of identity, and at the commencement of the U.S. entry into World War I (when Indian reformers were fighting for Indian people to be recognized as full members of American society and were subsequently disillusioned),[46] Eastman uses the linear, progressive format of *From the Deep Woods* as a subtle critique of the failure of European Americans to live up to their own perceptions of their "fully evolved," providential "civilization." While a repertoire of identities that includes a sustained affiliation—no matter how mediated or problematic—with Dakota people and Indian communities can be less than empowering for Eastman, he nonetheless struggles to articulate this multiplicity. The final paragraph of *From the Deep Woods* most strongly belies the "progression" suggested in its title. Eastman concludes this later version of his life with the statement: "I am an Indian; and while I have learned much from civilization, for which I am grateful, I have never lost my Indian sense of right and justice. . . . Nevertheless, so long as I live, I am an American."[47] Murray describes Eastman as "vacillat[ing] from one spurious identity to another" in this passage, but it seems he is instead (and at times uncomfortably) displaying a repertoire of identities that cannot—and need not—be synthesized into one, fixed, unified identity.[48] As Philip Deloria states in his brief but perceptive reading of Eastman in *Playing Indian*:

> "He lived out a hybrid life, distinct in its Indianness, but also cross-cultural and assimilatory. By channeling both a Dakota past and an American-constructed Indian Other through his material body—from mind to pen to paper to book to Boy Scout—Eastman

made it ever more difficult to pinpoint the cultural locations of Dakotas and Americans, reality and mimetic reality, authenticity and inauthenticity."[49]

The representative self that this complicated individual portrays in *Indian Boyhood* differs from the self he represents in the later autobiography, which continues to support a Christian worldview but begins to associate Christian behavior with Dakota culture in opposition to a European American culture, which continually falls short of Christian ideals. In one of his most forceful statements on this subject, in *The Soul of the Indian* (1911), Eastman proclaims: "It is my personal belief, after thirty-five years' experience of it, that there is no such thing as 'Christian civilization.' I believe that Christianity and modern civilization are opposed and irreconcilable, and that the spirit of Christianity and of our ancient religion is essentially the same."[50] Continuing to negotiate the tension between his Christian faith and Western education and his Dakota values and kinship, Eastman's writings throw into question the stability of the binary categories—Christianity, private ownership of property, English language literacy, and "civilization" in opposition to native religions and cultures, tribal land claims, ancestral languages, and "savagery"—that both the Friends of the Indian and subsequent literary critics have used to attempt to fix his identity and define his textual production. Through this deconstruction of binary categories (as Erik Peterson notes), Eastman's writing challenges "the moralistic charge of selling out often directed toward ethnic writers, particularly successful ones," and urges critics toward what Powell defines as "a [reimagined] scholarly relationship to writings by Indian peoples, one that hears the multiplicities in those writings."[51] A critical praxis that listens for and acknowledges Eastman's multiplicity will recognize that Eastman is choosing from among a repertoire of available forms to represent a situational identity. Eastman's various self-representations are not, therefore, contradictory but are deployed for differing purposes. Acknowledging this repertoire highlights Eastman's agency and reveals how *Indian Boyhood* entered the discourse on race and the future of the Indian at the turn of the century in a particular way and for the specific purpose of proving the Indian's potential for survival through assimilation in the years immediately following the horror of Wounded Knee.

ZITKALA-ŠA'S "IMPRESSIONS OF AN INDIAN CHILDHOOD" AND "SCHOOL DAYS OF AN INDIAN GIRL"

Eastman writes and publishes under his English name juxtaposed with his Dakota name (usually with "Ohiyesa" in parentheses following "Charles Alexander Eastman"), but Zitkala-Ša makes a different selection from her repertoire of identities when presenting herself as a writer. Although she uses Western forms, her decision to publish under her self-given Lakota name rather than under her birth name indicates that she is writing as a Sioux woman, attempting to identify herself more firmly with the continuation of traditional language, ideas, and people. Her act of self-naming asserts control over an "Indian" autobiographical form and is evidence that she was able to use tribal languages as meaningful and vital expressive codes.[52] The Lakota name on the by-line of an English-language autobiography is an early indicator of the representational complexities of Zitkala-Ša's work.

Zitkala-Ša passed her childhood in a world of accommodation to white presence. Her family's struggle to adjust to a changing world (they were successfully adaptive, though frequently bitter) forms an important theme in her representation of her childhood, and her mother's selective acceptance of Western material objects provides a model for Zitkala-Ša's active selection of Western literary forms. As she writes in "An Indian Teacher among Indians," for instance, although her mother "meant always to give up her own customs for such of the white man's ways as pleased her, she made only compromises."[53] Zitkala-Ša, too, is aware of the options available to her and chooses among them to please herself. One characteristic of European American autobiographical form that she selects for use is an emphasis on how childhood experiences mark the adult. Her childhood was full of fear of white aggression and expansion, as when Zitkala-Ša tells her mother in "Indian Childhood" that she looks forward to the day she will be grown-up enough to fetch water from the spring, and her mother replies, "'If the paleface does not take away from us the river we drink'" (9). Her mother's sadness and bitterness at what she and her people have lost clearly mark the child and impress her deeply. We see in her later autobiographical essay "An Indian Teacher among Indians" that many of the elements of this early scene of uncertainty about the land and disgust at the white invaders are replicated, as when she visits her mother, who shows her the new white settlements and warns her: "'My daughter, beware of the paleface. . . . He is the hypocrite who reads with one eye "Thou shalt not kill," and with the other gloats upon the sufferings of the Indian race'" (93–94). Her mother's powerful curses against the white settlers are an important part of her daughter's "inheritance of a marvelous endurance [that] enabled me to bend without breaking" (85).

We see throughout her essays how her dual inheritance of anger and strength empowers Zitkala-Ša to shape her representation of her adulthood into a response to her childhood uncertainty about the future of her land and her people. Zitkala-Ša is not using Western autobiographical forms to present a self that is assimilated and Westernized, however. Although she and her family have adapted elements of European American culture into their lives, they have not simultaneously discarded Yankton or "Indian" cultural markers and values. They have not experienced, in short, a zero-sum transformation of identity. Instead, they have incorporated Western accouterments into their repertoires of identity for the purposes of cultural survival. Just as her mother uses canvas to make a tipi when buffalo hide becomes unavailable, Zitkala-Ša uses these Western autobiographical forms to present a sympathetic and sentimentalized—though angry—Yankton self to an audience who understood and expected those forms, using the individual perspective as a means of resistance to assimilation.

Zitkala-Ša's autobiographical writings are certainly hybrid forms. Her essays are episodic and may, in some ways, follow the structure of traditional trickster tales, placing Zitkala-Ša in the position of Iktomi the wanderer who traverses worlds.[54] She does not, however, use traditional forms nearly as much as Eastman. One reason for this may be gender-related. Many pre-literate native autobiographical forms, such as coup tales and war and hunting stories, would usually—if not always—be told by men. Wong notes that, among the Sioux, the warriors would tell stories and then the women would make up songs about them, songs that honored the men and the tribe but did not retell the stories themselves.[55] Perhaps Zitkala-Ša found fewer traditional modes available to her. Her world is clearly a very female world. As she tells us, she and her mother lived alone while her brother, Dawee, was away at school in the East, and her father (who was white) and her maternal uncle were both absent or dead (10, 40). The warrior tradition itself is only marginally present in her life because of the dispersal of her family and her people. But these reasons alone are not enough to account for Zitkala-Ša's use of Western conventions in her autobiographical writing. Like Eastman, Zitkala-Ša knows that she has choices as to the forms she can use, and she is aware of the forms used in oral narratives. She did, in 1901, publish a volume of traditional trickster tales called *Old Indian Stories,* and she wrote a number of stories (unpublished during her lifetime) in Dakota and English that reflect and transform Yankton literary traditions.[56] Her autobiographical essays and letters do incorporate various traditional Sioux forms of autobiography, such as educational stories and naming stories, but she structures her overall autobiographical strategy in her published essays around Western sentimental autobiography. It seems that she, like Eastman, made conscious choices from a repertoire of representations and that she chose among them for a reason.

Eastman and Zitkala-Ša clearly make different choices from—what we might assume are—similar repertoires. Unlike Eastman, Zitkala-Ša does not shift her point of view but maintains an individual rather than a representational self. She always identifies herself as the first-person "I" of the essays and never refers to herself in the third person as Eastman does. This "I" is consistent throughout the three autobiographical essays she published, essays that covered her youth, school days, and adulthood. The narrative of these essays, while episodic and impressionistic, is more markedly chronological than in Eastman's *Indian Boyhood.* The generalized title of "Impressions of an Indian Childhood," which concentrates on the events leading up to her departure from the reservation to go to school, is again deceiving—for the childhood described is neither Dakota nor Pan-Indian but is unequivocally that of an individual. Rather than describing rites of passage common to all Indian children, Zitkala-Ša relates very personal and differentiating experiences of growth and maturation. Her story of the first time she noticed a relationship between herself and her shadow and chased it across the prairie, for example, portrays her realization of her distinct, though multiple, identities as an individual. Similarly, her anecdote about playing with a bag of marbles and noticing that the river ice contained the same rainbow hues certainly has metaphoric implications but portrays a subjective "spot of time" rather than a "representative" experience (38). Instead, Zitkala-Ša chronicles her unique moments of growth and development, those moments that give meaning only to her life. She refuses to collapse herself into a stereotype, using Western notions of autobiography to render herself as distinct and individual rather than as representative and generalized.

Another significant difference from Eastman is that Zitkala-Ša does not show an interest in ethnography. She does not view her project as salvage ethnography in the face of impending extinction. While she does talk about how her mother teaches her to bead and do quill work, this information is present to prove the existence of a Native system of education, a system that values the integrity and intelligence of the child more than the Western educational system: "The quietness of [my mother's] oversight made me feel strongly responsible and dependent on my own judgment. She treated me as a dignified little individual" (20). The choices Zitkala-Ša makes about which stories from her childhood to include have less to do with relating ethnographic detail than they do with an interest in foreshadowing. In the episode of "The Dead Man's Plum Bush," for example, Zitkala-Ša tells us she was on her way to a feast to honor a "strong young brave who had just returned from his first battle, a warrior" (31). Where Eastman described the Maiden's Feast in intricate detail, providing an account of the performance of the ceremony, the positioning of the guests, the social rules governing the festivities, Zitkala-Ša never describes the feast at all. Instead, she tells us; "The lasting impression of that day, as I recall it now, is what my mother told me about the dead man's plum bush" (33). Her mother cautions her never to eat the fruit from a particular plum bush, because it grew from the seeds that were buried in the hands of a dead man and therefore mark his grave. Rather than relating anything about burial customs, this anecdote serves a symbolic purpose, introducing the idea of forbidden fruit. Zitkala-Ša will later pick up on this concept when she describes how the missionaries tempt her to go to school in the East— the "red apple country"—and how she accepts the "forbidden fruit" of white knowledge, a move that will shut her out of her Edenic childhood relationship with her mother (41–45). This building and layering of tropes is used to enhance the emotional impact of the struggles she will face while trying to maintain an Indian identity, even as they replace an ethnographic mode of reporting that identity's constituent parts.

Zitkala-Ša uses tropes common in sentimental writing as tools in her self-representation. Laura Wexler has argued: "without the background of the several decades of domestic 'sentiment' that established the private home as the apotheosis of nurture, the nineteenth century interracial boarding school could probably not have existed, since it took as its mission the inculcation of domesticity in former savages and slaves."⁵⁷ As a product of the boarding schools, Zitkala-Ša was familiar with the domesticating project of sentimentalism and its accompanying literary tropes. In fact, she must have been aware of the ways in which the Carlisle Press used literary sentimentalism as a disciplinary tool in its portrayals of returned students like Fannie and Stiya, representing these transformed students as sentimental heroines whose virtues and sensibilities developed when they discarded their Indian identities. Wexler notes that "sentimentalism encourages a large-scale imaginative depersonalization of those outside its complex specifications at the same time it elaborately personalizes, magnifies, and flatters those who can accommodate to its image of an interior."⁵⁸ As a vigorous opponent of the depersonalization of Indians, Zitkala-Ša unsurprisingly chose to utilize a language and a system that would give her individual personhood, that would allow her to represent herself as a thinking and perhaps, more important, a *feeling* individual to a readership accustomed to valuing the sentimental. At the same time, Zitkala-Ša does not use this framework to indicate her acquiescence in the *values* of sentimentalism. Instead, she attempts to use the masters' tools to dismantle the masters' house, showing the way that institutions spawned by sentimentalism were injurious to Indians and urging their reform.⁵⁹

In her second essay, "School Days of an Indian Girl," Zitkala-Ša herself actively subverts the forces of domestic ideology in the boarding school. The episode of the turnip-smashing, an act of linguistic revenge, is also an act of rebellion against enforced domesticity. After having broken a rule that she felt was "very needlessly binding," Zitkala-Ša was told to mash turnips for dinner—both a punishment and a chore designed to teach the Native girls the values of sentimental domesticity. Instead of passively taking her lesson, Zitkala-Ša attacks the turnips "in [a] hot rage," pounding them so hard that she crushes the bottom of the bowl that holds them (60). After the turnips fall to the floor, Zitkala-Ša proudly celebrates "for having once asserted the rebellion within me" (95). Filled with rage, she turns the sentimental ideal on its head, refusing to be punished by the system that claimed to be her savior.

The best example of Zitkala-Ša's use of sentimentalism to undercut the institution of the boarding school is her description of the death of a classmate, also in "School Days":

Once I lost a dear classmate. I remember well how she used to mope along at my side, until one morning she could not raise her head from her pillow. At her deathbed I stood weeping, as the paleface woman sat near her moistening the dry lips. Among the folds of the bedclothes I saw the open pages of the white man's Bible. The dying Indian girl talked disconnectedly of Jesus the Christ and the paleface who was cooling her swollen hands and feet. I grew bitter, and censured the woman for cruel neglect of our physical ills. I despised the pencils that moved automatically, and the one teaspoon which dealt out, from a large bottle, healing to a row of variously ailing Indian children. I blamed the hard-working, well-meaning, ignorant woman who was inculcating in our hearts her superstitious ideas. (66–67)

In this stunning portrayal, Zitkala-Ša undermines one of the most effective tropes of sentimentalism—the deathbed scene of a young girl. Like Harriet Beecher Stowe's Little Eva, Zitkala-Ša's friend lies dying in her bed with her bible by her side. As Zitkala-Ša's commentary makes clear, however, the bible does not provide a source of transcendence for the dying girl. Instead, the book, the bureaucracy of the Indian school, and the religious and domestic superstitions of the "paleface" woman— all manifestations of sentimentalism's "civilizing machine" (66)—kill the girl rather than save her.

By presenting her own mistreatment along with the pain of other Indian children in this emotional language, Zitkala-Ša encourages her readers to feel with her, hoping that if her audience could feel her pain and subsequent anger, they would work to alleviate it, weeping as well as censuring along with her. This was, of course, the linking idea between sentimentalism and reform, the motivating factor behind *Uncle Tom's Cabin* itself.[60] The "reformers" that Zitkala-Ša attacks clearly feared the potential of her work, as the review published in the *Word Carrier* and reprinted in the June 1900 issue of the Carlisle Indian School's *Red Man*, indicates:

And our hearts swell with indignation as we see these unfortunates driven like a herd of buffalo many days and nights, while with every step the sick sister shrieks with the painful jar, until at last, when they reach the far Western country, on the first weary night she dies. It will relieve the sympathetic tension to remember that this is simply dramatic fiction. The same is undoubtedly true of the climactric [*sic*] scene when her mother discovers a new fire in the bluffs across the river where white settlers have made homes.[61]

The *Word Carrier* caricatures Zitkala-Ša's sentimental language—hearts swell, sisters shriek—in its flustered attempt to undercut her authorial integrity. Her autobiographical writing is so threatening because it builds "the sympathetic tension," using sentimental prose to excite the emotions of its readers, with the hope of instigating change. As Zitkala-Ša writes in a letter to the editors of the *Red Man* and published in April 1900: "To stir up views and earnest comparison of theories was one of the ways in which I hoped ["Impressions of an Indian Childhood"] would work a benefit to my people."[62] This "stirring up," she hoped, would be a catalyst for political action and reform.

Along with the boarding-school journalists, some contemporary critics maintain that Zitkala-Ša's essays are not properly "autobiographical," since Zitkala-Ša may have "fictionalized her own life" to a certain extent, "blurring the distinction between fact and fiction."[63] Both this contemporary critique and the criticisms in the *Word Carrier* raise the specter of the authenticity of Zitkala-Ša's autobiographical writing, though each has a different motivation. Contemporary critics such as Spack hope to reinforce Zitkala-Ša's writing as authentic even if not strictly "true" to the verifiable events of her life, whereas the *Word Carrier* seeks to discredit her by proving her a fraud. However, Zitkala-Ša—as an artist, activist, Dakota woman, and Western-educated autobiographer—is offering a *representation* of her life and is, therefore, shaping and molding her experiences to fit both literary conventions and her political agenda. Since "no one can dispute [her] own impressions and bitterness," no one can deny her own interpretation and portrayal of her life. Even her own terms—"impressions" and "bitterness"— convey her awareness of the uses to which she could put sentimental subjectivity and emotion in her self-representation. Viewing her autobiographical essays in their communicative context, as situational representations of situational identities, thus enables a reading of the texts that moves beyond the question of authenticity in order to examine Zitkala-Ša's communicative goals.

In both defying the domestic ideology of sentimentalism and utilizing its literary conventions to criticize the proponents of what Wexler calls "institutionalized sentimentalism," Zitkala-Ša puts a human face on the wrongs done to Indians at the turn of the century. This face is distinctly her own, the face of an individual, and her criticisms were pointed enough, and persuasive enough, to draw very personal attacks. As the unnamed author of the *Word Carrier* article further disparaged her: "By her own showing she is a person of infinite conceit."[64] Zitkala-Ša's vehement response to such criticisms by the boarding-school establishment emphasizes her sense of her own literary agency: "I won't be another's mouthpiece— I will say just what *I* think," she exclaimed in a 1901 letter to Carlos Montezuma.[65] The "utterly unthankful" Zitkala-Ša's autobiographical writings are proof that using a Westernized form leaves plenty of room for the expression of an Indian identity.

Her formal and thematic choices also demonstrate how writing about the boarding schools contributed to the American Indian literary tradition. In addition to providing a strong link to sentimentality, Zitkala-Ša's scene of the young dying girl recalls La Flesche's description of Brush's death at the end of *The Middle Five*. In both instances, the young, vulnerable boarding-school students physically succumb to the schools, but they also represent a much more complicated message of simultaneous accommodation and resistance. Brush urges La Flesche to continue his education, even as he affirms his Omaha language and identity; Zitkala-Ša's classmate's naïve faith reveals the deadly ignorance of the civilizing machine that pays no attention to students' needs, even as her story hijacks the form of literary sentimentalism to inspire pro-Native political action. La Flesche and Zitkala-Ša were not alone in representing the death of a boarding-school classmate in their autobiographies, nor in linking that death to the student's resistance to or rejection of the school experience—Charles Eastman and Luther Standing Bear, among many others, tell similar stories.[66] Most boarding-school students would have been exposed to the death of a classmate, as death rates at the schools were "alarming" according to David Adams.[67] The stories of these deaths—or of the authors' own near-death experiences—have been told repeatedly by Native writers representing the boarding-school experience, which points toward the development of a shared repertoire of tropes and signification that unites boarding-school writers in a common literary endeavor, building the formal elements of a pan-tribal literary tradition and defining what it means to write "Indian." Far from demonstrating her capitulation to the assimilative agenda of the schools, then, Zitkala-Ša's autobiographical essays point toward her championing of Native people and her centrality to a thriving American Indian literary and intellectual tradition.

Despite Zitkala-Ša's mutiny against the ideology and expectations of the Friends of the Indian, it would also be reductive to read Gertrude Simmons Bonnin as strictly a pro-tribal radical. The shift in names does not suggest schizophrenia but rather, the presence of a repertoire of representations visible in the accepted critical practice of identifying Bonnin as Zitkala-Ša when speaking of her authorial persona and as Gertrude Simmons Bonnin when referring to her activism, since this is how she identified herself in these arenas. Bonnin, though a prominent Indian activist, was not, in Robert Allen Warrior's language, a "traditionalist-nationalist."[68] Though she wrote to Carlos Montezuma that she was at odds with the boarding-school philosophy because "the *old folks* have a claim upon us" (original emphasis) and she worked to support the maintenance of many tribal values, she joined in a rather unholy alliance with Richard Pratt himself and a number of Friends of the Indian groups against peyotism circa 1918.[69]

Peyotism—a syncretic religion—was an important sign of cultural persistence for Francis La Flesche and for many former boarding-school students. Warrior states: "the groups that would later become the Native American Church managed to accomplish what the U.S. government was unwilling to allow politically and culturally: internal, self-determined adaptation to a new situation."[70] Although Bonnin's opposition to peyote arose from her concern for a particular tribal community (the Utes of the Uintah-Ouray Agency, among whom she and her husband, Raymond, had lived and worked for more than a decade), her decision to support federal legislation banning the use of peyote in Indian country worked against religious freedom and tribal self-determination. In her fight to pass the Hayden Bill into law, Bonnin demonstrated her acute awareness of the politics of representation as she constructed an Indian identity she could display before Congress. Dressing in pan-tribal regalia to lend the weight of insider status to her position, she joined Pratt and Charles Eastman, among others, in testifying before Congress concerning the perceived evils of the religion. She wore the Southern Plains–style garment—itself a material-cultural representational form—to "play Indian" for a white Congress, attempting to portray herself as visibly and authentically Indian in order to fight against Indian freedom of religion.[71]

Pratt and the Carlisle Press had attacked her writing, undermining her authenticity by urging readers not to view her as "the true picture of all Indian girls."[72] Bonnin now found her use of this different identity from her repertoire under fire for being "inauthentic" as well. Arapaho peyote activist and former Carlisle student Cleaver Warden denounced her anti-peyote testimony, calling her a "half-breed who [does] not know a lot of [her] ancestors or kindred" and proclaiming that a "true Indian is one who helps for a race, and not that secretary of the Society of American Indians."[73] Pro-peyote Anglo ethnologist James Mooney launched an angry attack on Bonnin's credibility, claiming that her regalia actually included (presumably unwittingly) a peyote fan commonly used in the very rituals she sought to outlaw. He disparaged Bonnin as someone who "claimed to be a Sioux woman" dressed in "woman's dress from some southern tribe" and a Navajo man's belt in addition to the peyote fan.[74]

Everyone involved in this testimony—from Mooney to Pratt to Warden to Bonnin—attempted to influence their congressional audience by constructing, manipulating, and judging Native self-representations based on readings of a supposed Indian authenticity, which cannot encompass the complexity of their politically charged deployment of identities. Mooney's attempt to inauthenticate Bonnin purposely overlooks the representative forms—visibly Indian, insider of a tribal community, Western-educated Indian expert, leader of a Pan-Indian organization, and so on—that she layered to build a situational identity, presented in order to reach a political goal. As Carol Batker points out: "Negotiating the tensions between tribal self-determination and full participation in U.S. society was a complex and difficult venture" for turn-of-the-century Native activist writers. It required multiple strategies of resistance.[75] Rather than randomly "oscillating" between positions and worldviews, Bonnin masters moving among the numerous strategic identities that make up her repertoire, varying representative codes to attempt to articulate a middle ground between a pure, all-encompassing tribalism to which she never had access and the genocidal policies of the boarding-school system and the Dawes Act (harsh realities that built upon the supposed loss of Indian culture).[76] Strongly disagreeing with Eastman that reservations contain only relics of the past and deeply questioning an uncomplicated equation of education with civilization, yet advocating policies that do not comfortably align with tribal nationalism, Zitkala-Ša put to use her education and the life-writing and literary conventions it made available to her to share a complicated and controversial understanding of sustained Indian presence and to fight tirelessly against many institutions that attempted to force Indian people to abandon their cultures altogether.[77]

Zitkala-Ša and Charles Eastman point toward the multivalent identities that so-called representative Indians inhabited at the turn of the century. Examining all of the identities in these writers' repertoires is beyond the scope of this study, but it is important to note that they later represented themselves differently than they did in the autobiographies studied here. Unwilling and unable to be classified as assimilated or tribal, these writers sought to create versions of Indian identity that would enable them to achieve (sometimes provisional) reforms without locking them into a single essentialized identity. For Eastman, this meant highlighting the capacity of "the race" to adapt to the values and institutions of hegemonic American society. He felt this way because he believed that his education had served him very well and provided a life for him off the reservation and away from the cultural stagnation and physical danger he saw there. And yet, Eastman reversed the trajectory indicated in the title of *From the Deep Woods to Civilization* later in his life. He spent his last years living in a cabin in the woods of Ontario, removing himself from the integrated social setting he had advocated for his people.[78] Zitkala-Ša, on the other hand, saw the representative Indian as an Indian wronged and demanding retribution. Finding the educational policies identified with the government boarding schools she both attended and worked for to perpetuate and perpetrate injustices, she incited her readers to "question whether real life or long-lasting death lies beneath this semblance of civilization."[79]

These writers lived during a time of accelerated change. Rather than being trapped between worlds, they inhabited several worlds simultaneously. By refusing any simple classification and by choosing expressive codes to represent themselves situationally, Eastman and Zitkala-Ša encourage us to question our own critical assumptions concerning Indian identity and its representation in autobiography. An exploration of the complexities of Indian self-representation provides a fertile ground for intertextual comparisons of the sort provided here. As scholars such as Robert Allen Warrior persuasively argue, this type of analysis is central to the development of an American Indian intellectual history that seeks to prevent "an ossifying of American Indian existence" by avoiding either "unmitigated praise" or "unbridled criticism" of Indian authors, related to an obsession with their authenticity.[80] At the same time, Warrior's analysis of the group of turn-of-the-century Indian writers referred to here as the representative Indians, is itself essentializing in its broadness. For example, he lumps Eastman and Zitkala-Ša together as writing "from similar political commitments and affiliations . . . to gain sympathy from white audiences for the difficult, but to the authors necessary, process of becoming American citizens . . . [and supporting] the advancement of the policies of the U.S. government."[81] He elides the nuanced—but significant—differences between them. Warrior's reminder, that "understanding the literary output of the period requires an acknowledgment of how closely the authors related to each other politically and how much the work they produced was guided by the political landscape they inhabited," serves as further support for a model such as the repertoire of representation, which deploys a critical praxis moving beyond issues of authenticity as it resists a simplistic linkage of form and identity.[82] Such praxis can aid critics in a more fruitful study of American Indian autobiography that displays an understanding of the racist and culture-killing past in which these authors wrote without replicating that ideology in scholarship. By reading each text in its communicative context with an understanding of identity and representation as situational and negotiated, critics can respect the complexity of American Indian identity and life-writing by explicating exactly when, why, and how autobiographers represent themselves as they do, without falling into the tired practice of brokering Indian authenticity.

CHAPTER 5

RUNAWAYS, REBELS, AND INDOLENT BOYS IN CONTEMPORARY RE-VISIONS OF BOARDING-SCHOOL NARRATIVES

Educators and students used representations of the Indian boarding-school experience for differing political ends. Marianna Burgess designed representations of Indian students in the Carlisle newspapers, for example, to serve as a model of what "good" (or assimilating) students should strive to become, whereas Zitkala-Ša's essays provided images of angry, pain-filled students, whose plight challenged white educators' justifications of the boarding schools. Once we acknowledge, however, that students and educators deployed identities and literary forms situationally in their representations of schools and students, we must also recognize the need to ask when, how, and why particular representations of Indian boarding schools emerge in contemporary texts.

In the late twentieth century, boarding-school stories and students appear frequently both in non-Indian-authored texts, such as Rinaldi's *My Heart Is on the Ground,* and in poetry, short stories, drama, and novels by American Indian writers. Craig Womack asserts that, through the 1930s, many Native writers "were uncertain or hesitant about whether a Native voice, Native viewpoint, the narration of tribal life, or even a Native future was possible."[1] Certainly the Native authors we have examined here considered those issues in their work and responded in a variety of ways, emphasizing strategies of survivance. Native authors at the end of the twentieth and beginning of the twenty-first centuries build off that earlier writing, which, Womack continues, "has come a long way toward legitimizing tribal experience as an appropriate subject for writing and, most importantly, toward assuming tribal life will continue in the future."[2] As Frederick Hoxie explains, shifts in government policy in the early part of the twentieth century ironically assisted this process: "The assimilation effort, a campaign to draw Native Americans into a homogenous society helped to create its antithesis—a plural society."[3]

Policymakers in the first decades of the twentieth century, losing much of the reforming zeal of Pratt's generation and believing less fervently that Indian people possessed the intellectual capacity for becoming civilized, "grew more tolerant of traditional practices," inadvertently providing the "cultural space" that, Hoxie argues, enabled tribal members to "take advantage of their peripheral status, replenish their supplies of belief and value, and carry on their war with homogeneity."[4] Much contemporary American Indian literature and scholarship, coming out of this mixed legacy of governmental neglect and ongoing tribal commitment to survival, draws on the intellectual inheritance of the Native literary tradition and has become even more explicit about the relationship between writing and the continuation of tribal life. As Lakota novelist and critic Elizabeth Cook-Lynn has stated, one of the most important questions we can ask today of Native literatures is "What role do American Indian literatures play in today's struggles to defend and clarify tribal sovereignty?"[5] The contemporary authors studied here ask this question in different ways, but all of them reconsider the figure of the boarding-school student and the significance of the school experience and its legacy when narrating their answers.

Paula Gunn Allen notes that many Indian writers "publishing between 1900 and 1965 were either [the boarding schools'] products or were raised by parents and grandparents who were," but the schools' influence on American Indian authors does not end in the mid-1960s.[6] Many contemporary authors have personal or family ties to the institution. Silko's Aunt Susie, Grandma A'mooh, and Grandpa Hank, for example, were students at Carlisle and Sherman; Louise Erdrich lived on the campus of the Wahpeton, N.D., Indian School, where her parents taught during her youth.[7] N. Scott Momaday's mother (a Haskell student) and father both taught at an on-reservation Bureau of Indian Affairs (BIA) school at Jemez Pueblo.[8] While mid-twentieth-century American Indian literature portrays the boarding-school experience as alienating and deadening—in Allen's words, "focusing on cultural and psychic dissolution"—many late twentieth-century texts tend to concentrate on boarding-school student resistance, portraying students as integral members of a tribal community who contribute to the maintenance of a nationalism that emphasizes legal, intellectual, and rhetorical sovereignty.[9]

D'Arcy McNickle's *The Surrounded* (1936), for example, describes Salish boarding-school students who try to escape; but their uncle, Archilde Leon, a graduate of those institutions, realizes that "somehow or other he would get them away from the Fathers—but what would he do then? He might turn them loose in the mountains, like birds let out of a cage, or like a pair of buffaloes turned out of the government reserve; he had no doubt that they would survive. But there ought to be something better."[10] Archilde himself has returned to the Flathead Reservation profoundly distanced from both his Salish mother and his Spanish father and cannot find a good answer to the troubling question of whether a boarding-school student has any ability to resist schooling—any chance of finding something better than a life imprisoned or on the run. After spending a full year striving to reintegrate himself into his family, Archilde is arrested for a crime he did not commit, and the last scene of the novel depicts his capture. As the Indian Agent arrests Archilde, his nephews slip off into the woods to avoid being returned to school. Agent Parker swears: "'Why those little fools! How far do they expect to get? . . . It's too damn bad you people never learn that you can't run away. It's pathetic—'." The last sentence of the novel reiterates this defeat through Archilde's silence: "Archilde, saying nothing, extended his hands to be shackled."[11] Those who attempt to elude culture-killing pressures will find themselves, according to McNickle's text, surrounded by insurmountably oppressive disciplinary power, darkening even the hope that the next generation can manage to escape.

In contrast, Louise Erdrich's poem "Indian Boarding School: The Runaways" uses this subject matter in one of the author's earliest literary explorations of her American Indian identity. As she explained to Joseph Bruchac: "'Runaways' is one of the first poems that came out of letting go and just letting my own background or dreams surface on the page."[12] What surfaces in the poem, like the "frail outlines" on the school's pathways, is the memory of the boarding-school experience as an important part of what it means to be Indian today.[13] Although the children's faces are supposed to become as hard and as pale as the cement they scrub, they remember their homes, and because of this memory they continue to run, continue to resist. "Riding scars/ you can't get lost. Home is the place they cross," the poem explains, acknowledging that shared pain can sometimes strengthen knowledge of or longing for home. The last lines of the poem, in which the recaptured runaways remember, even in carrying out their punishment, "delicate old injuries, the spines of names and leaves."[14]

The cycle of running and being returned, even if it does not allow the students to gain freedom, allows their memories to surface. Erdrich's reference to "the spines of names and leaves" resonates in several ways. The "spines of names" are the markings of students' tribal identities and languages that remain beneath the English names they have received. "Spines of leaves" refers to the natural world, to the imprint of organic material that remains in a fossil or in cement when the rest is washed away, suggesting that students hung on to something of themselves and to an awareness of the landscape even within the boarding schools' culture-eroding lessons. But this image also suggests the persistence of literature, of stories—and, even more specifically, books, constructed of spines and leaves—emerging from the dialectic between school and the irrepressible longing for home. Many, many Indian people hold a personal experience at boarding school, or family stories about the experiences of ancestors, as part of their personal and collective identities. Boarding-school narratives—especially stories of surviving the genocidal aims of the schools—are shared texts that act as markers of understanding and solidarity among contemporary Indian people in both the tribal and Pan-Indian registers. K. Tsianina Lomawaima explains:

> The petty, tyrannical details of a regimented life were linked at every turn to [students'] identity as Indians. It follows logically that the details of their resistance to regimentation are also now linked inextricably with their identity as Indians, specifically, as alumni of an Indian school. Personal reminiscences and shared stories . . . are powerful symbols of identity today not because of some Indian cultural content (in some externally defined ethnographic sense), but because they are the chronicles of Indian experiences told by Indian people.[15]

Autobiographies of Indians who attended boarding school from the turn of the century to the present abound. In addition to the works we have seen, the autobiographies of Don Talayesva, Asa Daklugie, Polingaysi

Qoyawayma, Mourning Dove, Helen Sekakwaptewa, Reuben Snake, Esther Burnette Horne, and many others include discussions of the authors' years at boarding school.[16] While these autobiographies have various kinds of literary and historical significance, my focus here will extend Lomawaima's analysis by looking at fictional texts in which contemporary Indian authors reinvent boarding-school students as characters, in order to demonstrate how Indian people today attempt creatively to make sense of the institution that affected Indian life and identity so deeply. In literature, boarding-school students and their stories appear both in the background as a marker of the Indianness of a text—or in the foreground as a primary subject of reflection and reimagination. Integral to these reinventions, as with Erdrich's poem, is a focus on resistance, on running away from the school and running toward home. Joseph Bruchac suggests that "The Runaways" is "a metaphor for the things that are happening with American Indian writing and culture in general. People have been dragged into the twentieth century, European/American culture and frame of mind and running away from that means running not away, but back [home]."[17] Kate Shanley explains that while "home" certainly relates to a homeland, a particular tribal territory, "'home' also functions metaphorically to refer to a future place of self-esteem (on the individual level), and self-governance, cultural maintenance, revitalization, and sovereignty (on the collective level)."[18] Contemporary writers' return "home" is often a turn toward examining the boarding-school experience as a component of both a tribal-nationalist identity, which, in Womack's words, "roots literature in land and culture" and emphasizes self-determination and cultural integrity, and a pan-tribal or indigenist identity, a politicized group identity that recognizes shared experiences, values, and goals and has enhanced Indian political power in the last quarter of the century.[19] Since both of these identities support tribal life and resistance to anti-Indian U.S. government policies, contemporary Indian authors tend to reimagine the boarding school as a site of resistance, and boarding-school students as rebels and culture heroes. The figure of the runaway appears frequently in contemporary American Indian literature, as authors who are well aware of the historical reality of resistance to boarding-school education also build on the textual resistance of boarding-school narratives by troping on the figure of the defiant student.

The boarding-school experience thus acts as a shared narrative that undergirds Native experience, and it need not be the central focus of a text to have an impact on its characters and plot. Louise Erdrich's characterization of Lulu Lamartine, who inhabits *Love Medicine*, *Tracks*, and *The Bingo Palace*, is one example of boarding school as subtext. Lulu 's time at boarding school, though never narrated in any of Erdrich's novels, shapes who Lulu is and even how she speaks. Erdrich stated in an interview:

> This doesn't appear in the fiction, but [Lulu] is sent to a boarding school, and in government boarding schools during the time she would have been going to school, children would have been punished for speaking native languages. So she has a very lyrical and very unconventional way of speaking. . . . [Lulu was] punished for being [her] most fluent and absorbing and interesting self, because self and language are so much the same [and there is a strong connection between] what you express and who you are. [Being forbidden to speak Ojibwe at boarding school] had to have been an act that destroyed the self. We really have very few people who talk a lot about what that was like.[20]

Erdrich's novels give Lulu a voice, converting her linguistic displacement into lyrical language as a labor of love and commemoration. In order to understand Lulu's character, her distinctive narrative voice, and her continual search for connection to the community from which she was exiled while at school, we need to understand what boarding school was like, and the kinds of restrictions students faced under its culture-eradicating ideology. The brief references in *Tracks* to Lulu's time away at school, from which she returns in the "shabby and smoldering orange [dress] . . . that any child who tried to run away from the boarding school was forced to wear," sparely suggest a rich source of understanding and character development.[21] These references would surely not be missed by a Native audience or any informed audience, who could fill in the gaps Erdrich leaves with their own historical knowledge fully to understand and appreciate the audacious Lulu, who genetically links the disparate factions of her reservation community and, in her old age, fights for the reclamation of wrongfully taken Turtle Mountain land from a position of cultural power.

Clifford Trafzer also demonstrates the importance of the figure of the boarding-school student to contemporary American Indian literature by making Agnes Yellowknee, the fictional tribal librarian who introduces his collection *Blue Dawn, Red Earth: New Native American Storytellers*, a former

Carlisle student. Trafzger explains that this character is a "composite of people I have known and respected":

> Agnes Yellowknee was a tribal personality, a one-of-a-kind woman of the old-time mind. She spoke the ancient language, but she had taught herself to read and write English. She did so after running away from Carlisle Indian School, where white teachers and matrons tried to destroy her word shadows and trickster temperament. . . . She kept tribal stories about the reserve, even though she never thought of herself as a reservation Indian. She knew the remembered history of the People, traditions and stories that unlocked secrets about ourselves, the very stories the matrons tried to beat out of her at Carlisle Indian School.[22]

Trafzer's Agnes serves only as a device to introduce this anthology of stories by young American Indian authors, but her position as the repository of tribal information, the woman who shares culture-sustaining stories with the tribe's youth both orally and through books, both in the tribal language and in English, is suggestive of the ways in which many contemporary authors reimagine boarding-school students in their work. On the reservation, Trafzer's culturally knowledgeable former student fosters and encourages a new generation of Indian writers to produce literature. Agnes's time at Carlisle, like Lulu's sojourn at school, is marked by her rebellion—a runaway, she does not even credit Carlisle with teaching her English. And it is also marked by her successful retention of the old stories, the lifeblood of tribal identity, despite—or more likely *because* of—the violence with which Carlisle tried to erase history and identity. Today, the Indian boarding-school student remains representationally evocative. Rebels, runaways, repositories of tribal history and knowledge maintained against the odds, these characters demonstrate how contemporary authors often place the boarding-school experience at the center of American Indian literature, simultaneously reinforcing both tribal-national and indigenous identities.

IMPLICIT RESISTANCE IN
LUCI TAPAHONSO'S "THE SNAKEMAN"

Running away from school was not the only way to express resistance to the cultural metamorphosis demanded by the educators, as demonstrated in "The Snakeman" (1979), a short story by Diné (Navajo) writer Luci

Tapahonso, who was herself a boarding-school student at the Fort Wingate school on the vast Navajo reservation.[23] "The Snakeman" impressionistically portrays life in a girls' dormitory, where the girls build their own community and develop syncretic explanations for the fears and dangers that threaten them, displaying at once their isolation, loneliness, and fellowship. The story opens with a young girl sliding down the fire escape in the middle of the night. We learn that she leaves the girls' dorm every night to visit with her mother, who is buried in the graveyard at the school but who materializes after dark to hold her and call her "shiyázhí," or "little one" in the Diné language. The other girls comment on her nightly visits with a combination of understanding and longing. They, too, wish to be with their mothers every night, and it is the exquisite irony of the story that only the girl whose mother is dead is allowed this kind of comfort. Instead, the girls concentrate on evading the authority of the dorm matron, who cannot seem to catch them at their nighttime activities and who is nothing like a mother to them. They also worry about issues as various as "how the end of the world is really going to be," the shadowy figure of a man they believe lives in the attic and will throw evil powder on anyone who gets too close to the door, and the snakeman "who sometimes stole jewelry from them."[24] Together, the girls pray, remember, and comfort one another, as the cycle repeats itself night after night. While the story clearly draws upon Tapahonso's personal experience and Diné culture, the timelessness of the setting, the longing for mothering portrayed in so many boarding-school narratives (including Zitkala-Ša's), and the repetition of the girls' actions also suggest a cyclical experience, shared in common across generations and tribes.[25] In "The Snakeman," Tapahonso portrays boarding-school students as implicitly resistant, concentrating on their own community and the connections that tie them to both their past and their present. Their fellowship gives them comfort and provides them with antidotes to boarding-school life, allowing them to reach for the distinctly Diné value of *hózhó*, or balance.[26]

Tapahonso's storytelling is rooted in her Diné language, which she both speaks and writes. She has explained that her poems and stories begin in Navajo, and that writing them in English is a process of translation, which suggests that this former boarding-school student has an internal monologue in Navajo, a fact that completely contradicts Marianna Burgess's depiction of Stiya's easily readable, stridently English-language inner voice.

Tapahonso's philosophy of storytelling exists within a Diné worldview, in which "a person able to 'talk beautifully' is well thought of and considered wealthy" and is believed to have been "raised right" by his or her family.[27] The Diné love of words and attention to the precision of their meanings and resonances apply to their use of English as well as Navajo. While social evolutionary educators (and literary critics, see Chapter 4) insisted that facility in English would result in narratives that express assimilation and acquiescence in a European American cultural system, Tapahonso asserts that Diné linguistic and expressive values have only grown stronger after contact with English and contemporary Western influences such as radio, television, and video. These innovations have not lessened "the value of the spoken word" for the Diné. Rather, they seem to Tapahonso to have "enriched the verbal dexterity of colloquial language" capable of giving voice to Navajo culture and values in both languages.[28] Finally, it is significant that Tapahonso asserts the importance of writing for Diné people who live off the reservation or who are somehow separated from their communities, whether by choice or by force, such as boarding-school students. She declares that "writing is the means for returning, rejuvenation, and for restoring our spirits to the state of 'hohzo' [sic] or beauty, which is the basis of Navajo philosophy. It is a small part of the 'real thing,' and it is utilitarian, but as Navajo culture changes, we adapt accordingly."[29] Far from acting as a marker of the eradication of Navajo culture, writing in English assists Navajo people in achieving an important cultural goal. If anything, Tapahonso believes that her writing makes her more, rather than less Navajo, and the boarding-school students she portrays likewise forge connections to Navajo culture through storytelling even as they experience the anti-Navajo boarding-school curriculum.

Student resistance in "The Snakeman" appears in the students' successful placing of their own community at the center of their lives, even within the tightly regulated boarding-school system. The action in Tapahonso's story takes place entirely within the confines of the girls' dorm, with the dorm matron (the only school employee ever mentioned) existing merely to be outwitted, though the girls bear the brunt of her anger and violence when they fail to evade her surveillance. The narrator relates that one night when the girls were particularly frightened by the man in the attic, whom they heard walking down the stairs to the hallway door, "They all slept two to a bed, and the bigger girls made sure all the little ones had someone bigger with them. They stayed up later than usual, crying and praying. No one woke early enough to get everyone back to their own beds, and the dorm mother had spanked all of them. It was okay because nothing had happened to any of them that night, they said."[30] Certainly the boarding-school environment terrorizes and enervates the girls, but they cope with their fears and longings as a community, not needing or wanting the comfort and guidance of the educators who were supposed to serve as their role models. And within their own community, the little girl who climbs down the fire escape to meet her mother is the strongest and most admirable of them all, since she has contact with her mother—if only in the graveyard at night—and she moves past boundaries and restrictions established by the educators, evading their watchful disciplinary gaze. Tapahonso does not portray these actions as angry acts of political rebellion, but in their own quiet way, the girls continually resist the school's attempts to transform them.

This resistance is neither perfect nor unanimous. If the students are able to avoid the gaze of the matron herself, they are not always able to escape the enforcement of the ideology and norms of the educational system, which several of their peers have internalized and incorporated. Two of the girls, for instance, "empty their pockets of small torn pieces of paper and scatter them under the beds" each morning. The bed skirts hide these bits of paper from the casual observer, and "this was how they tested the girl who swept their room. In the evenings, they checked under the beds to see if the paper was gone. If it wasn't, they immediately reported it to the dorm mother, who didn't ask how they were so sure their room hadn't been cleaned." These students have placed themselves in the position of a Man-on-the-Band-stand, testing and oppressing one another in exactly the model the Carlisle Press worked so hard to demonstrate and dissemi-nate in its literary productions. Nevertheless, even though some students administer the examinations that make the boarding school a space of domination, the girls (even, Tapahonso suggests, those who do the testing) value a student solidarity built on the shared experience of isolation from home. "Late in the night," the narrator reports, "someone always cried, and if the others heard her, they pretended not to notice. They understood how it was with all of them—if only they could go to public school and eat at home every night." While students may test one another as a means of building and enforcing a hierarchy based on acquiescence in the disciplinary mechanisms of the school, they also recognize, understand, and respect each other's desires to maintain a connection with their tribal communities.[31]

Like Francis La Flesche and his Middle Five gang, Tapahonso's students use the space they create for themselves outside of the social evolutionary continuum as a middle ground for the production of a syncretic student worldview, which blends Navajo philosophy with the realities, limitations, and lessons of the boarding school. The ritual of holding the window open and swinging it in and out while the girl climbs down the fire escape, as well as the belief in both the man in the attic and the snakeman, in many ways directly responded to the particularities of boarding-school life, in which students needed to evade authority and where they—especially the girls—rightfully feared the presence of men who might do them harm. The man in the attic suggests the Man-on-the-Band-stand because he always watches their actions; unlike the Man-on-the-Band-stand, however, the man in the attic also possesses the characteristics of a Navajo-style witch, throwing dangerous dust on those who come too close to forbidden territory.[32]

Tapahonso further highlights students' practical, creative response to their situation when she claims that the girls "just gave [the snakeman] that name" without reference to Christian or Navajo beliefs.[33] Of course, as an adult writing and remembering the story, Tapahonso allows the snakeman to accrue metaphorical weight from its connotations in both Christian and Navajo cultures. Embodying both the evil, dangerous knowledge of the Christian devil serpent and the strange but beneficial powers of the snakeman in the Navajo Beautyway, the snakeman is a hybrid figure who balances the forces of good and evil and brings the girls together in their common fears and beliefs.

Allen notes an even stronger tie between the students' constructed culture and Navajo culture when she claims that Tapahonso's entire story is modeled after an ancient Navajo abduction story: "According to that tradition, it was during a conflict long ago that two young women were abducted from their village by the enemy." Separated from one another, each was forced to spend the night with one of their abductors, and each found, upon awakening, that she slept next to a corpse. One of the corpses turned into a snake, and "the woman taken by Snakeman was compelled to follow him to his land among the supernaturals, where she lived with his mother. . . . But although she was undisciplined and inattentive, she eventually gained the old woman's approval and was given a Yei-bei-chi, a chantway, to take to her people so they could restore their bond to the sacred and regain peace."[34] That chantway became part of the Beautyway, the primary Navajo ceremonial and healing ritual, which enacts and restores balance and health. Although the abduction initially separated the woman from her community, she eventually returned with new knowledge that inspired her people and encouraged their connection to one another and to Dinétah, the Navajo homeland. Through her claim that Tapahonso's story is "an offshoot of the main ceremonial tradition of the Diné," Allen uncovers the ceremonial underpinnings of the girls' syncretic world.[35] Thus, Tapahonso places her boarding-school student characters within a Navajo worldview, which recognizes that even knowledge gained through an abduction may be put to good use, and relates their experiences to the Beautyway, making them agents of the tribe's achievement of *hózhó* or beauty and balance. Yet clearly, in this story, the snakeman is not a benevolent force. He steals the girls' jewelry, and his presence frightens them, because of both his maleness and his supernatural qualities. The presence of mothers—even ghost mothers—is comforting in a way that the snakeman is not. But this vaguely malevolent force, too, connects to Navajo tradition, as Allen's analysis indicates. And as such, the snakeman provides an element of balance in the lives of the boarding-school students. Their abduction is specific to their time and place, but their reactions meld myth and actuality, much as Silko's "Yellow Woman" does, bringing together contemporary and ceremonial realities in a fashion that would be incomprehensible to the linear thinking of turn-of-the-century boarding-school educators (as well as today's hegemony).

Just as the abducted woman brought back a chantway, which she taught to the tribe, Tapahonso's students teach one another, providing an alternative education geared toward survival away from home and strategies for maintaining and reasserting their connectedness to each other and to their nation in the midst of a hostile, constantly threatening environment. The story ends as all of their nights end:

> They talked [about the snakeman] until they began looking around to make sure he wasn't in the room. The bigger girls slept with the little ones, and they prayed together that God wouldn't let the man

in the attic or the snakeman come to them. They prayed that the world wouldn't end before their parents came to visit. As the room became quiet and the breathing even and soft, the little girl got up, put on her housecoat, and slid soundlessly down the fire escape.[36]

The little girl's visit to her mother's grave emphasizes that the safeness generated by the girls is not wholly adequate to protect and comfort them, but these ritual acts of quiet—even soundless—resistance keep them safe enough from evils both real and imagined to survive the experience, to move, even perilously, toward balance. Because Tapahonso's story is partly autobiographical, her text has an added valence. By creating and writing the snakeman, making him the focus of a story about her boarding-school experience, Tapahonso represents herself and her fellow students as innovative, syncretic survivors. She successfully writes herself and the other girls into *hózhó*, bringing them into alignment with the rhythms and imperatives of the Diné world. Surviving at the school, nurturing and remembering their Navajo-ness, supporting each other, resisting the white rules, the girls in "The Snakeman" display students' repertoires of identity as did characters and self-representations in turn-of-the-century texts.

While Tapahonso designs her story to produce *hózhó* through the process of writing and reading, Kiowa playwrights N. Scott Momaday and Hanay Geiogamah in their dramas about the boarding-school experience produce feelings of empowerment or catharsis in their casts and audiences alike as their vastly different plays actuate stories of boarding-school student resistance. Momaday's *The Indolent Boys*, an unpublished play written circa 1992, takes for its subject the story of three runaways from the Kiowa Indian Boarding School in 1891.[37] Geiogamah's *Foghorn*, first performed in 1973 just after the American Indian Movement (AIM) attempted reclamation of Wounded Knee, places the boarding-school experience within the context of Indian activism and resistance from 1492 to the Red Power movement.[38] Both plays deal very differently with the subject matter, and each stages its vision in its own unique manner, but each enacts student resistance and allows Indian actors to play boarding-school students who are placed in positions of power that few, if any, students were able to experience at the turn of the century. The dramas thus allow a cathartic release and celebrate students as keepers of the culture, representing educators as violent abusers and farcical fools—light-years removed from the educators' representations of themselves a century earlier. In these dramas, we see a different sort of transformation than the schools intended. Instead of changing into "imitation white men," Momaday's and Geiogamah's students become Indian culture heroes.

REPLAYING THE RETURNED STUDENT IN MOMADAY'S *INDOLENT BOYS*

Momaday sets *The Indolent Boys* in 1891, the same year Marianna Burgess published *Stiya*. Yet the two works could not be farther apart in their representations of Indian boarding-school students and their responses to their education. Momaday writes the story of "the frozen boys," three young Kiowas named Mosatse, Koi-kahn-hodle, and Seta (known at school as Jack, Arch, and Sailor) who ran away from the school after a severe beating and perished in an unexpected winter storm as they traveled toward their parents' camps. Although the frozen boys are the focus of the play, they are not among the cast of characters, appearing only as bundled corpses in the dream sequences. Instead of tracing their actions step by step, Momaday concentrates his attention on the differing interpretations and representations of the runaways' actions by tribal members, fellow students, and school officials. Deeply aware of educators' desires to control the representations of boarding-school students, Momaday purposefully shapes the story of these Kiowa boys, illuminating the turn-of-the-century contest over representation and arguing, by portraying the boys as heroes and ceremonial agents serving the continuance of Kiowa culture, that Marianna Burgess's depiction of boarding-school student complicity, for example, was propagandistic and inaccurate. Drawing on the conventions of traditional dramatic storytelling, Momaday creatively enacts this story of boarding-school students as Kiowa history. The play becomes a ceremony of teaching, healing, and mourning, re-presenting "the indolent boys" for a contemporary audience, and integrating their story into the corpus of American Indian literature.

Momaday states in the introductory notes to the script that the story of the frozen boys "is marked in the pictographic calendars of the Kiowas, and it remains fixed in the tribal memory."[39] These pictographic calendars, maintained by Kiowa chroniclers and historians for generations, denoted each year with a drawing of the significant event or events of the year or the season. The events illustrated by the drawings named the year and became the annotations by which the Kiowa kept "track of their tribal and family affairs."[40] Ethnologist James Mooney explains, for example, that the tribal leader Sett'an would tell people he "was born in 'cut-throat summer' (1833), and his earliest recollection is of the 'head-dragging winter' (1837–8)."[41] These names and pictographs represent stories that locate the Kiowa as a people. According to Mooney:

> It is customary for the owners of such Indian heirlooms [as calendars] to bring them out at frequent intervals during the long nights in the winter camp, to be exhibited and discussed in the circle of warriors about the tipi fires. . . . At these gatherings the pipe is filled and passed around, and each man in turn recites some mythic or historic tradition, or some noted deed on the warpath, which is then discussed by the circle. Thus the history of the tribe is formulated and handed down.[42]

Drawing upon the story associated with the winter of 1890–1891—"schoolboys frozen"—Momaday brings about his own history-telling and history-shaping in the performance of his play.

The pictograph for January 1891 in the monthly calendar of the Kiowa chronicler and artist Ankopaáingyadéte, commonly referred to as the Anko calendar, shows the boys who ran away from school. In this image, the two wear Western clothes and hold out a book atop the black line that indicates winter according to the conventions of Kiowa calendar art (see Figure 13). This story obviously held deep significance for the community. The incident of the frozen boys is so well known among the Kiowa, Anko explained, that although his pictograph only included two runaway students, "'everybody knows there were three.'"[43] Mooney notes that the calendars afford "a good idea of the comparative importance attached by the Indian and the white man to the same event. From the white man's point of view many of the things recorded in these aboriginal histories would seem to be of the most trivial consequence, while many events which we regard as marking eras in the history of the plains tribes are entirely omitted."[44]

This is certainly the case with the story of the frozen boys, which does not make it into U.S. history books but remains a defining moment in Kiowa history, explaining and referencing an entire year. The traces of this story that do remain in U.S. historical documents represent the government

Fig. 13. "Tépgañ P'a—Schoolboys Frozen." Illustration from the Anko Monthly Calendar (Kiowa) and reprinted in James Mooney's *Calendar History of the Kiowa*. National Anthropological Archives, Smithsonian Institution.

educators' perspective. Momaday explains that the story of the runaways is still "very much alive in the tribal memory. I grew up hearing about the frozen boys. The people tell the story."[45] In fact, he was surprised to find that the Oklahoma Historical Society and the National Archive contained written material about the incident.[46] Through his dramatization of the event, which privileges tribal history as more accurate than documentary records, Momaday presents a truly tribal story, a chronicle that holds a significance within the Kiowa nation that it lacks for outsiders. At the same time, Native people from other tribes have their own community stories about boarding-school runaways who perish in the attempt to return home. Zitkala-Ša, for example, wrote a story called "Search for Bear Claws, the Lost School Boy" that recounts a community's mournful, visionary winter search and is quite similar to the Kiowa story, establishing the narrative as pan-tribal in a very particular way.[47] These narratives are not blandly Pan-Indian, and devoid of tribal specificity, but instead are stories of the mobilization and mourning of many particular tribal communities with distinct cultures and philosophies. In other words, their Pan-Indian prevalence emphasizes and supports the tribal specificity of each story.

In *The Indolent Boys*, Momaday tells the Kiowa story by drawing from an extensive repertoire of representation to combine tribal storytelling forms with the structure of contemporary American drama. Critic Jeffrey

Huntsman claims that contemporary American Indian theater is closely tied to traditional tribal drama, a link readily apparent in Momaday's work.[48] While Momaday's script is certainly meant to be produced on a conventional stage, and he provides directions for lighting, sound, and set design that mark the text as a piece of American theater, Momaday also integrates Kiowa dramatic standards into these theatrical conventions, creating a hybrid form that effectively achieves the communal history-shaping objectives of previous Kiowa historians while sharing the history with Pan- and non-Indian audiences as well.[49] As Huntsman explains: "the lack of a clear boundary between audience and performer and a focus on the timeless moment of the center" (that is, a ceremonial presence and space) are two of the most important characteristics of traditional Indian drama, and Momaday's play incorporates both of these elements.[50]

Through the presence of the school children as a "kind of silent chorus" and his use of Mother Goodeye as a storyteller/narrator, Momaday breaks down the division between audience and performer, incorporating the audience as a responsive, active element of the production.[51] Momaday's instructions for the spatial design of the stage further dismantle the boundaries between performers and audience through his inclusion of a liminal schoolroom space containing several small desks, which will be filled with children throughout the course of the play. "At times this space appears to be inside the classroom, at others outside," he specifies (iv). The children, on stage throughout the play, act as a bridge positioned between actors and audience. They literally inhabit a middle ground, and their response to the action on the stage allows them to share their own reading of the events, inhabiting the simultaneous roles of insiders and outsiders and thus displaying a repertoire of identities. Mother Goodeye accomplishes audience participation even more effectively, beginning with her prologue. As she tells the audience the runaways' names, she encourages them to repeat the words, making them part of the dialogue of the play: "Mosatse. Eh, neh, neh. It's a funny name, isn't it—Mosatse? Say it, why don't you? MO SAT SE." Momaday's stage directions indicate, "She beckons to the audience; it speaks the name." And Mother Goodeye responds, "Yes, MO SAT SE. Yes, that's right" (1). From the first lines of the play, then, Mother Goodeye establishes the context of the dramatic event, that of communal storytelling. After encouraging audience response, Mother Goodeye, like any well-versed storyteller who sees the connections among stories, further explains that Mosatse got his strange name because his father was a Mexican man who called himself Muchacho, and who was stolen by the tribe and incorporated into the community. She begins to go off on a bawdy tangent about how Mexican captives contribute to the Kiowa community—"Their men show our women how to do it. And their women show our men how to do it! New way! Goddam! Eh neh, neh, neh!" (2). She dances and sings, executing two other forms of traditional performance, before bringing herself back to the story at hand, apologizing—"But that is another story. I tell it to you sometime" (2). This brief digression suggests that we should view Mother Goodeye's performance not as an unusual event but as a regular, consistent part of community life. She possesses a repertoire of stories, which she has performed for the members of the community before and which she will continue to relate in the future.

Momaday's inclusion of ceremonial space also connects his work to a tribal dramatic tradition. Momaday uses the image of the Medicine Wheel (hanging on a wall throughout the play) along with dream sequences to integrate ritual into performance of the play. According to the description of the setting: "a large wheel, crudely drawn on the blackboard [or a drawing hung on the wall] is a central icon, always visible on stage. Even in blackouts it is dimly illuminated. All the characters react to it, each in his own way. It is a likeness of the Bighorn Medicine Wheel in Wyoming" (iv), which symbolizes both religious rites and community relations to the Kiowa. The Medicine Wheel artifact located in northern Wyoming's Big Horn Mountains, a huge two-dimensional stone blueprint for the medicine lodge used in the Kiowa Sun Dance, is believed to have been constructed by the Kiowa between 1700 and 1760. The Medicine Wheel symbolically displays the elements of the sacred Sun Dance lodge: a central stone cairn marks the location of the lodge pole, while twenty-eight spokes radiate from the central cairn to the rim of the wheel. "Each radiating rock line or 'supporting pole' represents one of the twenty-eight Kiowa family groups then existing," reports Maurice Boyd.[52] Additional cairns mark the locations of the drum and of the head priest during the ceremony. The Medicine Wheel maps both a sacred space and a schematic diagram of community relations—ceremonial patterns and family groupings. In the play, the drawing of the Medicine Wheel reminds the Kiowa characters of the correlation between the location of the sacred and the interrelatedness of members of the many family groups in the tribe. Huntsman explains this type of configuration as a "dimensionless sacred place, the center of the universe and the locative counterpart of the ever-present time."[53] As Momaday indicates in his notes, characters' responses to the Medicine Wheel vary, measuring and displaying their connection to or distance from Kiowa community and metaphysics. John Pai, the "good student" at the boarding school, is constantly aware of and attentive to the Medicine Wheel's presence while he is on stage. In contrast, the school's disciplinarian describes the Wheel with disdain, calling it "an image drawn upon the skin of an animal, a Kiowa drawing, a pagan thing. . . . To me, frankly, it's superstition, paganism. Such things are sacrilegious, I believe" (5–6). The Wheel thus acts as the play's sacred and moral center, giving shape and meaning to the words and actions that spin around it.

Huntsman notes the religious or spiritual aspect of much traditional tribal drama, and Momaday's play illustrates the integration of this element because the play enacts a ceremony as it scripts tribal history, uniting history and ritual as does the Medicine Wheel. Ceremonial elements enter the play during two dream sequences. In the first, the final scene of act 1, the dreamer is John Pai, the "good student" upon whom the educators pin their hopes and reputations. Mother Goodeye and Emdotah, Seta's father and a boarding-school employee who was sent to recapture the runaways, participate in and comment on John Pai's dream as the bodies of the three boys, "like mummies or body bags," rest at the dreaming student's feet (33). Emdotah, the mourning father, prays over the bodies, "placing [his] words upon" them: "In my mind's eye, and in my heart, I see you moving into the camps. Not the poor camps, not the camps of the time when the ponies were killed, not the time of the camps when the buffalo were gone. But the camps of the Gaigwu [Kiowa], the coming-out people, in their gladness, in their dignity, in their glory." As Emdotah continues his prayer of reintegration, Mother Goodeye, John Pai, and the chorus of children join in, responding "Aho" ("thanks") to his prayer to the timeless darkness— the state of eternity and silence, the "above, below, beyond" that now encloses the children. The father's sadness is mitigated by a belief that his children are with their ancestors, free to be Kiowa in a way that Emdotah himself longs for—"When I come [into the darkness] . . . I shall be who I am then. I shall not be then an agency Indian; I shall not wear these ugly, branded clothes. And I shall not hunt down my children! I shall have lived as I could, and I shall be with you in the right way, in the right spirit" (34).

Emdotah's moving words clearly express the community's loss and speak the comfort that the dead children will be embraced by the Kiowa ancestors. In the second dream sequence, in the middle of the second act, Emdotah, significantly wearing Ghost Dance regalia, explains the ceremonial aspect of dreaming: "Haw! We are a tribe of dreamers. . . . Let us dream one story, and let us be whole and honorable and true to our dream, and ourselves in it" (60). Thus the dream sequences delineate a Kiowa spiritual space in which the play resolves its healing ritual, both a process of mourning and a reassertion of Kiowa values and philosophies. Played out in the context of the Ghost Dance, which came to the Kiowa in 1891 as a way to free their world from white presence, this ritual connotes the Kiowa's power to dream their own reality ceremonially, refusing to allow white explanations and representations to define them.

Use of tribal theatrical forms is, however, only one aspect of this affirmation. Momaday also vigorously articulates a tribal representation of the actions and motivations of the young boys, in direct contrast to the school's version of events.[54] The play's action begins once Mosatse, Seta, and Koi-kahn-hodle have run away after enduring severe physical punishment and humiliation at the hands of the disciplinarian, Barton Wherritt. From the first scene, we see that Wherritt and G. P. Gregory, the school's superintendent, are working to formulate an explanation of the boys' behavior and escape that will exculpate them and the school from any blame for the children's flight. Wherritt, aware that his actions will fall under scrutiny, writes a report that denotes his responsibilities as disciplinarian. He explains to Gregory: "I simply wanted to . . . express *my* reading, *my*, ah, interpretation of the manual" (7). Thus Momaday immediately establishes interpretation and representation as contested and important elements in the play. Wherritt asserts that Sailor, at age fifteen the oldest of the boys, received a whipping because he "deliberately violated the rules of the school" by kicking a younger, sickly boy (10–11). Sailor, or Seta, is particularly troublesome to the educators because the Kiowa believe that he possesses strong spiritual power, marked by his pure white hair. Mother Goodeye describes him as "an original boy, a boy priest, perhaps too a warrior. . . . And Seta talks like an old man, foolish and wise like Saynday [the Kiowa trickster], like a medicine man" (3). The Kiowa view Seta as powerful, important, and brave according to tribal cultural standards, so he is a target for the educators, who seek to destroy his legitimacy and integrity among the students and the larger community. By the first scene of act 2, after it has become apparent that the boys have perished in the winter storm, Wherritt and Gregory further manipulate their representation of Sailor, determining that his youthful participation in a ceremony, during which his hair turned white, made him "very cowardly, especially after night," and "when badly frightened, he seemed perfectly wild" (39). Gregory asserts that it was "Sailor's great fright" that made the boys lose their way as they traveled to their parents' camps, and Wherritt insists in the report he is preparing, that "Judging from the *frequency* with which the *boys in question* ran away, I consider the principal incentive that led to their departure, was identical with former instances, that is; [sic] they wanted to go to camp, preferring to reside there in indolence, rather than at school, leading a life of activity and usefulness" (39). Wherritt, therefore, uses the logic of social evolutionary thought to blame the boys' demise on their refusal to progress from their lives of "savage" indolence toward productive "civilization," barely mentioning the fact that he beat the boys severely.

Throughout the play, Kiowa characters challenge the educators' representations of the runaways, asserting their own representations of the actions and motivations of the boys and refuting and ironizing the moniker of "the indolent boys," an obvious misrepresentation guided by the educators' racist ideology and drive for self-preservation. As John Pai indicates in a discussion with Carrie, a young white teacher, students frequently had very good reasons for running away. Even though they faced danger from the elements and their pursuers, running away was worth the trouble.[55] Carrie is shocked to learn that her prize pupil himself was once a runaway, but as John Pai says:

> When I reached my mother's camp it was as if I had returned from the dead. I was so glad to be there, and everyone was so glad to see me. . . . And it didn't matter that I would be hunted down and taken back, because the time being was everything I ever wanted. It was all that my heart could hold. The old free life of the Gaigwu was there, just *there*, and it was mine, as it had been when I was born. I was simply, wholly, joyfully alive for the first time in years. My spirit had been caught and caged, and I had set it free again. Do you know how? By running away, like those three boys, by returning, by going home. Just the sheer physical exertion of running, of moving like a wild animal over the earth, across rivers and creeks, through woods,

on the long, rolling plain—that was to be alive, that was to be who I am and where I ought to be. (27)

If the very process of running was to feel free and alive, John Pai's capture by the Indian police and his return to the school "was as if I were mourning my own death" (28). Through his description of his own experiences, John Pai suggests that, although the boys physically perished in their flight, they were more alive in their escape than they had ever been at school. Echoing Zitkala-Ša's claim that boarding schools forced their students into a "long-lasting death" that masqueraded as "a life of activity and usefulness," John Pai represents the frozen boys far differently than do the educators.[56]

Likewise, Emdotah, comforted by his belief that the boys have in death been welcomed into the camps of the proud, thriving Kiowa of generations past, reads the details of their flight as signs of strength and bravery rather than indolence and savagery. Most of John Pai's second dream sequence consists of Emdotah and Mother Goodeye's explanation of the events surrounding the boys' deaths—a representation of those events that directly contrasts Wherritt's and Gregory's statements. Beginning with a song, which Emdotah sings in Kiowa and John Pai translates into English for the audience, Emdotah, John Pai, and Mother Goodeye begin the boys' story with the story of the origin of the Kiowa people, who named themselves the "Kwuda," or the "coming out" people after they emerged into this world through a tree trunk. John Pai connects Seta to his namesake, the legendary Kiowa warrior Set-angia. Stories about Kiowa ancestors, named and unnamed, clarify who the runaways were by explaining who the Kiowa people are. As the dream continues, Emdotah begins to narrate the events that led to the children's death. Mother Goodeye explains: "They are homesick, they are going to the camps, they are camping," establishing that the boys were not troublemakers who perversely refused to progress but, rather, homesick students who missed the families and community that nurtured them. Wherritt and Gregory insinuate that Seta led the others to their deaths and stole their clothes in a selfish effort to keep himself alive, but according to Emdotah, Seta "could be far ahead, out of danger, but he has kept to the slower pace of the children" (64). Rather than stealing Mosatse's clothes, he "removes the uniform and ties it round the small body in a dignified manner, like a coup string, like the captured possessions of a strong enemy" (65). When Koi-kahn-hodle dies, "my son removes the uniform, tears it, defiles it with dirt and mud, and puts it on like a trophy, as if it were the war shirt of a best enemy." He greets his own death with bravery, with "a death song, the song of a warrior. His song was his shield." When John Pai protests in sorrow, "there was not glory in his dying," Emdotah responds, "He earned his death. That is a better thing than glory" (65). The dreams ritually make sense of the tragedy and interpret the actions of the boys within a tribal context—asserting what Jace Weaver calls "hermeneutical sovereignty," in which "the community itself 'stands at the very center'" of the interpretive system and is affirmed and reinforced in the process of interpretation.[57]

The contrasting explications of the Kiowa and the educators collide in Wherritt's final dialogue with John Pai. Wherritt, who desires John Pai's admiration to affirm his own role in the student's educational transformation but who also dislikes the student because he views him as a rival for Carrie's affections, congratulates John on his acceptance into an eastern seminary, saying, "John, John, we are so very happy for you. You know, I envy you the long train ride through the countryside" (54). John informs the disciplinarian that one of his uncles rode on a train as one of Richard Pratt's prisoners, becoming the subject of Pratt's initial "experiment" in Indian education. Wherritt views the train ride as the boy's opportunity to "have a real look at America," whereas John Pai associates the train with incarceration and abduction. Wherritt expresses his sympathy for the families of the frozen boys, claiming that "the boys were very dear to me." "And they, Mr. Wherritt, were always mindful of you," replies John Pai, implying that student obedience did not signify affection. Wherritt insists, "Yes. We seem to have established a rapport, a real bond." Playing with his words, John Pai returns, "They knew of bonds." When Wherritt claims that Seta had a "disability," John Pai explains that Seta was different because "He was old, one of the old people" (65). Misunderstanding, Wherritt says, "Exactly. It is a disease. . . . There are cases in which children have become senile, and they have died of old age." But the boy points out: "It seems Seta died of the cold, and perhaps of shame," reminding the teacher that the humiliation he inflicted on the students through his physical and emotional punishment caused them to flee and to meet their death. Wherritt insists, "It is clear that Sailor acted imprudently, irrationally. He, well, he acted cowardly, it is sad to say. We must all agree that he led his little expedition into. . . into. . . . " While Wherritt searches for the words that fit his meaning ("peril and destruction"), John Pai interjects, "Into the Valley of the Shadow of Death. An *expedition*, as you say, I like that. *The Harm's Way Expedition*. Yes, they were a war party, a children's crusade. It is so." Purposefully filling in the blanks to suit his own interpretation rather than the administrator's, this "good student" verbally spars with the ideologue of the institution that taught him literacy in English. At the close of their interaction, after accusing Sailor of "stripp[ing] the little ones of their clothing," of stealing their meager protection against the cold because "he simply couldn't help himself," Wherritt, who fears reprisal from angry Kiowa parents, says, "It is very important to me that you understand how sorry and sympathetic I am and that you tell your people. Very important." John Pai gets the last word, replying, "I think I have it, Mr. Wherritt. Mr. Wherritt is a very sorry man" (56–57). John Pai's verbal play is not lost on Wherritt, who is "done in" by the end of the dialogue, breaks out in a cold sweat, and requests a leave of absence from the school. In this confrontation of representations, Momaday writes John Pai as the victor in the sparring match. The teacher cannot match the verbal dexterity of his student, and John Pai's representation of the runaways—based on his own experience of boarding-school life and his understanding of Kiowa culture—stands elevated as truth. Momaday's character is the antithesis of the *Indian Helper*'s paper Indians, coming out on top in a dialogue that undercuts the boarding-school ideology of "progression" and transformation.

Momaday is, therefore, taking on not only representations of the story of the frozen boys but also representations of boarding-school students in general, responding one hundred years later to the pervasive and insidious version of boarding-school student transformation found in the publications of the Carlisle Press. John Pai is Momaday's answer to Stiya; he is a "good student" who has not turned away from his culture. Through this character—whom the educators wish to send to divinity school and who would return as "the Reverend John Pai," a missionary for Christianity and Western education among his people (a version of Zitkala-Ša's disturbed Soft-hearted Sioux)—Momaday displays the complexity of boarding-school identity and highlights a focus on student resistance characteristic of most late-twentieth-century representations of boarding-school students.[58] Despite his imminent attendance at divinity school, John Pai has clearly not discarded Kiowa spiritual beliefs but has instead developed a collection of situational identities. Each time he comes on stage, he orients himself in relation to the Medicine Wheel, "taking a kind of customary observation" of the icon (53). At the same time, he has mastered his lessons at the school, becoming eloquent in English and conforming to the disciplinary mechanisms of the institution. John Pai uses English not to repeat the propaganda of the schools, like the paper Indians, but to engage in a type of wordplay doublespeak that exemplifies the "riddle" of his identity (22). When his teacher Carrie compliments him on his command of the English language, he responds, "Imagine. I am eloquent, and it isn't even my native language." Carrie replies, "But you have taken possession of it, appropriated it, made it your own, as if you were born to it." Carrie means by this that he has been able to comprehend and reproduce the lessons in civilization that he has been taught at the school. She tells him, "You will make a fine preacher, John. You will spread the gospel, as they say. You will glorify the word of God." But when John Pai responds by saying "I *was* born to words, truly, ma'am—very old words, from the time when dogs could talk," suggesting that his eloquence is a Kiowa characteristic rather than an effect of English literacy, he puzzles her. And when he inverts her statement about glorifying the word of God, stating that he will glorify instead, "the word of dog, the voice of the turtle," Carrie says with exasperation, "If we can get past your impertinence! Your riddling is . . . out of place. Remember yourself," she commands. With a glance at the Medicine Wheel, John Pai insists, "I *do* remember myself: I was a camp child, a child of the cloth, trade cloth. I preached to the dogs in the name of the Sailor [Seta], the dragonfly [Koi-khan-hodle], and the muchacho [Mosatse]. Amen" (22). Preaching to the Kiowa (in whose mythology the dog—and the "giant dog" or horse—plays an important and respected role) in the name of the three frozen boys, keeping them alive by sharing their story with the people, John Pai sees himself with a far more complicated mission and repertoire of identity than his teacher claims for him.[59]

This teacher-student relationship is also nothing like Marianna Burgess's depiction in *Stiya*. Where Stiya views her teacher as a "school mother" whose wishes she obeys and whose comfort she seeks, John Pai recognizes the sexual tension that exists between himself and Carrie. The teacher is certainly not a mother figure when she "closes her eyes and places her hands in the hollow of her skirt, draws them up to her breasts" telling him, "it's just that I wanted for so long to find a student who, who could make use of me, total use, whose mind and sensitivity I could shape and sharpen,

who would justify and fulfill me, who would confirm me in my purpose . . .
in my person and . . . vocation. It is what every . . . teacher dreams of, John.
And I found you" (23). Carrie's satisfaction with John's performance as a
student—"You're our entry, John, and our offering, our dearest sacrifice.
You are what we've got to show for all the disappointment and frustration
of this place"—becomes mixed with her attraction to the male Indian body,
seen in her recollection of a picnic the previous summer, when John and Seta
were playing a game and "you were, well, you were young men running,
and you had taken off your shirts—against the rules—and your bodies were
young and hard, and I don't know—rippling, . . . and I was somehow a girl
again, and there was in you a wildness, a kind of life I had never seen" (59).
Carrie's dreams of civilizing the savage become erotic fantasies of Indian
masculine wildness tamed by her "shaping and sharpening," a savagery to
desire sexually but to eradicate culturally.

Carrie's affection and desire for John Pai fool her into thinking that she
knows him completely. She firmly believes that "we are often of a mind,
John Pai and I. We see eye to eye on most issues" (46–47), but she certainly
does not understand the complexity of his identity, since, according to
Momaday's notes, he remains "inscrutable" (53). As Carrie and John speak
of the frozen boys and of his imminent trip East, John Pai writes on the
chalkboard:

Matthew		Sailor
Mark	John	Arch
Luke		Jack

By placing his own name in the middle ground between the Christian
Evangelists and the Kiowa runaways, John Pai indicates his position as a
cultural broker, able to write his way into both worlds. Touching his name
with a Kiowa gaming stick, he tells Carrie that he is "counting coup,"
showing his bravery by touching the enemy, a traditional Kiowa practice.
The audience might also recognize Momaday's allusion to the autobiography
of Luther Standing Bear, a Lakota member of the first class at Carlisle in
1879 (see the Introduction to this volume). With this intertextual reference,
Momaday links his character to a broader heritage of boarding-school-
student self-representation and asserts a literary solidarity for American
Indian authors based on shared subject matter. Just as Standing Bear's
action claimed a European American name as it asserted a continued

identification with Lakota culture, John Pai bravely displays the identities in his repertoire, continuing to represent himself as a complicated person who does not conform to a zero-sum view of identity formation. At the end of the play, we learn that John Pai has broken the linear trajectory of his progressive education by once more becoming a runaway. Leaving the train that was to take him east, in the direction of civilization, the "Reverend John Pai" returns to his people, not as a missionary but as a member of the community, where he will, perhaps, take part in the Ghost Dance, which was gaining popularity and significance among the Kiowa.[60]

The play ends with Mother Goodeye offering a humorous vision of healing and renewal through telling the story of the boys' burial. While everyone was crying and mourning "a strange thing happened, one of those things that are so unexpected and so deep in the center of life that they become a part of the story, you see" (76). As the wagon driver, "a dignified man," got down from the wagon at the burial site, the army coat he was wearing caught on the wagon brake, and "Luther hung dangling there, his feet well above the ground, his arms and legs thrashing. Well, it was an astonishing sight! They couldn't get him down until someone cut off the brass buttons, and then he fell on his ass like a sack of corn." The beleaguered community began laughing in the midst of their sorrow. Mother Goodeye explained: "There was crying, you see, and then there was laughter. And one was not greater than the other, neither more unaccountable or appropriate. When I think about it, you see, I believe it is a matter of balance. Even the stars are balanced, you see, and when they stray or fall, it is all right, for they will seek and find their balance in the great wheels of light. Well, for us, in the camps, that is how to think of the world. Eh neh neh neh!" (76). By placing the terrible loss of the boys within the tribe's cyclic understanding of joy and sorrow, life and death, the play's cycle of continuance demonstrates a healthy alternative to boarding-school ideology, which dichotomized the world through its either/or constructions of culture and identity. By staging a boarding-school story, Momaday shares Kiowa history and metaphysics with his audience, representing boarding-school students as complex individuals and community members, whose stories likewise demand intricate retellings.

Momaday's representation of the runaways as culture heroes is undoubtedly tied to the way the boarding school functioned as a marker of Indian identity in his family. His mother, Mayme Natachee Scott, was born in 1913 to a white mother and a father who was one-quarter Indian, through his maternal grandmother, a Cherokee woman also named Natachee. Momaday's mother strongly identified with her Cherokee great-grandmother and chose to identify herself as an Indian. Momaday recounts in *The Names:*

> In 1929 my mother was a Southern belle; she was about to embark upon an extraordinary life. It was about this time that she began to see herself as an Indian. That dim native heritage became a fascination and a cause for her, inasmuch, perhaps, as it enabled her to assume an attitude of defiance, an attitude which she assumed with particular style and satisfaction; it became her. She imagined who she was. This act of imagination was, I believe, among the most important events of my mother's early life, as later the same essential act was to be among the most important of my own.[61]

In order to claim the Indian identity she urgently desired, "She went off to Haskell Institute, the Indian school at Lawrence, Kansas."[62] Mayme Natachee Scott *chose* Indian boarding school as a way to choose Indianness. And in strengthening her Indian identification through school, she was not unique. As Paula Frederick concludes, "while Indian boarding schools were designed to acculturate Indians to dominant society, they often served the ironic purpose of strengthening the Indian identity of biracial Indians."[63] To Scott, as to her son and to other late-twentieth-century Indian writers, the boarding school signified Indianness rather than assimilation—an Indianness associated with defiance. To attend the school was to assert her right to call herself Indian and was also a way to surround herself with Indian people. Through her Haskell roommate, a Kiowa girl, Natachee met Al Momaday, who became her husband. In a very real sense, N. Scott Momaday is a product of the boarding schools' legacy of intertribal marriage, a principal component in the growth of Pan-Indian identity.[64] It is in this context that Momaday's representation of the runaway students— both the frozen boys who became an important part of Kiowa history and John Pai, Momaday's fictional character whose running away is very clearly a running *toward* tribal vitality and cultural life—must be understood as a memorial to the importance of the boarding-school experience to tribal history and contemporary American Indian identity.

Momaday also conceives of an activist role for *The Indolent Boys*, making the play an important component of his nonprofit foundation, the Buffalo

Trust. As its website explains, the Buffalo Trust works for "the preservation, protection and return of their cultural heritage to Native peoples, especially children, and [is] founded on the conviction that the loss of cultural identity—the theft of the sacred—is the most insidious and dangerous threat to the survival of Native American culture in our time. . . . The Buffalo Trust is concerned to enable Native American children to know their cultural inheritance, instill confidence in that identity, and to claim their place in the world."[65] The Indolent Boys educational project, a major trust activity, cultivates those same goals by "teach[ing] children about the history of Native American boarding schools and . . . foster[ing] dialogue between children and elders in tribal communities about personal boarding school experiences."[66] Momaday's foundation, in which productions of *The Indolent Boys* play a crucial role, thus uses stories of the boarding-school experience to promote cultural education and the continued strength of tribal communities, another act of hermeneutical sovereignty that weds community and activism to promote what Weaver calls "commutitism"—literary production with a "proactive commitment to Native community" that "participate[s] in the healing of the grief and exile felt [in response to colonialism] by Native communities and the pained individuals in them."[67]

CATHARTIC RELEASE AND PAN-INDIAN DEFIANCE IN GEIOGAMAH'S *FOGHORN*

While Momaday's play portrays a boarding-school story as a moment in a specific tribal history, Kiowa playwright Hanay Geiogamah's *Foghorn*, first performed in 1973, centers a Pan-Indian boarding-school scene in his satirical drama that charts Indian resistance to white colonization from Columbus to AIM. Geiogamah's play, written in response to Indian activists' assertions of Native rights, positions the occupation of Alcatraz as an event that came out of continuous Indian resistance and rebellion, from Pocahontas's time through the boarding schools and into the Red Power era. Emphasizing the continuity of defiant Indian response to assimilationist and genocidal challenges, Geiogamah portrays a strong Pan-Indian identity through his humorous reinvention of potentially tragic scenes.

Hanay Geiogamah is perhaps the most prolific contemporary American Indian playwright, and his involvement in both the scholarship on and production of Indian theater is unparalleled. In 1972, Geiogamah founded the Native American Theater Ensemble (NATE), a troupe of sixteen Indian artists who performed his and other Indian playwrights' plays throughout the United States and in Berlin between 1972 and 1976, when NATE disbanded.[68] Though NATE was short-lived, the group "spawned a number of theatrical offshoots," many incorporating former NATE members who returned to their homes across the country and founded such Indian theatrical companies as the Navajo-Land Outdoor Theater, the Spiderwoman Theater, and the Red Earth Performing Arts Company.[69] Geiogamah is also a founder and artistic director of the American Indian Dance Theater, professor of Theater Arts and American Indian Studies at UCLA, and interim director of UCLA's American Indian Studies Center (AISC). Currently, he is deeply involved with Project HOOP (Honoring Our Origins and People through Native Theater, Education, and Community Development), a multidisciplinary collaborative program of the AISC and Sinte Gleska University whose purpose is "to advance Native American Theater and to develop the next generation of artists."[70] Geiogamah's work as playwright, director, teacher, and scholar of contemporary American Indian drama has been groundbreaking and has significantly defined the genre and its conventions.

Like several of Geiogamah's plays, *Foghorn* was written with an Indian cast and an Indian audience in mind. Geiogamah explains that "the most important function of the Indian dramatist is to communicate with his own people. The major questions are: Does the play speak effectively to Indians? Can Indians understand what is happening on stage? If there is a message, is it communicated clearly and effectively in Indian terms? Are the characters and dialogue culturally authentic?"[71] As these issues and questions indicate, Geiogamah shares the concern of Leslie Silko and others about accurate, nonstereotypical representations of Indian people, created and produced by Indian people. Clearly, too, as his word choice reveals, Geiogamah is interested in appealing to and representing a broad, Pan-Indian audience, and as *Foghorn* and his other plays demonstrate, he is less concerned than Momaday with tribal specificity, instead concentrating on understanding and exploring issues and experiences that many Indian people share in common—those occurrences and characteristics that an Indian audience will recognize and acknowledge as "Indian"—to "promote an Indian theater whose significance is not restricted to one tribe."[72] Geiogamah accomplishes these goals by using dramatic forms from a variety of tribal traditions, including song, dance, and storytelling—(as in his play

Coon Cons Coyote, which incorporates a Caddo Bell Dance Song, a Salish Gaming Song, a Navajo Riding Song, and Skokomish, Taos, and Apache melodies into a retelling of a Nez Perce Coyote story).[73] But Geiogamah also draws from European theatrical styles—Annamarie Pinazzi notes "the indisputable affinity of Geiogamah's theater to the Euro-American theater of the 1900s, particularly the avant-garde of the 1960s"—effectively using his repertoire of representations to explore Indian identity.[74]

Critics have noted commonalities between Geiogamah's work and Brechtian political theater, and Brechtian elements of *Foghorn* make it appropriate that NATE first performed the play in Berlin in October 1973, two months before its U.S. debut. Geiogamah acknowledged that, as he was writing *Foghorn,* he read a study of Brechtian theater, paying particular attention to Brecht's use of alienation devices and coming to understand that "what was really interesting about Brecht was the attitude" behind such devices.[75] Indeed, *Foghorn* does not engage in most Brechtian techniques, such as projecting captions to explain or comment on a scene, or actors stepping out of character (techniques Geiogamah found "corny"), but the play does make use of the basic attitude behind the alienation effect, where actors do not identify with their roles, and instead portray a reading of their characters.[76] This detachment allows for the catharsis that occurs as Indian actors portray non-Indian people who have perpetrated serious crimes against Natives throughout the history of white-Indian contact. The title of the play refers to the disruptive foghorns that the U.S. government blasted continually at Indian occupiers of Alcatraz in 1969, and, according to Huntsman, "metaphorically it represents the playwright's awakening call to Indian people about the dangers that stereotypes pose."[77] Indeed, Geiogamah says in his author's note: "Almost all the characters in this play are stereotypes pushed to the point of absurdity" (49). The production consists of a series of scenes, joined to one another by interludes of drilling sounds and "visuals of earth being drilled" (49). The play opens with a procession of people, suggesting "a forced journey, such as the Trail of Tears, spanning the centuries from 1492 to the present and stretching geographically from the West Indies to Alcatraz Island" (51). Voice-overs of statements by various colonizers, including a Spanish sailor on one of Columbus's vessels, male and female "settlers," and a U.S. senator express a European American philosophy of racism and land hunger as they articulate the dual messages of Indian savagery and white Manifest Destiny. A scene set on Alcatraz follows. Reclaiming the land of the Americas for Indian people, the troupe sings a Zuni Sunrise Chant and proclaims the Alcatraz declaration:

> We, the Native Americans, reclaim this land, known as America, in the name of all American Indians, by right of discovery. We wish to be fair and honorable with the Caucasian inhabitants of this land, who as a majority wrongfully claim it as theirs, and hereby pledge that we shall give to the majority inhabitants of this country a portion of the land for their own, to be held in trust by the American Indian people—for as long as the sun shall rise and the rivers go down to the sea! We will further guide the majority inhabitants in the proper way of living. We will offer them our religion, our education, our way of life—in order to help them achieve our level of civilization and thus raise them and all their white brothers from their savage and unhappy state. (55–56)

Beginning with this reversal of the language of colonialism, the occupiers stage the remainder of the play as a reclamation through inversion, subverting and undermining scenes of oppression through their assertion of collective strength and resistance while the drilling sounds and visuals denote an upheaval of the very land, swept clean of white presence in a manner suggestive of Ghost Dance philosophy (though simultaneously describing the way that colonial actions have damaged the continent). The characters thus recover not only land but also spiritual and psychic health and cultural integrity through their humorous yet deadly serious play.

Geiogamah places the boarding-school scene at the center of the drama, after a vignette in which a nun, leading an Indian altar boy who carries a cross covered with paper money, screams "If we did not find you, your souls would burn! Burn forever, for eternity! In HELL!" (58) as she is attacked by a group of Plains Indians. The boarding-school scene occurs before scenes in which Pocahontas makes fun of John Smith's impotence, Tonto cuts the throat of the Lone Ranger, an Indian with a camera kills the First Lady in the course of photographing her, and a federal agent clumsily attempts to infiltrate a radical Indian group. The location of the boarding-school scene at the heart of the action of the play suggests the impact of the school experience on the lives of Indian people, and the urgency with which Indian revolutionaries wish to exorcise this particular demon.

The scene is set "circa 1900," the year Zitkala-Ša and La Flesche were publishing. The stage directions stipulate: "A clownish schoolteacher dances onstage, [wearing a garish 'stars and stripes skirt'], ringing a bell, carrying a bundle of small American flags, singing 'Good Morning to You.' She has been preceded by a group of very young Indian students who run onstage playfully, taking seats on two wooden benches. They respond to the teacher with awe, surprise, mild defiance, and fear. The teacher is snobbish, nervous, rude, feisty, and blusterous" (58). This caricature of a school-teacher upends the Carlisle teachers' self-representations, poking fun at their sanctimoniousness and uncovering the racism beneath their patriotism and philanthropy. She says good morning to the students, and when they ignore her she angrily calls out, "G—ood morning, savages!" and "busily arranges them in 'order'" (59). Her speech consists of plain, unrepentant, unobscured statements of social evolutionary rhetoric, and her actions mirror incidents common to the boarding-school experience. She "pummels" a girl who made a gesture in "Indian sign-language," forbids the use of any sort of Indian language in the classroom, and warns the girl, "I'll rap your knuckles hard if you do that again. . . . It'll be the dark room for you." She pauses and adds, "That's one step out of savagery for you" (59).

After expressing her disgust toward the children's dress and hair, she begins to sing "The Star Spangled Banner," but she stops when she sees the girl make another gesture. Shaking her as she screams, "This is not the reservation, child! This is not that awful place you came from where you all run around half naked, filthy, living in sin!" the schoolteacher regurgitates the thoughts and words of educators like Burgess without the cloak of sentimental prose to blunt or soften the vicious racist and anti-tribal state-ments. Once she has pushed the little girl into a dark closet, the teacher lectures the others:

> No more of that in his [sic] classroom, do you hear me? You are going to forget all of your Indian ways, all of them. You can start erasing them from your minds right now, right here, right this instant. No more of your disgusting sign language. No more of your savage tongue. No more greasy, lousy hair. No more blankets. You are going to learn the English language. . . . The most beautiful language in all the world. The language that has brought hope and civilization to our people everywhere. The one true language, OUR language! (61)

With this outburst, the schoolteacher represents the boarding-school philosophies of zero-sum identity transformation, and cultural erasure, asserting that knowledge of the English language will provide proof of assimilation. She has reduced the essence of the boarding-school philosophy to one angry diatribe.

The teacher proceeds to teach the students their first word of English, "the one word you must know first to become civilized," the word which will let white people "know that you are being relieved of your savage, uncivilized ways"; the word, ridiculously, is "hello" (61). Insisting that "the American way begins with hello," the teacher loudly repeats the word again and again, until the syllables become separated into "hell" and "oh," forming a mantra that begins to sound like "o hell o hell o hell" (61). Finally one of the children "timidly tries the word," and the exuberant teacher drags her to the front of the room and makes her wave an American flag while repeating the word and encouraging the rest of the class. It is significant that only this one word is uttered by a student, for the furious monologue of the educator allows for no discussion or dialogue. Despite their enforced silence, however, Geiogamah's students do get their say. As the scene ends, "The students ape the teacher with strong gestures as she continues to instruct the remaining students. The teacher soars on her success. The pupils form into a tight group, fists clenched, close in on her, and attack. The lights fade on the drilling sound, earth visuals" (62). After the teacher's excessive expressions of racism and violence, the students' attack provides a release, acting out what was, undoubtedly, the impulse of generations of Indian boarding-school students, made possible by the inversion of the power structure enabled within the play.

Geiogamah explains, "The audience loved *Foghorn*. The actors would really get into it. We'd turn up the sound just as loud as we could without breaking the limits. We had the visuals as big as we could magnified in zoom reverse. Everything was wild, absolutely wild, and it got wilder and wilder."[78] He identifies this as "buoyancy," which results from cathartic release. "I think vicariously a lot of Indi'ns were playing the Lone Ranger, along with the actors, playing the First Lady, playing that nun, playing the schoolteacher. Once again, the hardest scene, the cruelest scene is the schoolteacher scene, and the audience just laughed, and laughed, and laughed. She couldn't hardly get her lines out. That was just recognition."[79] Through recognition of the pain of these experiences—turned upside down

by Indian actors mocking the oppressors through their outrageous caricatures—the audience responds with laughter, bouncing back from the pain.
The action gets "wilder and wilder," itself an "anti-progressive" assertion
of resistance. Ken Lincoln comments: "The humor [in *Foghorn*] lies in . . .
'playing' out the hurt, as the play celebrates what it means to be alive
today in Indian America."[80] Scenarios of oppression, scripted by an Indian
playwright and played out on stage by Indian actors, are dismantled.

The play continues, as "the satire proceeds by playful mockery rather
than bitter denunciation," comments Geiogamah. "A production should
aim at a light, almost frivolous effect (the basic seriousness of the play will
emerge all the more effectively if the heavy hand is avoided)" (49). The
wild laughter builds, as a girl in pigtails reads the names of treaties off a
list written on toilet paper, while an actor wearing a bull's head "also holds
a roll, and unwinds enough tissue to wipe his behind each time a treaty is
called out" (75). The culminating musical number, a song and dance
enactment of a Wild West Show, ends with several of the Wild West Show
Indians falling dead to the floor in a "tableau" called "TRIUMPH OF THE
WHITES" (78). The scene shifts, as rifle fire sounds and "vistas of the terrain
around Wounded Knee, South Dakota" are projected on the backdrop.
Geiogamah's directions indicate that "the visuals stop on a single picture
of a marshal peering through a rifle scope that is aimed toward the performers and the audience" (79). The celebration of Indian persistence has
turned deadly serious. A drummer performs the AIM song, surrounded by
the entire cast, until a shot rings out, hitting the drummer and silencing
the song. The performing group carries the drummer off-stage and then
returns, all of them handcuffed, while the voice of a U.S. Marshal notifies
them that they are being arrested "on the charge of unlawfully trespassing
on private property" (80). As they walk toward their criminal trials,
individual members of the troupe step forward and announce their tribal
affiliation: "I am Pawnee," says the first; "I am Winnebago," and "I am
Sioux," or "I am Creek, . . . Apache, . . . Ojibwe" affirm the others. As the
voice of the Spanish Sailor is heard once more, telling Columbus
"¡Capitán! . . .¡Ellos son los indios!" the narrator states with finality and
compassion "I am . . . NOT GUILTY!" as the light slowly fades. This is a final
insistence of Indian innocence—the activists are not trespassers, nor
vicious savage fools. They proclaim their innocence of what Pinazzi calls
"some unspecified crime that seems to consist essentially in not meeting

the conqueror's expectations."[81] The seriousness of their resistance and rebellion comes out of the centuries of abuse they have experienced at the hands of anti-Indian individuals, policies, and institutions. These defining moments, the play argues, justify their cause. According to Geiogamah, to be Indian, whether one is Pawnee, Winnebago, Sioux, or Creek, is to experience this pain, and to rebel against it, resisting assimilation, conversion, obliteration. The final moments of the play, in which this sense of shared Indianness is achieved by the articulation of membership in many individual Native nations, emphasize the importance of a tribal-national identity as a foundation for pan-tribal Indian resistance.

When the play was first performed, in late 1973, it would have been particularly important for Indian activists to trace out a shared history of resistance, a vision of continuity that would empower them and reinforce their sense of identity with the cause, activating their strengths, as Geiogamah explains, in "the right kind of way—instead of *mis*activating them in the sense of militancy, and racism, reverse racism, and blame, blame, blame."[82] This message of solidarity and renewal still electrifies *Foghorn*'s audiences, sounding a call to action through a representation of past rebellion. As do Tapahonso and Momaday, Geiogamah strives to invoke balance. He explains: "I see the Indi'n capacity for humor as a blessing. And I see it as one of the fundamental miracles of our lives. It's a miraculous thing that's pulled us through so much. . . . You've always got to try to balance everything, know where that factor fits into the way you conduct your life."[83] Being Indian, then, is to be a boarding-school student, and to survive the experience as an Indian, adding a politically charged Pan-Indian identity to your repertoire. Through *Foghorn*'s contemporary enactment of scenes that define Indianness, in both its pain and its triumphs, Geiogamah writes the Indian boarding-school experience as a moment in which today's Native people can bear witness to their historical oppression (noting in that shared recognition a pan-tribal solidarity), and beat it down with laughter.

LEARNING TRIBAL COSMOPOLITANISM IN SILKO'S *GARDENS IN THE DUNES*

Tapahonso, Momaday, and Geiogamah represent Indian boarding-school students as keepers of Indian and tribal identities, but Leslie Marmon Silko takes these representations one step further in her latest novel, *Gardens in the*

Dunes (1999), which radically reinvents turn-of-the-century "Indian education" and revises the trope of the boarding-school runaway, to cast the heroine,
Indigo, a member of the fictional Sand Lizard tribe, as both student of tribal
cultures and teacher to the Europeans and white Americans she encounters.
Indigo's flight from the Sherman Indian Institute in Riverside, California,
is not an immediate escape from the institutions of Eurocentric education.
She runs directly into the heart of social evolutionary ideology when she is
taken in by a wealthy white couple who decide to keep her for the summer
and "educate" her on a tour of Europe. Despite her grand tour of European
civilization with Edward Palmer, a collector and broker of rare plants, and
his "heretic" wife, Hattie (the kind of journey that turn-of-the-century European American literature depicts as refining and "civilizing"), Indigo is not
transformed by her contact with European American and European culture.[84]

Instead, she seeks out and learns about the pagan and early Christian
beliefs of the Old Europeans, which reinforce and coincide with her Sand
Lizard culture and the tenets of the Ghost Dance, in which her family
(particularly her mother) participates. Throughout her circuitous journey
home, Indigo continually reaffirms her tribal identity and develops strategic pan-tribal alliances as she gathers seeds from across the United States
and Europe that she will bring back to grow in the gardens of her desert
homeland. Yet, as Kate Shanley has written: "'Home' may not be a 'place'
indigenous people have ever been before—the global economic structure
requires new forms of culture and governance. The drive to go 'there'
nevertheless urgently continues."[85] Indigo returns home, bringing useful
lessons with her, and incorporates them into Sand Lizard practices to
create a culture that is new and yet still distinctly grounded in Sand Lizard
identity and cultural traditions. The notions of nationalism and a very
specific sort of cosmopolitanism therefore come together in Indigo's education, in order to articulate a kind of "tribal cosmopolitanism"—a recognition
of shared traditions, political interests, and values that preserves space for
distinct claims of indigenous nationalism, sovereignty, and autonomy. This
stance acknowledges strategic global connections in the interest of coalition-
building, but always with the nationalist goal of the retention of tribal land,
culture, and identity. The educational curriculum she designs enables Indigo
to sustain herself in her Sand Lizard culture because it makes her an active
agent of hybridity.

Lakota scholar Elizabeth Cook-Lynn has asserted that cosmopolitanism is the "enemy of resistance literature," because it is "the exploration in literature of the tastes and interests of the dominant culture" and attempts to "transcend national affiliations" and "legitimize hybridity."[86] In contrast, she defines the discourse of sovereignty and tribal nationalism as "a concept in the arts that argues for nation-specific creativity and political unification in the development, continuation, and defense of a coherent national mythos."[87] These definitions seem to set nationalist and cosmopolitan discourses as binary opposites. Cosmopolitanism, in this iteration, lacks anchor, seeks to transcend (which implies "to devalue, to leave behind") ties to the nation, and is unable to consider indigenous or tribal sovereignty meaningfully.

This definition of cosmopolitan literature as the exploration of the tastes of the dominant culture may capture the tendencies of some literature written by privileged border-crossers such as V. S. Naipaul or Salman Rushdie. But it may not fully encompass recent attempts of postcolonial scholars to extend the definition of cosmopolitanism, beyond a universality that arises out of detachment, to incorporate transnational experiences or connections that are particular and not universal, arising from very specific cultural and historical circumstances. Such specific cosmopolitanisms— "vernacular," "postcolonial," and "rooted" cosmopolitanisms—open space for considering, in the words of critic Bruce Robbins, that "like nations, cosmopolitanisms are now plural and particular. Like nations, they are both European and non-European. . . . And like the nation, cosmopolitanism is *there* . . . habits of thought and feeling that have already shaped and been shaped by particular collectivities, that are socially and geographically suited, hence both limited and empowered." As Robbins further explains: "For better or worse, there is a growing consensus that cosmopolitanism sometimes works together with nationalism rather than in opposition to it."[88]

In *Gardens in the Dunes,* Silko examines the particular form of cosmopolitanism that arises from the experience of turn-of-the-century Indian education. Silko has said in an interview about *Gardens* that "The old time people were way less racist and talked way less about lines and excluding than now. So that way of being in the world and in the Americas is not forgotten, we've got to be reminded of how the people used to see things."[89] The coexistence of tribal and Pan-Indian identities within a repertoire, according to Silko, is a reiteration of the lessons she learned from the elders

of her Laguna Pueblo community. By coming to understand the significance
of tribal cosmopolitanism, then, Indigo and her older sibling, Sister Salt,
successfully complete a tribal education and learn what they need to know
in order to maintain their tiny community amid threatening change.

  Gardens in the Dunes voluminously documents the Sand Lizard education
Indigo and Sister Salt receive from their Grandma Fleet. Grandma impresses
upon the girls the importance of family and community, the necessity of
using every available resource for survival, and the obligation to respect
and honor the land that nourishes both the body and the spirit. Grandma
Fleet and her daughter, the girls' mama, have survived the violations and
hardships that came with the white colonial presence through their selective adaptation—by participating marginally in the capitalist economy,
selling baskets to tourists or cleaning rooms at a hotel, and by joining the
syncretic Ghost Dance and never losing their abiding connection to their
ancestral gardens in these accommodations. Silko, in fact, created the Sand
Lizard tribe based on extensive research on Colorado River tribes, because
she wanted to "imagine a people who had characteristics that made others
remark they were different—characteristics that, in being who they were,
it set them up to be destroyed."[90] Her Sand Lizard people, then, possess a
distinct and unique tribal culture, which distinguishes them from others
and marks them as targets for programs of cultural genocide. Grandma
Fleet, the one remaining tribal elder, passes the community's unique vision
to her grandchildren.

  Although Grandma Fleet dies when the girls are young and Mama
disappears with the Ghost Dancers and the Messiah, who are fleeing from
both police and soldiers, we are assured that "Sister Salt remembers everything."[91] What Indigo does not remember from her youth, Sister teaches
her in the months they live together in the gardens alone following
Grandma's death. Indigo and Sister Salt have learned how to respond to
anything they encounter in accordance with Sand Lizard values, customs,
and practices. It is only when they are captured by tribal police and taken
forcefully to school—Indigo to the Sherman Institute and Sister Salt to a
"school" that is nothing but a work camp—that the girls are forced to
encounter other philosophies and cultures that aggressively attempt to
displace their Sand Lizard lessons.

  While *Gardens in the Dunes* determines to investigate and challenge
representations of turn-of-the-century Indian education, the novel spends

very little narrative time in the schoolroom itself, instead using the grand tour of Europe as a stand-in for the boarding school. Indigo spent three months at Sherman, but her time at the school takes up only two of the almost five hundred pages of the novel (and, in fact, one of those two pages primarily discusses her train ride to the school) (69–70). In these two pages, we see that Indigo does not become part of a student community at Sherman, as she is unable to conceive of Pan-Indian community early in the novel. Instead, the schoolgirls "hated her because she already knew English words and she had never been to school" (69). Native employees, too, share no sense of solidarity with their charges. When Indigo attempts to justify her street-wise English to the Pomo matron, saying: "Hey, Lady! What's the trouble? I'm talking English—see. God damn! Jesus Christ! Son of a bitch!" (70), the matron washes her mouth out with soap. Then the Mission Indian janitor locks her in a closet when she spits the soap at the matron's eyes. The matron, the janitor, and the docile, obedient girls who enforce the school's rules with new arrivals, indoctrinating them into the school's web of disciplinary power, offer no hint of resistance or repertoires of identity.

Perhaps Silko avoids the detailed narrating of Indigo's experience at Sherman because she views the boarding school as an unrepresentable space, too full of repression to allow a rebellious Indian voice to speak from within it. But perhaps Silko's silence about Indigo's time at Sherman is generative. It is not the silent capitulation of McNickle's Archilde Leon, but rather the silence that might provide narrative space in which Indigo's story may be heard.[92] According to Momaday: "In the Indian world, a word is spoken or a song is sung not against, but within the silence. In the telling of a story, there are silences in which words are anticipated or held on to, heard to echo in the still depths of the imagination."[93] Silko intends for the words of her story to be held within a silent knowledge of the boarding-school experience, creating a dialogic experience for conversant readers. The parts of the story she does tell us should resonate with the unspoken historical realities faced by Indian children at school, generating layers of intersections and interstices, the connections and gaps, presences and absences, that constitute the web of story. She incorporates her Grandpa Hank's stories about his years at Sherman into her brief representation of the school, particularly the incident in which Indigo watched "three girls from Alaska stop eating, lie listlessly in their beds, then die, coughing blood" (70). Echoing the deathbed scenes related by La Flesche and Zitkala-Ša, this incident impresses a similar message of resistance onto Indigo. In a dream, "the girls did not speak to her, but she knew what their message was: she had to get away or she would die as they had" (70).

. Words are not needed to express this invocation to flight. Certainly Indigo's escape offers Silko narrative opportunities and grants Indigo the ability to elude the coercive gaze of a Man-on-the-Band-stand. Moving the narrative action off campus also allows Silko to play with the concept of an education in "civilization." If exposure to European culture should transform Indian students within the grim confines of the boarding school, an Indian student who journeys to the heart of Victorian society should assimilate even faster and more completely, and lose her tribal identity almost immediately, in the face of a clearly "superior" culture and its ordering mechanism of social evolutionism. By placing Indigo's education outside the school, Silko causes Indigo's resistance to be read as even more heroic, given the intensity of the ideological inundation she must overcome and the dangers she rebuffs as a runaway. Silko's silence about the middle ground of the boarding school therefore focusses our attention on Indigo's multiple, complicated responses to Western culture.

Silko's representation of the philosophy behind the boarding schools is unambiguous. The novel clearly and consistently articulates a critique of social evolutionary thought, which championed a European American civilization into which Indian people must be educated and assimilated. Edward Palmer embodies this social evolutionary ideology within the novel. A gentleman naturalist, Edward Palmer's interest in Indigo stems from "the notion that the child might be the last remnant of a tribe now extinct, perhaps a tribe never before studied by anthropologists" (113). Like the Friends of the Indian, Edward appreciates her "savagery" for scientific purposes but nevertheless recognizes that such traits must be eliminated, because Indigo must lose her Indianness to "adjust to the world she was in now" (304). Edward was "satisfied Hattie was teaching the child geography and reading and writing on their journey, but a docile willingness to serve must also be cultivated" (311). Indigo must be "civilized," but integrated into "the white man's world" only in an appropriate social status. Although others may "progress," for Edward the apex of civilization ultimately remains the domain of the white man.

A modern imperialist in search of financial gain, Edward "traveled to places so remote and collected plants so rare, so subtle few white men ever saw them before. He added these rare treasures to his growing collection of roots, stalks, leaves, and most important, when possible, seeds. His ambition was to discover a new plant species that would bear his name" (80). Indigo's Grandma Fleet urged her and Sister Salt to follow the very different Sand Lizard philosophy of gardening: "to collect as many new seeds as they could carry home. The more strange and unknown the plant, the more interested Grandma Fleet was; she loved to collect and trade seeds. Others did not grow a plant unless it was food or medicine, but Sand Lizards planted seeds to see what would come; Sand Lizards ate nearly everything anyway, and Grandma said they never found a plant they couldn't use for some purpose" (86). Edward's acquisition of and trade in tropical plants serves no apparent practical purpose at all but rather feeds the "gardening fashion"-frenzy of his sister, Susan, who, like other Eastern socialites, remakes the land in the image of the current trend, with no interest in sustenance or sustainability (192).

Edward's specimens, one of which—"a single shriveled stalk with fragments of dried plant material"—is particularly illustrative, bespeak the sterility and impotence of his ideological and political position, a characterization enhanced by the "wound" he suffered while on an orchid-collecting trip to Brazil. Linking his fortunes with financiers who also desired disease-resistant rubber plant seedlings to prevent the loss of "supplies of cheap natural rubber" for England and the United States (part of a trade in rubber and other plants built upon the torture, slavery, and death of Indian laborers [135]), Edward is double-crossed and abandoned by his business associates when one of them torches the habitat of an already-rare orchid in order to increase the value of his specimens. Escaping, Edward falls, and his heavy camera (in his hands signifying the eye of colonial surveillance) crushes his leg and renders him literally impotent (143). Edward ultimately dies because of his belief in pseudo-scientific experimentation. He allows Dr. Gates, his unscrupulous business partner in a mining concern, to swindle him out of his estranged wife's money and then kill him with experimental treatments for pneumonia. Edward's death—the result of a greedy, fatal faith in unhealthy "scientific" endeavors—highlights the lack of integrity behind supposed scientific "objectivity."

The scientist who collects plants without thought for the protection of their habitats and who mines meteorites without recognition of their sacredness to Indian cultures, is a pathetic, profit-driven figure.[94] With philosophy

neither compelling nor particularly effective, Edward does not even achieve
the status of a villain. Unlike Geiogamah's schoolteacher, an overblown
stereotype designed to elicit the audience's disgust, neither the reader nor
Indigo hate the scientist. Instead, Indigo is plainly indifferent to him, his
philosophies, and his actions. Through her connection to unconventional
women such as Hattie's Aunt Bronwyn and her friend, the Professoressa
Laura, Indigo distances herself from Edward and his ideas. When she hears
of his death, Indigo merely shrugs her shoulders: "She had not thought
about Edward since they said good-bye. . . . Except for the big glassy eye
of his camera, Indigo thought he wasn't a bad man. 'Poor thing. I guess he
was old,'" she says simply (441). In Silko's novelistic world, the white
educator is pushed out of the center and replaced by Indigo, the dynamic
and voracious student, who draws to herself the lessons she wants and
needs, expressing only indifference to social evolutionary thought and the
tenets of "civilization."

With Edward Palmer removed from the center, other strains of European thought become visible, revealing that the European and Indian
worlds are not at root diametrically opposed as "civilized" and "savage."[95]
In Europe, for example, Indigo follows signs of the annual migration of
the Messiah, whom she knows through her family's participation in the
Ghost Dance, searching for her mother and reaching for a better understanding of a system of beliefs that promised the return of ancestors and
the elimination of European influence from the face of the Americas. The
pan-tribal, syncretic Ghost Dance mirrored elements of traditional Sand
Lizard religion, such as praying to and depending on the spirits of
ancestors, and also offered the hope of a universal faith that would unite
disparate cultures—Indians, Mormons, and even the followers of the
pagan Old Europeans. When the Messiah and his mother appeared at
Needles, "all the dancers could understand them, no matter what tribe
they were from. . . . In the presence of the Messiah and the Holy Mother,
there was only one language spoken—the language of love—which all
people understand . . . because we are all the children of Mother Earth"
(33–34). Not only Indian people but also white Mormons danced and
found the words of the Messiah mutually intelligible.[96] The Messiah's
philosophy of language is strikingly different from the English-only
policy of the boarding schools, privileging no one language over the
others to mark it as the language of salvation and civilization. Instead,

the shared faith is communicated to the Dancers in mutually intelligible but culturally specific languages, offering the vision of cross-cultural communication without imposed monolingualism.

Hattie's Aunt Bronwyn likewise understands the connection between the Messiah and the religious rites of the Old Europeans.[97] While Hattie worries that her aunt would "confuse . . . the child with superstition," Aunt Bronwyn tells the girl about sightings of a group of dancers in England, and "Indigo and [Hattie's] aunt exchanged smiles; yes, the Messiah and his dancers were safe" (264). Hattie, Indigo's educator, is deeply disturbed by this exchange, exclaiming: "Why, her aunt had left the church altogether! . . . Hattie did not want [Indigo] to become confused—certainly not by the notion that old stones should be worshipped!" (265). Although Hattie worries that Aunt Bronwyn is leading her protégé astray, Indigo and the older woman share a heartfelt bond based on a common understanding of the spirituality at the base of both their cultures.

Similarly, Indigo and Aunt Bronwyn's Italian friend Laura, the professoressa, recognize a shared belief system reflected in the Old European figures that the professoressa shelters in her gardens. In the garden of tall, black gladiolus, when Indigo sees a snake-headed terra-cotta figure, cradling snake babies to her human breasts, she brings to mind Grandma Fleet's teachings: "Grandma Fleet used to talk to the big snake that lived at the spring above the old gardens; she always asked after the snake's grandchildren and relatives and sent her best regards" (299). While Edward Palmer views these figures as "grotesque madonnas far more monstrous than the centaur or minotaur," Indigo easily integrates them into her Sand Lizard beliefs, recognizing their power (299). Hattie and Edward, shocked by a large stone phallus and the snake-people statues in the garden, fret about what she has learned in Italy: "The child was from a culture of snake worshipers and there was no sense in confusing her with the impression the old Europeans were no better than red Indians or black Africans who prayed to snakes (304). Clearly threatened by lessons that dismantle the social evolutionary racial hierarchy that boarding-school education sought to ingrain in its students, Hattie and Edward nonetheless cannot stop the alternate education revealing itself to Indigo throughout her travels. The lesson Indigo takes from her encounters with Aunt Bronwyn and Laura is one of transcultural solidarity and equality, of reciprocal education, along with a simultaneous reaffirmation of Sand Lizard teachings.

Silko's characters reap what they sow. Edward's botanical imperialism is punished when he is shamed, impoverished, and incarcerated for stealing citrus saplings from Corsica to grow for profit back in California. Indigo, in contrast, heads back to the Southwest, her valise stuffed with seeds, gifts from Aunt Bronwyn and Laura, full of knowledge and memories of Old European statues and visions of the Messiah. Edward alarmingly notes that "her demeanor was that of a sultan, not a lady's maid" (310). Indigo has never once doubted that she will return to her gardens in the dunes, to be reunited with Sister Salt and her mother. She sees herself in her Victorian dresses not as an "imitation white man," but as a "Sand Lizard girl . . . loose in the white people's world" (161). Although she at times forgets "how dark she was because all around her she saw only lighter faces," and she knows that "Grandma Fleet would really laugh and Sister Salt probably would pinch her and tease her for becoming a white girl, not a Sand Lizard girl," she never questions the continued presence of her Sand Lizard identity within her growing repertoire (287). "Wait until they saw all the seeds she gathered and the notebook she brought back with the names and instructions and color sketches too," she anticipates, planning her return home to plant her seeds in the gardens of her ancestors, using her newly acquired knowledge in the service of the continuance of Sand Lizard culture (287).

While Indigo's travels with Hattie (and their eventual alliance) teach her about the shared values of Old Europeans and Sand Lizard people, the most important affiliations Indigo forms are with Indian people from other tribes, though at first neither Indigo nor Sister Salt understand the need for them. Indigo clearly feels no sense of solidarity with the other girls at boarding school, nor with the Indian police who break up the Ghost Dance and bring Indigo to Sherman with her hands and feet bound. When she stops with Hattie and Edward Palmer in Albuquerque on their way to New York, and Hattie asks her if she would like to speak with the Indian women who sell crafts at the train station, Indigo contemplates: "What did Hattie think? Those women were strangers from tribes Indigo knew nothing about; what was she supposed to say to the Indian women?" (126). But when she wanders away from Hattie's parents' estate in New York, the farmers who catch her in their fields do not think of her as Sand Lizard. To them, she is simply Indian, and she belongs with the only Indians they know, in the Matinnecock settlement near Manhasset Bay. In the brief period of time she spends in the settlement, Indigo plants the seeds of her Pan-Indian identity. After sharing a meal with the Indians, Indigo asks a Matinnecock woman, "Where are your gardens?" In response, "the woman looked at the hills for a long time, and Indigo understood her silence as her answer; the land where their gardens used to grow was taken" (173). With this exchange, as silence resonates with mutually understood meaning, Indigo begins to realize that Indian people across the continent share similar concerns and have faced similar wrongs. She carries everywhere a mother of pearl button that the Matinnecock woman gave her, "because the button was her first gift from another Indian," a sign of her growing awareness of a politically significant pan-tribal connection (182).

Sister Salt, too, adds a Pan-Indian identity to her repertoire, developed as she washes laundry alongside the Colorado River in the work camp "school" at Parker. She builds friendships with strangers from many tribes and gives birth to the child of Big Candy, a man of African and "Baton Rouge Indian" heritage. Sister Salt, who is clearly of mixed racial heritage, knows that among Sand Lizards "sex with strangers was valued for alliances and friendships that might be made" (204). Such alliances do not diminish the strength of Sand Lizard culture since, "Sand Lizard mothers gave birth to Sand Lizard babies no matter which man they lay with; the Sand Lizard mother's body changed everything to Sand Lizard inside of her" (204). Sister Salt's baby, born through her alliance with Big Candy, links her not only to him but also to her Sand Lizard ancestors. She calls the infant, who looked to Sister like "a tiny shrunken old man," the "little black grandfather" (343). Her link to her past—an ancestor come back to guide her—and her hope for the future, Sister Salt's baby literally embodies the positive aspects of cross-tribal allegiances. The child is a cross-cultural alliance that enhances rather than diminishes a sense of connection with the Sand Lizard nation. Sister Salt also comes to know and respect Delena, a Mexican Indian revolutionary who steals Big Candy's money to fund an indigenous army whose goal is to retake the land. Through Big Candy, who unwittingly transports the weapons purchased with his life's savings across the Mexican border, Sister Salt and her child join in a larger Pan-Indian alliance that stretches across national boundaries.

By linking Indigo and Sister Salt's growing awareness of Pan-Indian solidarity to the Ghost Dance and the Mexican revolutionaries (both of which promise liberation from colonial occupation), Silko represents Pan-Indian identity as an explicitly political identity that comes directly out of their "educational" experiences on the grand tour of Europe and at Parker work camp, thus arguing for a radically revised representation of Indian education that emphasizes the girls' agency and their recognition of shared Indian concerns and beliefs. The grand tour of Europe, substituting for the boarding school, bears as fruit Pan-Indian resistance to white colonialism in the Americas. Joane Nagel explains:

> Although the decades since 1960 represent the real period of American Indian ethnic mobilization, Indian activism and the resurgence of Indian culture and identity cannot be understood except within a larger historical context. The American Indian ethnic renewal of recent decades arose in reaction to, and thus in many ways was dependent on, trends in Indian affairs that were mainly assimilationist in character and intent.[98]

Silko tells the story of a boarding-school-student runaway who takes from her educational experience not only a reinforced tribal identity but also a powerful Pan-Indian identity rooted in concerns about the land—what Kate Shanley calls, in a different context, the "paradox" of "pan-Indian defenses of cultural distinctions."[99] It is significant that the Ghost Dance is one of the primary examples of intercultural connection within the text, because the Ghost Dance, even in its pan-tribal performance, is intimately connected to the reclamation of land that makes nationhood possible. The way the alliance between Indigo and Hattie plays out with respect to the Ghost Dance makes clear Silko's vision of tribal cosmpolitanism.

Hattie Palmer learns from Indigo (who takes on the role of her teacher) to reject the values of her culture—unmasked as patriarchal and violating— and leaves behind her own position as de facto schoolmarm whose educational mission was cultural indoctrination. Hattie decides she would "rather wander naked as Isaiah for years in the wilderness than go back" to the European American society she has come to find empty and oppressive (454). After a white man rapes and beats Hattie near the town of Needles, where the white townspeople feel she has challenged the boundaries they seek to maintain between their own "civilization" and the surrounding "savagery" by consorting too closely with Indigo and her family, Hattie does in fact wander in the desert, making her way to the river where Indians are once again gathering to dance for the Messiah's return. Silko resists representing Hattie's metamorphosis as the mirror image of boarding-school educators' vision of Indian student identity change. Hattie does not become an "imitation Indian," which would ultimately be appropriative. Instead, Hattie's final transformation comes when she recognizes that her presence at the Ghost Dance is drawing unwanted attention from the police who join her parents to search for her, and she makes the decision to burn down Needles and leave the United States to return to live with Aunt Bronwyn who has "gone native" in England (254). Through her actions, Hattie enacts the Ghost Dance, which Silko posits as the ultimate reversal of Eurocentrism. Hattie herself attempts to wipe the land clean of white presence and to take her proper place as an ally—off of Indian land and back in her own ancient homeland of Europe, in frequent contact with the affirming practices of those who follow the ways of the Old Europeans (254). Her movement outside of the confines of her culture teaches her to redefine her own sense of nationalism, respecting the boundaries of her relationship with Indigo even as she reaches across them.

Recognition of connections beyond tribal boundaries clearly bears fruit for Indigo and Sister Salt as well, as they return to the gardens and thrive even while maintaining contact with others they have come to know while away from their home. The novel ends with the sisters and the little black grandfather (along with a monkey and a parrot) once more within the gardens, and it is through the metaphor of the garden itself that we can see what is at stake in tribal cosmopolitanism. Of all the seeds Indigo brings home, none is more surprising and useful than the gladiolus corms she brings from Laura in Italy. The gladioli are hybrids, crosses of African and European plants, and Indigo sows them in rows that mimic the colors of corn varieties native to her garden. As Indigo discovers, the corms themselves are tasty and nutritious, providing nourishment as well as aesthetic appeal. This hybrid, then, does not transcend national use. Instead, it can be incorporated into systems of knowledge and meaning in order to nourish and sustain national initiatives such as a return to the garden, for as a Sand Lizard woman, Indigo is a gardener, and as Grandma Fleet taught, "Sand Lizards . . . never found a plant they couldn't use for some purpose" (84).

Indigo and Sister Salt's education in the effectiveness of alliances brings them back together with a child to raise in their tribal home, and the signs of rebirth abound in the ancient tribal gardens in the dunes, proven by the return of a snake to the garden spring, a prediction that Indigo, Sister Salt, and the little black grandfather will flourish because of their new knowledge. The snake's welcome return to the garden invokes the formal hybridity of Silko's gardens as well—the gardens in the dunes work metaphorically by allusion to the biblical story of the Garden of Eden, as well as by their connection to tribal beliefs about the sacredness of snakes and the reclamation of land. Furthermore, the return to the garden suggests an inversion of Zitkala-Ša's boarding-school allegory written nearly one hundred years before Silko's novel. Where Zitkala-Ša viewed a boarding-school education as the "forbidden fruit" that could banish her forever from her childhood tribal Eden, Silko uses her rebellious, resistant characters to change the paradigm altogether, representing her boarding-school student as a moral victor, one who was able to taste the fruit of knowledge, hybridize it to grow in her own climate, and then tend her gardens on her ancestral lands.

Through Indigo, we can see how Geiogamah's representation of rebellious Pan-Indian identity in *Foghorn* and Tapahonso's and Momaday's assertions of students' maintenance of extremely strong tribal identities in "The Snakeman" and *The Indolent Boys* are really two sides of the same coin, displaying choices from among a repertoire of options and articulating different, but not mutually exclusive, political statements about the persistence of both the tribal and Pan-Indian identities of these characters—a tribal cosmopolitanism that develops despite the boarding schools' design to eradicate any sense of indigenous identity. This model of the repertoire of identity allows for the possibility of pro-tribal, pro-Indian political action, by acknowledging the ability of Indian people to respond to assimilative pressures outside of the social evolutionary linear vision of progress, breaking down the Friends of the Indian's oppositional definition of "traditional" and "assimilated." Significantly, the late-twentieth-century texts examined here deemphasize (though they certainly do not prohibit) switching among identities within a single text. Instead they highlight rebellion over repertoire to suit the authors' representational objectives and assert strong cases for the vitality of tribal nations. In many cases, contemporary authors rewrite the story to allow students to possess a degree of radicalism and freedom that would have been very difficult for an actual turn-of-the-century boarding-school student to achieve. Choosing to deploy these rebellious identities, contemporary writers re-create boarding-school students even as leaders of a revolutionary assertion of the primacy of both tribal and Pan-Indian cultures and a reclamation of the land of the Americas. Achieving rhetorical sovereignty through the use of repertoires of identity and representation, American Indian authors are writing boarding-school stories that are narratives of Indian liberation—narratives that Richard Henry Pratt and the Friends of the Indian would have deemed impossible one hundred twenty-five years ago, when they began to generate their narrative of oppression in their desire to kill the Indian to save the man.

BOARDING-SCHOOL REPERTOIRE AND THE AMERICAN INDIAN LITERARY TRADITION

"The history of American Indian education can be summarized in three simple words: battle for power," writes K. Tsianina Lomawaima. "In Indian America, power means sovereignty, and sovereignty means self-government, self-determination, and self-education."[1] Although boarding-school education attempted to strip power and sovereignty from American Indian people by remaking Native children as imitation white men, in large and small ways the body of writing that has come out of the Indian boarding-school experience attempts to reclaim that power for the purposes of rhetorical self-determination and literary self-education. The model of the repertoire of representation articulated in this study emphasizes the ability of individual authors to draw from a collection of formal choices in order to reflect a wide range of situational identities and individual political and artistic goals. It is important to be attentive to differences in representational choices made by a single author in various situations as well as to different representational choices among authors. And yet, by reading texts that concern themselves with the boarding-school experience alongside one another and by looking for commonalities, we can see the outlines of a shared formal repertoire that contributes to the building of a literary tradition. This Indian boarding-school repertoire has manifested itself in three related ways: shared forms, shared language, and intertextuality.

Of these three, the one examined most closely here is how boarding-school narratives rework literary form in order to represent the complexities of student identities and experiences. For example, both Hanay Geiogamah and N. Scott Momaday bring together indigenous dramatic forms with the conventions of Western theater. Leslie Marmon Silko and Zitkala-Ša meld aspects of the sentimental tradition with Indian subjectivity in order to move their characters to voice and their readers to action through their formal choices. The boarding-school experience has, moreover, contributed new literary forms to a shared repertoire. Letters home, renaming stories, stories of running away, deathbed encounters, and student resistance narratives (to name a few examples), all arise out of the specific experiences that Native people faced within the schools and expand the repertoire of representations that constitutes American Indian literature. Both students and educators were well aware of the power that accrues to storytelling. Boarding-school stories map the struggle over this narrative power that took place in the schools as students fought the educators' paper Indian scripts in order to represent themselves in ways that acknowledged their complexity and humanity. The narratives produced by students and their descendants seek to protect and encourage student agency by demonstrating that American Indian writers can and do draw from a wide range of literary forms. There is no single "boarding-school form." Rather, these works build narrative authority and dismantle cultural evolutionary ideology through their awareness of the possibilities and limitations of a variety of literary forms, positioning themselves to speak in particular communicative contexts. It is this variousness, this particularly rich repertoire of options alongside a decoupling of form and identity, that boarding-school narratives contribute to the American Indian literary tradition.

Boarding-school narratives also contribute to what it means to write "Indian" on the level of language. William Leap identifies a distinctive "boarding-school English" in use at the schools that drew upon both English and ancestral language structures and built a vocabulary responsive to student experiences within the school setting.[2] When Zitkala-Ša writes in "Impressions of an Indian Childhood" of the red, red apples that the missionaries offer her if she will go east to school, she not only references biblical cosmology but also speaks boarding-school English. To accept an apple from the missionaries means to put oneself in danger of becoming an "apple"—

red on the outside, white on the inside—and succumbing to the schools' assimilating efforts.[3] By working with imagery that holds meaning in more than one literary tradition, Zitkala-Ša both rewrites biblical narratives, challenging the educational power structure by naming the missionaries as tempters, and creates a new allegory that speaks particularly to Indian people who have experienced the civilizing machine of the schools and who began to constitute a Native audience for American Indian literature written in English at the turn into the twentieth century. Nearly one hundred years after Zitkala-Ša published her essay, Laura Tohe's story "So I Blow Smoke in Her Face" refers to a student nicknamed Apple Annie because she is the head dorm matron's favorite.[4] Linked not merely by subject matter but also by a culturally charged use of the English language, Tohe and Zitkala-Ša work from an overlapping repertoire of representational choices. Together, they write "Indian."

Tohe's story demonstrates the importance of a boarding-school vernacular to student survivance. Vida, the narrator, is nicknamed Wishbone by her peers, because of the bowed legs she proudly accentuates with her jeans, proof of her prowess and experience as a horseback rider. She prefers the student-generated nickname to "the names the school has labeled me, troublemaker, incorrigible, dumb Indian."[5] A resistant student who resents the power plays of the matron, Mrs. Harry, who "has a reputation for being a mean woman even though she's an Indian, a Heinz 57, an Indian who's from several different tribes," Vida understands that the extra work details she is given are "their way of shaming you, their way of taking control of you. They want you to know who's in charge, who's the authority."[6] Vida subverts this institutional authority linguistically by becoming fluent in the student language and culture, becoming an insider in a student-centered representational system in which it is the students who assign meaning rather than being constantly under surveillance and evaluated according to school standards. Vida and her companions joke about "bedchecks"—"an expression that we use to make a joke. Just something to laugh about, living in these government boarding schools"—and note the distinction between "bear meat" (Salisbury steak) and "rubber meat" (roast beef).[7] And the laughter that accompanies this process of recoding their school experience is powerful. Having built a sense of linguistic solidarity with her companions, who speak boarding-school English alongside Diné, Vida eventually rejects the school's labeling systems entirely, blowing cigarette smoke into the face of the matron and returning home, where she is continually reminded of how she is connected to ancestry, landscape, and Diné art forms such as her mother's weaving. Tohe's entire book is a larger-scale version of Vida's linguistic subversion. By taking control of language, claiming the power of naming, Tohe stands in solidarity with the generations of boarding-school writers who preceded her like Zitkala-Ša and Silko's Aunt Susie, who embedded "boarding-school words" like "precipitous" in Laguna stories, transforming the English language in their own image and forming a distinctive linguistic community.[8]

Tohe's purposeful use of the "letter home," or Momaday's retelling of a Kiowa school story and his reference to Luther Standing Bear's account of receiving an English name, takes this solidarity one step further, signifying on elements of previous works and demonstrating how contemporary American Indian boarding-school narratives are self-consciously intertextual. Such "acts of formal revision can be loving acts of bonding," explains Henry Louis Gates, Jr.[9] Recurring figures and events such as the runaway, the deathbed scene, the returned student, and the linguistic rebellion are no coincidence. Native writers are working within an awareness of and appreciation for both tribal and pan-tribal literary traditions, troping on other representations of the boarding-school experience. This engagement with each other's ideas exemplifies the intellectual sovereignty that Robert Allen Warrior's work values.[10]

In addition, awareness of and reference to other boarding-school narratives can function as acts of healing that move toward other assertions of sovereignty and Indian rights. Canadian First Nations survivors of the boarding-school system (called residential schools in Canada) are currently engaged in writing their own counternarrative to the schools' pedagogy of oppression, employing representations of the school experience in a legal battle to gain justice and compensation for abuses inflicted in federal residential schools, which operated in conjunction with the Catholic and Anglican churches and the United Church of Canada.[11] As of September 1, 2004, more than 12,440 individuals have filed Indian-residential-school claims against the government of Canada, according to the Indian Residential Schools Resolution Canada (IRSRC), a department of the Canadian federal government that is dedicated to addressing residential school issues.[12] Among the allegations claimants have made, one of the most frequent was physical abuse (93 percent), with allegations of cultural loss (90 percent) and loss of language (84 percent) also motivating a large majority of the former students who have filed claims.[13] Although claims for loss of language and culture have been categorized as "noncompensable," former students, by entering the legal discourse, have brought these issues to international attention and have explicitly named as crimes the pedagogical goals of the schools.

Survivors of the residential schools are telling their own stories in legal briefs, to tribunals, on the internet, and in the mainstream media, to fight for justice and to counter ethnocentric and inaccurate portrayals of the schools. Gilbert Oskaboose (Ojibwe), claimant and journalist, has insisted that First Nations people must not leave it

> to the social scientists and writers of the future to determine the impact of those infamous residential schools on our nations. . . . [We must] make the connection between that dark chapter in our history and the dysfunctionalism in our communities today. . . . It's not enough to dismiss this as ancient history or as "water under the bridge," as one aging Blackrobe tried to do recently. We are human beings, not water flowing serenely under a bridge. It's what we were and what we've become.[14]

Oskaboose issues a call for residential-school-student self-representations, acknowledging the importance of written representations to political action. Residential-school survivors are meeting this challenge daily, evidenced by the internet sites that link these narratives in a web of intertextual testimony.[15]

Contemporary Indian writers are not the only ones whose writing is being used in support of the Canadian lawsuits. James M. Craven, a judge on the Inter-tribal Tribunal on Residential Schools in Canada, cites Charles Eastman (referring to him only as Ohiyesa) as one of the thinkers behind "some principles of aboriginal life and law guiding my inquiry and findings" (Craven). Citing passages from Eastman's treatise *The Soul of the Indian*, Craven uses Eastman to prove the legitimacy of the tribal tribunal and its "sacred and fundamental imperatives" of "Truth, Justice, Healing, Reconciliation, and Prevention of Future Abuses." Eastman wrote: "Before there were any cities on this continent, before there were bridges to span the Mississippi, before the great network of railroads was even dreamed of, we Indian people had councils which gave their decisions in accordance with the highest ideal of human justice."[16] Craven uses these words to illustrate that an "Indian Trial or Tribunal is a sacred and a spiritual event as well as a secular one," possessing both sacred and secular authority to administer justice, in this case gathering evidence of residential school abuse.[17] Craven further quotes Eastman's thoughts on truth-telling: "Because we believed the deliberate liar is capable of committing any crime behind the screen of cowardly untruth and double dealing, the destroyer of mutual confidence was summarily put to death, that the evil might go no further."[18] Craven's intertextual references to Eastman's work support the tribunal's search for accurate articulations of criminal wrongdoing on the part of the residential schools. The written words of Eastman, a "representative" Indian, are now being used to support the cases of former students who are seeking retribution rather than demonstrating, as Jessie Cook argued in 1900, the schools' efficacy as assimilating institutions. Through this important contemporary example of intertextuality, Eastman's writing has come full circle from being read as a sign of his assimilation to being used as a call for justice and support for the sovereign authority of Native institutions of governance, like the tribunal.

Indian writing about the boarding-school experience, as the example of the Canadian claims demonstrate, has spoken out for justice and self-determination for over a century. Whether overtly and aggressively protecting tribal sovereignty or, rather, seeking to ease the pain of an individual survivor, Indian boarding-school narratives have become a central part of what it means to write "Indian" today. Laura Tohe ends *No Parole Today* with a poem called "At Mexican Springs," which reaffirms the power of language and the continuance of tribal nations: "I relive visions of ancient stories . . ." she writes, "and I will live to tell my children these things."[19] Tohe's words, at the end of her volume of literature that specifically addresses the boarding-school experience, demonstrate the role that language and storytelling have played in fighting the schools' genocidal agenda to eliminate community connections and Indian nationhood. By learning to write "Indian," American Indian writers have found a way to bear witness to the legacy of the schools, claim their languages, land, rights, and stories, and pass a rich literary legacy to the next generation.

NOTES

INTRODUCTION

1. Tohe, *No Parole Today*, ix.
2. Ibid.
3. Ibid., xii.
4. See, for example, Prucha, *Americanizing the American Indians*, 261.
5. Ibid., 193–94.
6. Pratt, *Battlefield and Classroom*, xii. See also P.B.S., *In the White Man's Image*. Information on Pratt's career can be found in his memoir, *Battlefield and Classroom*; and another contemporary source on his life and his founding of Carlisle is Elaine Goodale Eastman's adulatory biography, *The Red Man's Moses*. The P.B.S. documentary *In the White Man's Image* provides a wealth of visual images and a late-twentieth-century analysis of Pratt and the founding of Carlisle. Another helpful source on Carlisle's history is Barbara Landis's article on the Carlisle Indian Industrial School history web page: <http://home.epix.net/~landis/>.
7. For more information on Hampton's Indian education program, see Lindsey, *Indians at Hampton Institute*.
8. Pratt, *Battlefield and Classroom*, 265–66.
9. Noriega, "American Indian Education," 382.
10. Qtd. in Hoxie, *A Final Promise*, 190.
11. Ibid.
12. Tohe, *No Parole Today*, 2.
13. Ibid., 3.
14. Ibid., 2–3.
15. Ibid., 3.
16. Ibid.

17. Ibid., xiii.

18. See also Harjo and Bird, eds., *Reinventing the Enemy's Language*.

19. Leap, *American Indian English*, 162.

20. Richard Pratt, qtd. in Prucha, *Americanizing the American Indians*, 269.

21. Kroskrity, *Language, History, and Identity*, 207–209.

22. Prucha, *Americanizing the American Indians*, 275.

23. A debate over the issue of agency has claimed a prominent role in Indian studies, especially in considering the boarding-school experience, and particularly in Canada. See Trevithick, "Native Residential Schooling in Canada," for more on this issue.

24. See Hertzberg, *American Indian Identity*.

25. See Horne and McBeth, *Essie's Story*, which explains, from the perspective of Horne (who both attended and taught at a variety of boarding schools), the role that Bronson played in teaching her about Indianness from within the boarding-school system. Horne, too, developed curricular models for teaching students about Indian culture during the middle years of the twentieth century.

26. Shanley, "'Writing Indian,'" 131–32.

27. Hoxie, "Exploring a Cultural Borderland," 280.

28. Lyons, "Rhetorical Sovereignty," 449–50.

29. Allen, *Voice of the Turtle*, 12–13.

30. Tohe, *No Parole Today*, 4.

31. Standing Bear, *My People, the Sioux*, 137. "Counting coup" refers to an act of bravery in battle, particularly the act of touching a live enemy with a stick and escaping without harm. Warriors would keep track of their coup, and counting coup was viewed as more brave than killing an enemy. See, for example, Waldman, *Word Dance*, 54–55.

32. My use of "signifies" draws on the work of Henry Louis Gates, Jr., for whom signifying "indicates a form of intertextual revision, by which texts establish their relation to other texts, and authors to other authors. The force of this revision is to establish a critical relation to previous discursive statement. In this sense, one signifies on a particular work, author, form, or tradition by copying central elements or practices, even while revising those in some significant way" (Andrews, Foster, and Harris, eds., *The Oxford Companion to African American Literature*, 665).

33. Tohe, *No Parole Today*, 7.

34. Child, *Boarding School Seasons*, xii–xiii.

35. Ibid., xii.

36. Spack, *America's Second Tongue*, 10.

37. See Duran and Duran, *Native American Postcolonial Psychology*, for an assessment of the impact of the boarding-school experience on contemporary American Indian mental health. Duran and Duran claim that the boarding schools have been particularly detrimental to the structure and functioning of Indian families and also play a role in alcoholism, abusive relationships, an so on, by contributing

to what they identify as "Intergenerational Posttraumatic Stress Disorder, as well as to internalized oppression." See especially pages 27–35.

38. See Zitkala-Ša, *American Indian Stories*, 45.

39. Momaday, *Man Made of Words*, 6.

40. Sarris, *Keeping Slug Woman Alive*, 70.

41. This book will focus on written representations and interpretations of and by the "representative Indians." It is also possible to see, however, that this talented group used other expressive and creative forms and tools acquired at the schools to produce complicated representations of identity. For example, Dennison Wheelock's musical compositions for the Carlisle brass band appear to reflect many of the identity issues and formal concerns discussed here. The same argument may be made for Charles Eastman's practice of medicine, Angel de Cora's artwork, even the Carlisle football team's transfiguration of the game of football into "deep play, . . . secular ritual" with "deep social or historical meaning" (Adams, *Education for Extinction*, 183–84; see 183–91 for more on Indian football). Cook also terms the Carlisle team "representative."

42. Prucha, *Americanizing the American Indians*, 193.

43. Tohe, *No Parole Today*, xii.

CHAPTER 1

1. Silko, *Yellow Woman and a Beauty of the Spirit*, 51.

2. Krupat, "The Dialogic of Silko's *Storyteller*," 190.

3. Silko, *Yellow Woman and a Beauty of the Spirit*, 57–58.

4. Silko, *Storyteller*, 1. Further references to this work will be given parenthetically in the text.

5. Taken from the program for the dedication of the Susie Reyos Marmon Elementary School, on March 11, 1990 (Carlisle Barracks Library vertical file, "Students"). The scheduled events exemplified Susie Marmon's inclusive teaching philosophy: astronomy, art, and literature exhibitions stood beside staging areas for Laguna storytelling, song, and dance. Leslie Silko participated in the event, which took place two years after Aunt Susie's death in 1988. The venerable educator died just eleven days short of her 111th birthday (Grammer, "Laguna Matriarch Dies," 1).

6. Silko, *Yellow Woman and a Beauty of the Spirit*, 54.

7. Ibid, 57.

8. Silko repeats the word "precipitous" several times in *Storyteller* (for example, pp. 147, 229).

9. Coleman, *American Indian Children at School*, 22.

10. Marr, "Making Oneself," 52.

11. Silko, *Yellow Woman and a Beauty of the Spirit*, 179, 176.

12. Lincoln, *Indi'n Humor*, 73–74.

13. Silko, *Yellow Woman and a Beauty of the Spirit*, 177–78.

14. Qtd. in Lincoln, *Native American Renaissance*, 224.

15. Ruoff, "Ritual and Renewal," 73.

16. Ibid.

17. Krupat, "The Dialogic of Silko's *Storyteller*," 195, 190.

18. Zitkala-Ša, letter to the editor.

19. Stocking, *Race, Culture, and Evolution*, 124.

20. Ibid., 81.

21. Ibid.

22. Ibid., 122.

23. Morgan, *Ancient Society*, 10–12.

24. Ibid., 31. Apparently, Morgan was either unaware of or ignored Indian "written" records such as winter counts, Anasazi cliff drawings, and so on, which approximate hieroglyphics.

25. Ibid., 30–31

26. Adams, *Education for Extinction*, 14.

27. Stocking, *Race, Culture, and Evolution*, 129.

28. Bieder, *Science Encounters the Indian*, 250.

29. Catholics, too, were interested in converting and "uplifting" Indian people, although Catholic goals for conversion differed significantly from those of the Friends of the Indian. In general, late-nineteenth-century Catholic missions were not as interested in removing Indian people from their homes and families. Catholic missionaries tended to value the role of the Indian mother far more than the Protestants did. Protestant reformers denigrated Indian mothers—whom they represented as dirty and evil—because of their association with cultural maintenance. Pratt and other Friends of the Indian frequently railed in print against Catholic educators. For a Catholic perspective on Carlisle, see the *Anishinabe Enamiad*, the newspaper of the Harbor Springs, Michigan, Indian Mission School. The March 1898 issue, for instance, asks the Catholic missionary, "which of these three things does more lasting damage among the Indians: *Drunkenness, Impurity, or Carlisle?* The two former corrupt the heart, but the third corrupts the mind and this with them leads to the other two" ("Captain Pratt vs the *Anishinabe Enamiad*"; emphasis in original). And an October 1899 editorial complains that the motto of a recent Indian Service Institute was "Great is Carlisle and Pratt is its prophet." The editorial goes on to denounce Pratt as "a gasbag," "a pedagogical fraud," and "the little god [and little idol] of Carlisle" ("What Uncle Joe Has to Say").

30. Tylor qtd. in Stocking, *Race, Culture, and Evolution*, 81–82.

31. Adams, *Education for Extinction*, 14.

32. For a closer examination of the shift in social evolutionary theory and assimilation policy that occurred between 1880 and 1920, see Hoxie, *A Final Promise*.

33. Prucha, *Americanizing the American Indian*, 268–69.

34. Coleman, *American Indian Children at School*, 112; Lomawaima, *They Called It Prairie Light*, 65–94.

35. Pratt, *Battlefield and Classroom*, 266. For more on the outing program, see in particular Lomawaima, *They Called It Prairie Light*, 5, and ch. 3; Coleman, *American Indian Children at School*, 43–44, 113; Adams, *Education for Extinction*, 156–63; and Pratt, *Battlefield and Classroom*.

36. McBeth, *Ethnic Identity*, 102.

37. Coleman, *American Indian Children at School*, 112, 115.

38. Lomawaima, *They Called It Prairie Light*, 66. Additional primary source evidence for this point of view can be found in papers given by Indian educators at the "institutes" held for Indian school employees, many of which are reprinted in the "Report of the Superintendent of Indian Schools" (Hailman, *Report 1895* and *Report 1897*). See especially Capt. W. H. Beck's 1895 paper on "Higher Education of Indians" and a series of papers on "Education for True Manhood and Womanhood in Indian Schools," reprinted in Hailman, *Report 1895*. Both Lomawaima and Wexler ("Tender Violence") give compelling evidence of how the Victorian sentimental constructs of "true manhood" and "true womanhood" produced a rationale for a racially determined underclass of manual laborers, institutionalized in the Indian schools.

39. Qtd. in Prucha, *Americanizing the American Indians*, 224–25.

40. See Hoxie, *A Final Promise*, 200 and ch. 5.

41. Prucha, *Americanizing the American Indians*, 224.

42. Hoxie, *A Final Promise*, 196.

43. Qtd. in Prucha, *Americanizing the American Indians*, 200.

44. Ibid., 198.

45. Ibid.

46. Ibid., 205.

47. Cobb, *Listening to Our Grandmothers' Stories*, 14–15.

48. Noriega, "American Indian Education in the United States," 374.

49. Konishi, "What He Would Have Said." The title of this article, along with the apparent slipup when Konishi refers to American statesmen as "our" statesmen, may be evidence that the editorial staff itself wrote Konishi's remarks. The statement is prefaced in the *Indian Helper* by the following: "While he writes very fair English he hesitates to speak. Had he been able to speak as he felt he would have said the following, which was handed to the Man-on-the-Band-stand by him." The Man-on-the-Band-stand was a figure that embodied school authority in the *Indian Helper* (see Chapter 2), and his appropriation—or invention—of Konishi's voice is not without precedent within the pages of this newspaper. Whether Mr. Konishi's statement consists of his own words or is the Man-on-the-Band-stand's invention, his comments send a clear message regarding the duties of the graduates to write positively about their experiences.

50. Board of Indian Commissioners qtd. in Prucha, *Americanizing the Indians*, 193.

51. McFee, "The 150% Man," 1098, 1096.

52. Prucha, *Americanizing the Indians*, 193.

53. The October 13, 1904, issue of *The Arrow,* a Carlisle newspaper "devoted to the Interests of the Progressive Indian," mentions that "Mrs. Jessie Cook, who has been field agent for girls under our Outing System for the past year, goes back to Riverside, California, as Principal Teacher, at Sherman Institute." Laurie Sisquak, a researcher at Sherman's museum and archives, provided additional information about Cook: she was a white woman, born in Connecticut in 1854, who spent much of her adult life in the Indian service. She was originally appointed as outing matron at Sherman in May 1892. She served alternately as outing matron and as teacher at Sherman, before transferring to Carlisle in 1903. Less than a year later, she returned to teach at Sherman. Cook and her husband, a minister, were stationed at Pine Ridge Agency in 1890 where they became good friends with Charles Alexander Eastman and his fiancée, Elaine Goodale. See Elaine Goodale Eastman, *Sister to the Sioux,* for more about this period of Cook's life.

54. Cook, "The Representative Indian," 80.

55. Though he was a Yavapai, Montezuma was often identified as an Apache, perhaps because hostile bands of Apaches still fought the U.S. troops while Montezuma was being educated in the East. The reformers frequently compared Montezuma to the legendary Apache warriors in an attempt to show that even the most "savage" Indian could be "civilized." Cook writes: "There are men who have fought Dr. Montezuma's tribe, and have suffered from its depredations not so many years since, who would laugh to scorn the suggestion that any good could come out of the Apache tribe. Dr. Montezuma is a living example of the possibilities of any one of his people under like conditions" ibid., (81).

56. Ibid., 83.

57. Hertzberg, *American Indian Identity,* credits Carlisle and Hampton with producing many of the leaders of and participants in Pan–Indian organizations: "This was by no means the intention of General Richard Henry Pratt," she writes (15). And yet, many of the leaders of the largest "reform Pan-Indian" organization—the Society of American Indians (SAI), in which most of the representative Indians were active, high-ranking members—had achieved a higher level of education than that provided by the boarding schools (ibid., 303).

58. Cook, "Representative Indian," 80; Berkhofer, *The White Man's Indian,* 96–103.

59. Cook, "Representative Indian," 80.

60. Ibid., 83 (emphasis added).

61. Ibid., 80.

62. Prucha, *Americanizing the American Indians,* 5.

63. Even today, a web page detailing the history of Carlisle is illustrated with the "before" and "after" photographs of Tom Torlino, a Navajo student at Carlisle. See <http://www.epix.net/~landis/main.html>. Torlino's photographs are also prominent on the back cover of Adams, *Education for Extinction.*

64. Malmsheimer, "'Imitation White Man,'" 54.

65. Malmsheimer notes that the children's skin even looks lighter in the "after" photographs—perhaps as a result of time spent indoors during long Pennsylvania winters (ibid., 66).

66. Ibid, 66.

67. Ibid, 56.

68. See Child, *Boarding School Seasons*; Trennert, *The Phoenix Indian School*; Archuleta, Child, and Lomawaima, *Away from Home*; Cobb, *Listening to Our Grandmothers' Stories*; Riney, *The Rapid City Indian School*; Spack, *America's Second Tongue*; Adams, *Education for Extinction*; Coleman, *American Indian Children at School*; Lomawaima, *They Called It Prairie Light*; Haig-Brown, *Resistance and Renewal*; Mihesuah, *Cultivating the Rosebuds*; and McBeth, *Ethnic Identity*.

69. Lomawaima, *They Called It Prairie Light*, 29.

70. Riney, *The Rapid City Indian School*, 217, 221.

71. Child, *Boarding School Seasons*, 7–8.

72. Archuleta, Child, and Lomawaima, *Away from Home*, 48.

73. Jones qtd. in ibid., 19.

74. Nagle, *American Indian Ethnic Renewal*, 114.

75. Ibid., 21. See also McFee, "The 150% Man," and Kroskrity, *Language, History, and Identity*.

76. I do not wish to suggest that a situational identity is equivalent to a postmodern understanding of identity as performance, with no core or coherence, echoing Clifton's construct of the "invented Indian" (Clifton, *The Invented Indian*). Situational identities are delimited by social constructs and attitudes, and many Indian people participate in tribes that foreground the importance of a *tribal* identity as a core identity and worldview. Krupat writes about Silko, for example, that "for all the polyvocal openness of Silko's work, there is always the unabashed commitment to Pueblo ways as a reference point. This may be modified, updated, playfully construed: but its authority is always to be reckoned with" ("The Dialogic of Silko's *Storyteller*," 197).

77. Kroskrity, *Language, History, and Identity*, 208–209.

78. Ibid., 207.

79. Ibid., 209.

CHAPTER 2

1. Freire, *Pedagogy of the Oppressed*, 120–21, [128], 121.

2. Ibid., 53.

3. Pratt qtd. from Prucha, *Americanizing the American Indians*, 268.

4. Freire, *Pedagogy of the Oppressed*, 51.

5. Littlefield and Parins, *Native Newspapers*, 1: xxviii.

6. This anonymous, untitled verse was published on page 4 of the February 7, 1890, issue of Carlisle's *Indian Helper*. Note its similarity to the longer poem below.

7. Gilcreast, *Richard Henry Pratt*, 86.

8. Littlefield and Parins, *Native Newspapers*, 317–18. The publication history of the Carlisle newspapers is complicated. According to Littlefield and Parins in their guide to American Indian and Alaskan Native newspapers, *Eadle Keatah Toh* first appeared in 1880 and acted both as a school paper (in addition to *School News*, which Littlefield and Parins regard as more of a newsletter but which Gilcreast considers a newspaper), and as a "means of proselytizing the concept of education on which the Carlisle school was based" (317). In 1882, the title of *Eadle Keatah Toh* was changed to the *Morning Star*. In 1883, it absorbed *School News* and served as both a paper for the students and a paper for a national audience. Toward the end of 1884, the *Morning Star* expanded to eight pages and made more of a commitment to covering Indian policy issues. Soon after this, in 1885, the *Indian Helper* was established to take the place of the defunct *School News* as a paper primarily for the students. The *Morning Star* continued until 1888, when its title was changed to the *Red Man*. In 1900, the *Red Man* was combined with the *Indian Helper* to form the *Red Man and Helper*.

9. Gilcreast, *Richard Henry Pratt*, 87.

10. Littlefield and Parins, *Native Newspapers*, 320.

11. Marianna Burgess was born in Pennsylvania in June 1853. Her parents, William and Mary Burgess, were Quakers. Her father knew the printing trade and served as the headmaster of Millville High School before being appointed as agent of the Pawnee Reservation in Nebraska in the summer of 1872. William Burgess hired his wife as matron of the agency's Manual Labor School and named Marianna as a teacher at the school. William Burgess served as Pawnee agent during the tribe's removal to Indian Territory, which was an extremely difficult time for the Pawnee, and Burgess's actions and decisions were frequently called into question. He was dismissed for financial improprieties in 1876. Marianna Burgess and Annie Ely, a friend and fellow teacher at Pawnee, came to Carlisle in 1880. Burgess was initially hired as a teacher but held the title of Superintendent of Printing for most of her tenure at Carlisle. Although commissioner of Indian Affairs Ezra Hayt criticized Burgess to Pratt, saying, "We have tried her in the agency service and had to discharge her. She is not a suitable teacher. You had better discharge her at once," Pratt refused to fire her and later reflected: "She remained at the school for more than twenty-five years and was among its ablest and most devoted helpers" (Pratt 236). Genevieve Bell reports that Burgess stayed at Carlisle until November 1904, when she left on her annual leave and never returned. Burgess remained involved in Indian affairs until her death in Pasadena, California on Easter Day 1931. For more information on Marianna Burgess, see Bell, "Telling Stories out of School," 105–107. For more on the Burgess family, especially William's work as Pawnee agent, see Blaine, *Pawnee Passage*; Milner, *With Good Intentions*; and Hyde, *The Pawnee Indians*.

12. In its role as "defender of the Right," the newspaper sought to portray itself as anti-institutional, the tyrannical institution being instead tribal authority.

It is for this reason that "The Song of the Printer" engages in what amounts to a rhetorical contortion, insisting that the printer is at once all-powerful and in opposition to "the tyrant."

13. Just because Burgess did not anticipate or encourage printers to subvert the power of the writer or editor does not mean that it did not happen. Littlefield and Parins point to numerous examples of Carlisle-trained printer-boys who went on to produce their own newspapers, which did not necessarily depict Pratt's "party-line" (*Native Newspapers*).

14. Foucault, *Discipline and Punish*, 194. Further references to this work will be given parenthetically in the text.

15. Ibid., 314, n. 1.

16. Pratt wrote: "The fitness [the Negro] had for [citizenship] he was given during slavery, which made him individual, English speaking and highly capable industrially. This was a lesson which in some way should be applied to the Indians" (*Battlefield and Classroom*, 214).

17. Littlefield and Parins, *Native Newspapers*, 182.

18. *Indian Helper*, March 9, 1888, 2.

19. *Indian Helper*, October 22, 1897, 3.

20. *Indian Helper*, March 9, 1888, 2.

21. Coleman, *American Indian Children at School*, 89.

22. See Adams, *Education for Extinction*, 121–24; Ball, *Indeh*, 150; Pratt, *Battlefield and Classroom*, 237; and the transcript of the 1914 Congressional investigation of the Carlisle Indian School.

23. "Who is that Man-on-the-Band-stand?" *Indian Helper*, November 29, 1889, 1.

24. The Grinnell family was closely associated with Carlisle for many years. Dr. Grinnell served as Carlisle physician; and after the family had left Carlisle, Marianna Burgess and a Carlisle entourage visited them on the West Coast in 1903, as she reported in a series of articles in the *Red Man and Helper*, including "Off to the Pacific Coast."

25. "Who is that Man-on-the-Band-stand?" *Indian Helper*, November 29, 1889, 1.

26. Montezuma, "An Apache," 1. In representing himself as an Apache, Montezuma is representing himself according to the reformers' view of him, displaying himself as what they needed him to be. (He was in fact Yavapai.)

27. Iverson, *Carlos Montezuma and the Changing World of American Indians*, provides a biography of Montezuma and discusses his relationship with Pratt, and with several of the other representative Indians. Most significant among these relationships was his brief engagement to Zitkala-Ša. They never married, probably because of their differing politics. See also Spack, "Dis/Engagement."

28. Montezuma, *An Apache*, 4.

29. There is extensive secondary criticism on sentimentalism and American literature, but one significant text to begin exploration of this topic is Tompkins, *Sensational Designs*.

30. "Home Difficulties," part 1, *Indian Helper*, September 16, 1887, 1.

31. Ibid., 4.

32. It is instructive to think of tribal culture and "civilized" culture playing the implicit role of suitors for Fanny's attention here, for, Tompkins points out, "the male figure, representing both divine and worldly authority, who marries the heroine in the end, is the alternative to physical death in sentimental fiction; he provides her with a way to live happily and obediently in this world while obeying the dictates of heaven. He is the principle that joins self-denial with self-fulfillment, extending and enforcing the disciplinary regimen of the heroine's life" (*Sensational Designs,* 183). Here, "civilized" culture, as the winning suitor, is intended to fulfill Fanny by denying her Native identity and enforcing Carlisle's disciplinary power to regulate her behavior and cultural expression.

33. "Home Difficulties," part 2, *Indian Helper*, September 30, 1887, 4.

34. Ibid, part 3, *Indian Helper*, October 28, 1887, 4.

35. Cook, "Representative Indian," 83.

36. "Home Difficulties," part 3, p. 4.

37. "Home Difficulties of a Young Indian Girl" is never set within an explicitly fictional framework, though Fannie is referred to as "our heroine." This type of language and the serialized format strongly suggest to readers that the piece is fictional. Other pieces of fiction—such as a dialogue between two Sioux boys (see below)—are presented almost as fact; again, there is no disclaimer mentioning that the pieces are fictional, and they contain few generic markers that would indicate to a young student that they are not "real." An adult reading these pieces would not doubt they were fiction, but students, however, might be confused and might assume that the voice of the "paper Indians" reflects the real feelings of former students.

38. Burgess, "Among the Dakotas," 1.

39. Ibid., 4.

40. Ibid.

41. "Two Carlisle Boys at Pine Ridge Talk Over the Sioux Bill," *Indian Helper*, August 31, 1888, 1.

42. Ibid.

43. Ibid., 4.

44. Ibid.

45. Ibid.

46. Wilson, *Ohiyesa*, 55.

47. "The Sioux Bill: Will the Indians Be Cheated?" *Indian Helper,* September 7, 1888, 2.

48. Ibid.

49. Wilson, *Ohiyesa*, 55.

50. "Boys, boys . . .," an untitled news item from the *Indian Helper,* September 7, 1888, 3.

51. The descriptions of the novel are taken from advertisements for the book that ran in the *Indian Helper*, appearing years after the novel's publication. The

novel is called "thrilling" in advertisements on May 21 and June 4, 1897. It is called "pathetic . . . but not overdrawn," in the June 11, 1897, issue.

52. This byline appeared beneath the title of all but the first installment of the serialized text (October 4–December 20, 1889).

53. Burgess, "How an Indian Girl Might Tell Her Own Story If She Had the Chance" (my emphasis).

54. See note 37.

55. *Indian Helper*, December 20, 1889, 1.

56. Sadly, this view of history still exists. In Rinaldi's 1999 children's book *My Heart Is on the Ground*, Rinaldi ends the supposed diary of a Carlisle student with the child's taking the role of a Pilgrim woman in the school's Thanksgiving Day pageant. Rinaldi asserts that this role honors the student by associating her with the strength and civility of the Puritans and by disassociating her from the Indians. Rinaldi's book enacts many of the same stereotypes and the social evolutionary ideology of these turn-of-the-century educators.

57. *Indian Helper*, November 29, 1889, 4.

58. *Indian Helper*, December 20, 1889, 1.

59. This message appeared on page 2 of the *Indian Helper*, November 22, 1889. A similar message appeared on page 2 of the November 29, 1889, issue. The emphasis is original.

60. This untitled letter, signed by "M.L.F., So. Bethlehem, PA," appeared on page 5 of the *Red Man*, March 1890. Bethlehem was long known as a Moravian settlement, serving as the headquarters of Moravian Indian missions (and even the home of a Moravian mission school for Mahegan and Delaware children) in the eighteenth century (Schutt, "Reading in Community"). One might anticipate, therefore, a non-Indian audience that would be very receptive to (or at least familiar with) the colonizing message of Burgess's story in that town.

61. *Indian Helper*, June 18, 1897.

62. Taken from an advertisement that appeared in the *Red Man* circa 1891.

63. Silko, *Yellow Woman and a Beauty of the Spirit*, 163. Silko's discussion of *Stiya* is based, as she says, on a reading of a copy of the book in the rare book room of the University of New Mexico library in Albuquerque. Many of her comments about the book suggest that the text was not fresh in her mind. She lists the author as "Marion Bergess . . . [who] wrote the novel under the fake Indian name Tonka" (Burgess, calling herself Embe, dedicates the book to a Tonké). Silko's other inaccuracies include an incorrect publication date (1881) and an incorrect publisher (the U.S. War Department—it was actually published by Riverside Press and Houghton Mifflin). Finally, she says that to her knowledge, the book was available only to Indian school students. Despite these inaccuracies, Silko's analysis is perceptive and useful. It is not certain whether all current and former Carlisle students were provided with copies of the book, but they certainly were a primary audience for the text.

64. Littlefield, "Catholics," 3.

65. For more information on Pratt's conspiracy theory regarding Jesuit involvement in the massacre, see ibid. Littlefield argues that assimilationists used ridiculous conspiracy theories to assign causes to nativistic movements among American Indian people because "nativistic revivals were somewhat embarrassing, for they might be construed as evidence that—at least in some segments of Indian society—the policy was not working" (ibid., 1). This interesting study also covers the 1917 Messiah movement and Collier's "Indian New Deal."

66. A personal conversation with Dan Littlefield on July 16, 1999, led to these ideas.

67. This information is taken from a paper given by Folsom at all three of the Indian Education Institutes in 1897, reprinted in Hailman, *Report 1897*, 36–37. Within the paper, Folsom cites and disseminates the information contained in her 1891 report.

68. Taken from the secretary of the interior's 1898 report, in U.S. Senate, "Education of Indian Children," 2.

69. Adams, *Education for Extinction*, 291.

70. U.S. Senate, "Education of Indian Children," 3.

71. See, for example, Littlefield's statement that, while only six of sixty-three returned Carlisle students had participated in the Ghost Dance, "those six had to be explained away" ("Catholics," 4). The educators' all-or-nothing views about identity and assimilation made it impossible for them to deal with the complexity of Indian response to their policies, or with the evidence of their own failure to eradicate tribal cultures and affiliations.

72. Carlisle's records are inconsistent and difficult to search. As Barbara Landis from the Cumberland County Historical Society (CCHS) Archives in Carlisle explains, the school's records remain in existence today only because, as the school was being closed in 1918, the wife of Disciplinarian Denny gathered up all the papers she could and sent them off to the National Archives and CCHS. Without her foresight and quick action, we would know even less about Stiya Kowacura. The records that remain are, however, incomplete and often un-indexed. Reference archivist Mary Frances Morrow from the National Archives reported that she searched all student names beginning with K "in ten different places," and while "there was a card in the index indicating a card report might exist," she did not find any card report for Stiya Kowacura.

73. See Luther Standing Bear's *My People, the Sioux*, in which he relates how his teacher Marianna Burgess gave her students English names (137). Another likely reason for Stiya keeping her name is that many Pueblo and California Mission Indians had received baptismal names of Spanish origin from the Spanish and Mexican priests who had inhabited the pueblos for centuries. Because these baptismal names were part of the church record and were already Europeanized, Pueblo people were not subject to the wholesale renaming that took place among other tribes such as the Lakota and Dakota. Charles Eastman was responsible for renaming much of the Sioux nation in the early years of the century (Wilson, *Ohiyesa*, 120–30).

74. This photograph, correctly identified as Lucy Tsisnah, Apache, appears in Witmer, *The Indian Industrial School.*

75. *Indian Helper,* January 29, 1888, 2.

76. *Indian Helper,* March 1, 1889, 2.

77. While Stiya's pueblo is not named, she tells her mother that her friend Annie lives in "Pa-hwa-ke village" (Burgess, *Stiya,* 62) (Paguate village), which is one of the several villages that make up Laguna Pueblo. Many Carlisle students—including, of course, the Anayas and the Marmons—came from Laguna.

78. Burgess, *Stiya,* 4. Further references to this work will be given parenthetically in the text.

79. See Babcock, "'Maids of Palastine,'" which argues that representations of Pueblo women potters and images of women with the oja or water jar were used in the service of "symbolic domination" (that is, domination of and by representation and signs) of Southwestern Indian people. See also Lewis Henry Morgan, *Ancient Society,* 11.

80. Burgess, "Off to the Pacific Coast."

81. Thomas Morgan, "Best Chance," 4.

82. Foucault, *Discipline and Punish,* 187.

83. Burgess, "Off to the Pacific Coast." Burgess also mentions in the same article that she saw Mary Natsawa [Natwawa] while at Laguna. Mary was one of the girls who performed on stage with Stiya Kowacura. Burgess notes that Mary wore "Indian dress" but only because she was too poor to dress in fashion. Burgess also relates that, when Mary was about to return to Carlisle after a visit home, her brother and an aunt plotted against her return and carried her off just as the train arrived to take her back east. Burgess laments: "With a few more years in the education and experience that go to make character, independence and social standing, Mary might as well now be occupying an enviable position among people of culture as to be held down by the bondage of conditions that dwarf. She deserves great credit, however, for doing as well as her friends give her credit" ("Off to the Pacific"). Mary's story, too, is made to match with Burgess's narrative of Indian bondage (and particularly Indian women's bondage) to tribal tyranny.

84. Silko, *Yellow Woman and a Beauty of the Spirit,* 163–64.

85. Not everyone at Laguna would have responded in the same way to *Stiya.* Paula Gunn Allen says, for instance, that some of the children of her great-grandmother, who was in Carlisle's first class, "spoke of 'Colonel Pratt' as though he was some sort of Saint. They probably would have so named him, but they were Presbyterians!" (personal e–mail, July 1, 1999). This variety of responses to Pratt and to Carlisle's mythology merely emphasizes the complexity of student response, despite the educators' constant attempts to force them into a simple, pro-assimilation position.

86. "Our World," *Southern Workman* (February 1885): 20.

87. Foucault, *Discipline and Punish,* 187.

88. "From Home Letters," *Indian Helper,* March 16, 1888, 4.

89. Ibid.

90. Ibid.

91. Stoltz, *The Dove Always Cried*, 29.

92. Ibid. Stoltz served as a teacher in the Indian service from 1928 to 1937. She did not teach at Carlisle, but her memoir illustrates the influence and tenacity of practices—like home letters—that had started at Carlisle decades earlier. Despite important changes in policy and differences in the way the policy was implemented at Carlisle and at its satellite schools, the Indian boarding-school experience remained surprisingly constant across distance and time.

93. Child, *Boarding School Seasons*, xii.

94. Wheelock, "Is It Right?" Both Wheelock's essay and the student letters home mention "Indian language." Of course, there is no one "Indian language." These references illustrate the complexity of the development of Pan-Indianism at the schools. They clearly show the efforts of the school to detribalize students, which was seen as an important step in assimilation, but they also indicate the formation of a new, Pan-Indian identity.

95. Wheelock, "Is It Right?" 1.

96. "Song of the Printer," Indian Helper, May 19,1899, p. 1, l. 15.

97. For more information on this, see the *Red Man*'s articles on Wheelock and the Carlisle band, such as "Press Comments on the Band," as well as the *American Indian Magazine*'s reports of SAI conference proceedings. (Wheelock was an SAI officer.)

98. Hawkins qtd from "What Our Pupils Think," *Morning Star* (December 1887): 8. Wheelock's essay is not reprinted in this article. Instead, the "pro" opinion is expressed in a letter from Clarence Three Star, a Lakota returned student who was working for the Pine Ridge Agency Dakota boarding school. Three Star is the only one of the writers to mention the continuance of tribal languages. He writes: "the Indian children can learn their mother's tongues even if they don't try to learn it [sic], so they better have only English taught in all the Indian schools."

99. Ibid.

100. This information comes from a handwritten notation of Wheelock's biographical information in the Carlisle Barracks' Library vertical file, "Students."

101. This was originally published in the *New York World*, and was reprinted in the April 1900 issue of the *Red Man*, in an article titled "Press Comments on the Band."

102. For more on the institution of the Indian school band, see Rayna Green and John Troutman, "'By the Waters of the Minnehaha': Music, and Dance, Pageants and Princesses," in Archuleta, Child, and Lomawaima, *Away from Home*. See also Katanski, "Victory Songs."

103. Articles in the *Sherman Bulletin* between 1909 and 1917 list these and other pieces as part of various Sherman Indian school band performances. The Sherman band appears to have been much less accomplished and ambitious than the Carlisle band in the first years of the twentieth century. Dennison Wheelock eventually

served as band director at Sherman (around 1917), and the *Bulletin* notes marked improvement in the band after his arrival.

104. Although I had hoped that the Cumberland County Historical Archives would have copies of Wheelock's scores, they did not. I am unaware of any located extant copies of these works.

105. "Press Comments on the Band," 8.

106. Rinaldi, *My Heart Is on the Ground*, author's note, 195–96.

107. See, for example, page 9, where Nannie is disgusted with her brother because he purposely used the word "ferment" incorrectly in class. Asa Daklugie tells of his indignation (and near whipping) for mistakenly using "ferment" incorrectly in a sentence. In his telling, Daklugie is sent to Pratt's office. When Pratt takes out a long whip, Daklugie grabs him by his collar, jerks him off his feet, shakes him, and tells him, "If you think you can whip me, . . . you are *muy loco*. Nobody has ever struck me in all my life; and nobody ever will. I could break your neck with my bare hands" (Ball, *Indeh*, 150). This startling scene is the only example I have found of a student who was able to challenge Pratt or other school officials physically. Rinaldi converts this charged moment of student power into an opportunity for Nannie to chastize her brother, whose reluctance to embrace Carlisle is, Nannie claims, an embarrassment to their family. Rinaldi retells Zitkala-Ša's turnip-smashing rebellion—but Nannie "feel[s] bad that I did this thing" (88), whereas Zitkala-Ša "whooped in my heart for having once asserted the rebellion that was within me" (*American Indian Stories*, 61). Rinaldi also reinterprets several of Francis La Flesche's experiences, including when the students let the pigs loose (Rinaldi 90; La Flesche, *Middle Five*, 67–68).

108. For a detailed review of Rinaldi's book, see "A Critical Review of Ann Rinaldi's *My Heart Is on the Ground*," by Reese, Landis, Atleo, Caldwell, Mendoza, Miranda, Rose, Smith, and Slapin. This review has been published on-line at <www.oyate.org/books-to-avoid/myHeart.html>. Oyate, which sponsors this web page, is an organization devoted to evaluating representations of American Indians in children's literature.

109. Silko, *Yellow Woman and a Beauty of the Spirit*, 165.

110. Allen, *Sacred Hoop*, 151.

111. Williams, "Documents of Barbarism," 238.

CHAPTER 3

1. Cook, "Representative Indian," 82.

2. Ibid.

3. See James A. Clifton's introduction to Clark and Webb, "Susette and Susan La Flesche," 137. Clifton coins the term "Franco-Ponca" and provides a brief (and cynical) discussion of the La Flesches' place within the Omaha community.

4. For biographical information on La Flesche, see Norma Kidd Green, *Iron Eye's Family*; Mark, "Francis La Flesche"; and Mark's biography of Alice Fletcher,

the ethnographer with whom La Flesche collaborated, *A Stranger in Her Native Land*. In addition, Liberty's two studies of La Flesche, "Francis La Flesche" and "Native American Informants," provide useful biographical facts as well as interpretations of his anthropological work. More recently, Sherry Smith's "World of Letters" and Ramsey's "'The Song of Flying Crow'" provide critical readings of La Flesche's work.

5. Fletcher and La Flesche, "The Omaha Tribe," 635.

6. Both Mark and Liberty discuss at some length La Flesche's uncomfortable position as an accomplished and knowledgeable anthropologist whose contributions to the work of Fletcher, especially, was never appropriately credited. Fletcher continued to regard La Flesche as her assistant, even when he suggested the focus of their research and gathered, interpreted, and transcribed most of the data. (See especially Mark, "Francis La Flesche," 505).

7. Qtd. in Littlefield and Parins's introduction to *Ke-ma-ha* (a posthumously published collection of La Flesche's short stories), xii.

8. Ibid.

9. Cook, "Representative Indian," 82.

10. Littlefield and Parins, Introduction in La Flesche, *Ke-ma-ha*, xix.

11. Fletcher's relationship with La Flesche was complicated, and there are definitely several other reasons she took an active role in the publication of his memoir. First, the two were constant companions, living in the same Washington, D.C., hotel for over twenty-five years and traveling and working together for even longer. Fletcher wanted La Flesche to succeed as an author because of her fondness for him. At the same time, whe sought to encourage La Flesche's literary career so that she would not have to share her prominence as an ethnographer with him. See Littlefield and Parins's introduction to La Flesche, *Ke-ma-ha*, especially pp. xviii and xix. For a more in-depth discussion of their relationship, see also Mark, *A Stranger in Her Native Land*.

12. Littlefield and Parins, Introduction to La Flesche, *Ke-ma-ha*, xvii.

13. "Indian Boys at School," *Red Man and Helper*, August 21, 1900. Because of Pratt's close surveillance over and involvement in the newspapers, one can assume that any editorial opinion expressed was Pratt's opinion. Unsigned articles in the Carlisle newspapers often indicate the article was written by Pratt himself. See Littlefield and Parins, *Native Newspapers*, 182, 320.

14. Angel de Cora attended the Hampton Institute and was appointed to teach art at Carlisle in 1906, becoming the school's first art teacher to teach and encourage tribal art. For more on de Cora, see her essay, "Angel de Cora—An Autobiography."

15. "Indian Boys at School."

16. Ibid.

17. La Flesche, *The Middle Five*, 132. Further references to this work will be given parenthetically in the text.

18. David A. Baerreis, Introduction to La Flesche, *The Middle Five*, ix.

19. This is not to say, of course, that it is only these differences in La Flesche's situation that make it possible for him to develop a repertoire of identities. Certainly

Carlisle students, as well, developed these complex relational identities. The proximity of La Flesche's school to a tribal community does allow him, when describing his identity, to use a vocabulary from outside social evolutionism. Zitkala-Ša, by contrast, seems compelled to take on the language of social evolutionism in order then to discredit it by describing her school experiences and her own formation of a repertoire of identity.

20. La Flesche and Fletcher translate the "I^{n}shta'çu^{n}da" into "the Sky people," and "Ho^n'gashenu" into "the Earth people." See Fletcher and La Flesche, *The Omaha Tribe*, 135. For extensive details on the various "gentes" and their subdivisions, see ch. 4, "Tribal Organization," (ibid., 134–98). La Flesche and Fletcher make clear that these various groups are not simply based on ties of blood, but are instead complex interweavings of relationships and religious rites that kept the balance between male and female, the earth and the sky (134–35).

21. Even with the great changes that allotment and other assimilative policies brought to the Omaha and forced on their tribal structure, La Flesche and Fletcher note that the Omaha maintained exogamous marriage patterns based on membership in the tribe's divisions, or villages. Tribal kinship relations were not replaced by the Western concept of the nuclear family (Fletcher and La Flesche, *The Omaha Tribe*, 135).

22. Coleman, *American Indian Children*, 156.

23. McFee, "The 150% Man," 1101.

24. See also, for example, Lomawaima, *They Called It Prairie Light* (especially pp. 96–99), a study of the Chilocco Indian school, which includes many examples of student culture that remained invisible to the educators.

25. This term invokes White's *Middle Ground* (x). White's influential paradigm of dynamic American Indian history extends in significance far beyond the way it's used here. His term is intended to refer to a specific period of history (1650–1815) and to a specific set of circumstances. Not all of the nuances of meaning he ascribes to the middle ground apply here.

26. Coleman, *American Indian Children*, 156.

27. Irrespective of whether the diction actually rendered Omaha patterns of speech into English, as opposed to stylizing the English usage to fit a white audience's expectations of Omaha speech, it served to represent a connection between the boys and Omaha culture and rituals. As an Omaha speaker and in his role as anthropologist, La Flesche frequently translated Omaha speech into English text.

28. Mikhail Bakhtin's understanding of the utterance—explained in "The Problem of the Text," in *Speech Genres and Other Late Essays* (103–31)—is useful to considering this situation. According to Bakhtin, a word's meaning changes with each utterance, because the context it is uttered in constantly changes. Therefore, Omaha words—even repetitions of ritualized formulas—take on new meaning when uttered in the context of the late-night meetings at the school.

29. Coleman, *American Indian Children*, 151.

30. Ibid., 68.

31. Bailey, *The Osage and the Invisible World*, 14.

32. McFee, "The 150% Man," 1100.

33. Ahern, "'The Returned Indians,'" 114. While, collectively, the La Flesche family was devoted to selective accommodation and cultural retention, the family was deeply divided about what to retain and how to accommodate. Francis's devotion to Alice Fletcher led him to support her policies, which were intended to work toward more complete assimilation, at least at first. (See Littlefield and Parins, Introduction to La Flesche, *Ke-ma-ha*, for more on Fletcher's changing attitudes toward allotment and assimilation.) On the other hand, his sister Susette Bright Eyes La Flesche Tibbles and her white husband worked for Indian citizenship and self-determination. Other family members moved between these two ideological positions, which were, in fact, very complicated. It would be incorrect to say that Francis was pro-assimilation while Susette was pro-tribalism. This is not at all the case. See Mark, "Francis La Flesche," and Littlefield and Parins's Introductin to La Flesche, *Ke-ma-ha*, for a more detailed analysis of the divisions within the La Flesche family.

34. Fletcher and La Flesche, *The Omaha Tribe*, 14.

35. La Flesche, "The Osage Tribe," 530–32.

36. Ibid., 532–38.

37. Ramsey takes up La Flesche's practice of ethnography in his article, "'The Song of Flying Crow'," which reads an unpublished, possibly autobiographical, essay found in La Flesche's files in the National Anthropological Archives as an analysis of his sense of himself as both an ethnographer and a tribal member. In the essay, La Flesche recounts the situation in which he learned a new Omaha song composed by a recently deceased friend who had been at boarding school with him, but who "learned very little of the instructions given in the schoolroom and much less of those given in the chapel. . . . Born a pagan he died a pagan, with the song of a pagan on his mind." Ramsey points out that learning this pagan song becomes important to La Flesche's need to belong to his community, and though he does not share the song itself in the essay (refusing to reveal this piece of continuing tribal culture to a reader), the song "is now so fixed in my memory that I shall never forget it even if I should live to be a hundred years old" (187). Here, a fellow boarding-school student teaches the Omaha ethnographer about the persistence and constant reinvention of his tribal culture. It is a lesson La Flesche never forgot.

38. Bailey, *The Osage and the Invisible World*, 18; Hertzberg, *American Indian Identity*, 174, 305.

39. Joane Nagel sees the Native American Church as "institution building," part of the community building necessary for collective ethnic renewal (*American Indian Ethnic Renewal*, 10). Hazel Hertzberg includes an extensive discussion of peyotism and the rise of the Native American Church as religious Pan-Indianism. While many former Carlisle students were leaders in the Native American Church and testified against anti-peyote bills in Washington, Zitkala-Ša, like Charles

Alexander Eastman and other SAI members, was deeply opposed to the church. She felt that the leaders of the Native American Church were shysters, exploiting their followers and injuring them by making them dependent on the drug (see chapter 4). Complicated identity issues come to the fore here, demonstrating again how impossible it is to make sense of Indian identity on a linear continuum.

40. Hertzberg, *Indian Identity*, 303, 315.

41. Ibid., 262.

42. Cook specifically mentions that the representative Indian must "raise his race with him" [*sic*], "Representative Indian," 83.

43. Bailey, *The Osage and the Invisible World*, 14.

44. Sherry Smith, "Francis LaFlesche and the World of Letters," 582.

45. Zitkala-Ša, letter to the editor, *Red Man* (April 1900), 8. Doreen Rappaport's "autobiographical biography," *The Flight of Red Bird*, is a good source on the areas of Zitkala-Ša's life that fall outside her autobiographical essays, especially her years on the Uintah and Ouray reservation in Utah. Likewise, P. Jane Hafen's (intro-duction to Zitkala-Ša, *Dreams and Thunder*, "A Cultural Duet") and Ruth Spack's (*America's Second Tongue*, "Dis/Engagement," and "Re-visioning Sioux Women") extensive archival work on Zitkala-Ša's life and writings provides important information about her life and analysis of her work. See also Willard, "Zitkala-Ša"; Warrior, *Tribal Secrets*; Hertzberg, *American Indian Identity*, and Wilson and Johnson, "Gertrude Simmons Bonnin," for information on her career as an activist, including her association with the SAI.

46. Fisher, *The Transformation of Tradition*, 16. According to Dexter Fisher, she was given the name of her mother's second husband, a white man named Simmons. Zitkala-Ša's biological father, a white man named Felker, had abandoned the family before her birth. Zitkala-Ša's mother was married to three white men but never learned to speak English, Fisher claims ("Evolution," ix).

47. Hafen, Introduction to *Dreams and Thunder*, xiv. Spack suggests that Bonnin's [Zitkala-Ša's] choice of a Lakota rather than a Nakota name indicated "that Zitkala-Ša wanted to link herself with the Lakotas—the last Sioux holdouts against the United States cavalry—rather than with the Yanktons, who were peaceful" (*America's Second Tongue*, 196, n. 16).

48. Zitkala-Ša, *American Indian Stories*, 67–68.

49. Susan Bernardin, "Sentimental Education," 221. For more on Zitkala-Ša's parentage, see Rappaport, *Flight of Red Bird*, 3. Rappaport reports that Gertrude was the ninth child born to Tate Iyohiwin ("Every Wind," her mother), and the only child she had with her third white husband. (Hafen says that Gertrude's mother was named Ellen Simmons or Táte I Yóhin Win, which she and Lakota scholar Agnes Picotte translate as "Woman Who Reaches for the Wind" [Zitkala-Ša, *Dreams and Thunder*, 154 n.2].) Zitkala-Ša's failure to mention her father's race in her autobiographical writing does not make her self–representation "false" in any way (see below).

50. Fisher, *Transformation of Tradition*, x–xi.

51. Adams, *Education for Extinction*, 311; Coleman, *American Indian Children*, 98.

52. Spack points out that Bonnin [Zitkala-Ša] attended "a Yankton Agency (Presbyterian, bilingual) day school for two years before entering boarding school at age eight. Between two terms at White's Institute (between ages eleven and fourteen or fifteen), she lived in Dakota Territory and for some of that time attended the bilingual Santee Normal Training School at the Dakota Mission" (*America's Second Tongue*, 144–45). In her essay, she leaves out her day-school experiences, a move that further emphasizes the juxtaposition between tribal education and boarding school.

53. Zitkala-Ša, *American Indian Stories*, 9. Further references to this work will be given parenthetically in the text.

54. Allen, *Sacred Hoop*, 82, 205.

55. See Cutter " Zitkala-Ša's Autobiographical Writings," for an extended (and slightly different) discussion of Edenic imagery in Zitkala-Ša's work (36–37). See also Okker, "Native American Literatures," 95.

56. Stocking, *Race, Culture, and Evolution,* makes it clear that the early social evolutionists were, in fact, responding to and arguing against degenerationist ideology (75).

57. "School Days of an Indian Girl," *Red Man,* 8.

58. Ibid.

59. Spack, "Re-visioning Sioux Women," 33.

60. "School Days of an Indian Girl," *Red Man* (February 1900): 8.

61. Zitkala-Ša, letter to the editor, *Red Man* (April 1900): 8.

62. See Littlefield and Parins, *Native Newspapers,* for a discussin of the *Word Camier,* a bilingual newspaper printed at the Santee Mission School; also Gilman and Schneider, *The Way to Independence,* 147, 352.

63. "Zitkala-Ša in the *Atlantic Monthly,*" *Red Man and Helper* (June 1900).

64. Spack, *America's Second Tongue,* 152–53 or "Re-visioning Sioux Women," 29. Spack explains that, in her analysis of Zitkala-Ša, she will "treat the texts as fiction, for I believe that such an approach allows readers to separate the loss of control of language that the first-person female narrator sometimes experiences from the rhetorical control that the author always maintains" (*America's Second Tongue,* 153). Despite Spack's reasoning, I continue to view these texts as autobiography, both because Zitkala-Ša's work engages in intertextual conversations with the American Indian autobiographical tradition and because recognizing the essays as autobiography emphasizes the process of self-fashioning that Zitkala-Ša engaged in.

65. "Zitkala-Ša in the *Atlantic Monthly.*"

66. In addition to moving east to write, Bonnin [Zitkala-Ša] became active in politics and became an officer in the Society of American Indians, eventually turning her literary talent to editing the SAI's important journal, the *American Indian Magazine.* For more on this journal, see Hertzberg, whose history of the SAI is as much about the journal as it is about the group itself.

67. "Indian Year in Literature and Art," *Red Man and Helper,* July 13, 1900.

68. Zitkala-Ša, *American Indian Stories*, 107. Originally published under the title "Why I am a Pagan," the essay is titled "The Great Spirit" *in American Indian Stories*.

69. Bruner, "Ethnography as Narrative," 144.

70. Littlefield and Parins, *Native Newspapers*, 320–21.

71. Ibid., 320–21.

CHAPTER 4

1. Lewis Henry Morgan, *Ancient Society*, 31.

2. Quoted in Littlefield and Parins's introduction to La Flesche, *Ke-ma-ha*, xiii.

3. Wilson's biography of Eastman, *Ohiyesa*, provides a detailed assessment of Eastman's publications. Elaine Goodale Eastman's memoir, *Sister to the Sioux*, depicts her own assimilationist ideology and recounts her experiences at Hampton Institute and her work on the Great Sioux Reservation. Among her accomplishments, Elaine spoke Lakota fluently and was a published author at age sixteen, when she and her sister, Dora, published their *Apple-Blossoms: Verses of Two Children*.

4. Use of the term "American Indian autobiography" here departs from the terminology Arnold Krupat standardized in his study *For Those Who Come After*. Krupat distinguishes between "autobiographies by Indians," or autobiographical texts written by Indian people who are literate in English and who bear the sole responsibility for authoring the text; and "Indian autobiographies," or the "bicultural composite" texts produced by collaborations between usually nonliterate Indians and white or mixed-blood editors or transcribers. Krupat uses the term "Native American autobiography" to encompass both categories. Since I do not use the term "Native American" frequently in this book, I am using "American Indian autobiography" where Krupat uses "Native American autobiography." The autobiographies I focus on here are what Krupat would call "autobiographies by Indians," but the line between his two categories is not always clear. For example, we do not know all of the details of the process by which Elaine Goodale Eastman edited her husband's work. The term "American Indian autobiography" here is meant to suggest that these texts are all of at least bicultural composition while stressing the importance of the agency of the Indian authors.

5. This search for authenticity is the verso of the assimilationist credo which insisted that Indian culture must be eliminated. After stating cultural genocide as a goal, and working to achieve that goal, assimilationists question those who still claim an Indian identity, charging them with not being Indian enough to count as Indian. This is not to suggest that contemporary literary critics share the political goals of the Friends of the Indian, but to assert that the contemporary critical praxis may reproduce elements of social evolutionary thinking.

6. Bieder, *Science Encounters the Indian*, 250.

7. Kroskrity, *Language, History, and Identity*, 207, 209, emphasis in original.

8. Ibid., 202. English is not, of course, the only multivocal expressive code. Kroskrity gives examples of Tewa who use Hopi at different times to indicate an affinity with the Hopi people, and to make fun of a Hopi attitude from the Tewa perspective (*Language, History, and Identity*, 199–202).

9. Wong, *Sending My Heart Back*, 13–15.

10. Krupat, *Anthology*, 4.

11. Krupat, *For Those Who Come After*, 29.

12. Wong, *Sending My Heart Back*, 12.

13. For example, not long before the publication of Brumble's book, Krupat held that, "unlike traditional Native literature, the Indian autobiography has no prior model in the collective practice of tribal cultures" (*For Those Who Come After,* 31).

14. Brumble, *American Indian Autobiography*, 22–23.

15. Ibid., 22; Wong, *Sending My Heart Back*, 24.

16. Brumble, *American Indian Autobiography*, 37.

17. Ibid., 17.

18. Sarris, *Keeping Slug Woman Alive*, 89.

19. Murray, *Forked Tongue*, 79.

20. Ibid., 79–80.

21. Ibid., 78–79.

22. Parks and DeMallie, "Plains Indian Native Literatures," 106.

23. Spack, *America's Second Tongue*, 112.

24. Sarris, *Keeping Slug Woman Alive*, 70.

25. See Hertzberg, *American Indian Identity*, 178–79, plate 3.

26. Charles Eastman, *From the Deep Woods*, 76. Further references to this work will be given parenthetically in the text.

27. See Utley, *Last Days of the Sioux,* and Brown, *Bury My Heart at Wounded Knee,* for more on the 1890 massacre.

28. Powell, "Rhetorics of Survivance," 400. Powell's article and Peterson, "An Indian . . . an American," are among the most helpful contemporary readings of Charles Eastman's autobiographical writing (in particular, *From the Deep Woods*).

29. Eastman's autobiographies remain the best known of his eleven books. This book references the University of Nebraska Press editions of these texts.

30. Eastman was clearly a well–educated and literate man, though questions have been raised about the extent to which his wife, Elaine Goodale Eastman, was involved in his writing. "Eastman's biographers tend to agree that Eastman was responsible for the ideas, while his wife was responsible for the editing," according to Wong (*Sending My Heart Back*, 141). It is important to remember, though, that Eastman was very literate, and he surely knew the conventions of both Western autobiography and Dakota storytelling and made choices about how to use them. Despite his wife's editorial input, I read him as responsible for the narrative structure of *Indian Boyhood*. In this I am in agreement with Ruth Heflin in *I Remain Alive,* who argues vigorously that "it is doubtful Elaine had as much of a hand in her husband's writings as she claimed, although she undoubtedly had some. His

earliest writings [including the pieces he identified as the beginnings of *Indian Boyhood*] were probably relatively untouched by Elaine" (56). For more on their collaboration and an analysis of Eastman's experimentation with genre, see Heflin, *I Remain Alive*, 53–58. For a contrasting opinion, see Carol Lea Clark, "A Cross-Cultural Collaboration."

31. Brumble, *American Indian Autobiography*, 148.

32. Charles Eastman, *Indian Boyhood*, dedication.

33. Josephy, *500 Nations*, 382; Hoxie, ed., *The Encyclopedia of North American Indians*, 341–42, 592; Wilson, *Ohiyesa*, 13–14. As Wilson points out, in retaliation for the Sioux Uprising, the U.S. government abrogated all treaties with the Santee, and their remaining annuity payments were given to white victims of the conflict. Charles Eastman later became involved in the Santees' claims case and represented the tribe in their attempt to recover the annuities (*Ohiyesa*, 16).

34. Charles Eastman, *Indian Boyhood*, 13. Further references to this work will be given parenthetically in the text.

35. Hertzberg, *American Indian Identity*, 2.

36. Ibid., 41–42. Pan-Indianism is thus a political identity, though at the turn of the century, especially for some members of the SAI, this identity was not as invested in self-determination as it became during the civil rights era (see Chapter 5).

37. Ella Cara Deloria, sister of Vine Deloria, Sr., and student of Franz Boas, wrote *Waterlily* during the 1940s. In 1944, she had completed the manuscript and edited it for publication, but it was not published until 1988 by the University of Nebraska Press. In addition to helpful materials included in the Nebraska edition, which contextualize Deloria's career and *Waterlily*, see also Rice, *Lakota Storytelling*, and Heflin, *I Remain Alive*.

38. Deloria, *Waterlily*, 138–41. *Waterlily* does not emphasize chastity as a moral virtue. Instead chastity is a status marker, because a virgin could be bought as a bride, which was an honor to her family and increased their social standing. Not all women were bought, however, and those who married in a different manner were not always permanently disgraced because of this difference (ibid., 12–14, 149).

39. Wong, *Sending My Heart Back*, 145, 144.

40. Wilson, *Ohiyesa*, 143.

41. Wong, *Sending My Heart Back*, 39.

42. Brumble, *American Indian Autobiography*, 162. For a detailed reading of Eastman's involvement with the Boy Scouts, see Carr, "The American Indian as Prototype," an unpublished paper presented at the October 1999 American Studies Association Conference in Montreal, Quebec. See also Philip Deloria, *Playing Indian*.

43. Brumble, *American Indian Autobiography*, 148; David Carlson, "'Indian for a While,'" 5.

44. Brumble, *American Indian Autobiography*, 161–62.

45. Charles Eastman, *From the Deep Woods*, 7.

46. See Hertzberg, *American Indian Identity*.

47. Charles Eastman, *From the Deep Woods*, 195.

48. Murray, *Forked Tongues*, 78.

49. Philip Deloria, *Playing Indian*, 123–24.

50. Charles Eastman, *Soul of the Indian*, 24.

51. Erik Peterson, "'An Indian . . . an American,'" 184; Powell, "Rhetorics of Survivance," 401.

52. As archival evidence shows, Zitkala-Ša was fluent and literate in Dakota, writing stories such as "Squirrel Man and His Double" first in Dakota and then shaping them into English (in this case as "The Witch Woman"). Hafen's important scholarship has brought to light these previously unpublished stories, which reveal entirely new aspects of Zitkala-Ša's artistry. See Zitkala-Ša, *Dreams and Thunder*.

53. Zitkala-Ša, *American Indian Stories*, 89. Further references to this work will be given parenthetically in the text.

54. For more on Zitkala-Ša as trickster, see Jeanne Smith, "'A Second Tongue,'" and Susag, "Zitkala-Ša (Gertrude Simmons Bonnin)."

55. Wong, *Sending My Heart Back*, 18.

56. *Old Indian Legends* has been reissued by the University of Nebraska Press in 2004 as Zitkala-Ša, *Iktomi and the Ducks and Other Sioux Stories*. See also Zitkala-Ša, *Dreams and Thunder*.

57. Wexler, "Tender Violence," 17.

58. Ibid.

59. Bernardin also notes Zitkala-Ša's complex relationship to sentimentality: "Having established herself as a sentimental heroine in the first installment [of her autobiographical essays], Zitkala-Ša systematically dismantles this role in the second installment through socially unacceptable revisions of the sentimental script" ("Lessons of a Sentimental Education," 224).

60. See Tompkins, *Sensational Designs*, ch. 5.

61. See "Zitkala-Ša in the *Atlantic Monthly*." The *Word Carrier* was a bilingual newspaper printed in English and Dakota at the Santee Mission School. It was extremely critical of Zitkala-Ša, as was Carlisle's *Red Man*. Boarding-school newspapers were used as tools of propaganda by school administrators to push their pro-assimilation, anti-tribal agenda. For complete descriptions and publication dates of both the *Red Man* and the *Word Carrier*, see Littlefield and Parins, *Native Newspapers*.

62. Zitkala-Ša, letter to the editor.

63. Spack, "Re-visioning Sioux Women," 29. Spack contends, for example, that "Zitkala-Ša revises or at least obscures her father's status. Rather than identify him as a white man who deserted the family before his daughter's birth, . . . she exoticizes him as a victim of white oppression" (ibid). Additionally, Spack explains, Zitkala-Ša downplays the level of success she attained at White's Manual Institute. In other words, Spack is contesting the identity Zitkala-Ša attempts to deploy in these essays, a stance that assumes there is a more authentic identity, which Zitkala-Ša somehow obscures through her autobiography. Spack acknowledges, for example, "the autobiographic truth in the writing, for these pieces may reveal the truth of the author's self if not exactly of her life" (ibid.). Spack does not have

the same motivation as the boarding-school journalist for challenging the events Zitkala-Ša includes in her essays, but the end result is the same type of authenticity-centered critique. See also Spack, *America's Second Tongue*, 153.

64. "Zitkala-Ša in the *Atlantic Monthly*."

65. Montezuma, correspondence with Zitkala-Ša.

66. See Charles Eastman, *Indian Boyhood*, 86; Standing Bear, *My People the Sioux*, 159; also Coleman, *American Indian Children at School*, ch. 9, "Rejection." Eastman briefly relates that his cousin, a close childhood companion, died because "she could not endure the confinement of the school-room" (86). Standing Bear talks about the death of Wica-Karpa, or Ernest White Thunder, who "complained that he did not want to go to [classes at Carlisle]. . . . The next day he complained that he felt sick. . . . The following day he died" (159). Standing Bear explains: "That was one of the hard things about our education—we had to get used to so many things we had never known before that it worked on our nerves to such an extent that it told on our bodies" (159). Adams, *Education for Extinction* provides more detail on Ernest's death and includes information about Pratt's attempt to discipline the boy in the pages of the *Indian Helper* just days before his death, which both Adams and Coleman read as a response to and a rejection of Carlisle.

67. Adams, *Education for Extinction*, 130.

68. Warrior, *Tribal Secrets*, 11.

69. See Zitkala-Ša's letters to Carlos Montezuma can be found in the Carlos Montezuma papers; the letter quoted here is dated February 20, 1901.

70. Warrior, *Tribal Secrets*, 12.

71. Doreen Rappaport provides a good summary of Bonnin's [Zitkala-Ša's] appearance at the congressional hearings on the Hayden Bill (*Flight of Red Bird*, 135–37). The transcript of the hearings provides the full text of the exchange between Mooney, Bonnin, and Warden and also includes the testimony of Pratt and Eastman (who joined Bonnin in support of the bill) and La Flesche (who joined Mooney and Warden against the bill). The transcripts will be cited here as U.S. Senate, *Peyote*.

It is important to note that Native people have had different reasons for supporting and opposing peyotism over the years. Zitkala-Ša's opposition to the religion draws on the arguments of white anti-peyotists, but she saw herself as responding to concern for a particular Native community's physical health. Members of the Navajo nation, on the other hand, have discouraged peyotism because they believe that its Pan-Indian bricolage of ceremony and its Christian elements undercut a vibrant practice of traditional Navajo religion. For more on the Navajo and peyotism, see Aberle, *Peyote Religion among the Navajo*, and Yabe, "Balancing Realities." For more general information on peyotism and the Native American Church, see Stewart, *Peyote Religion*, and Smith and Snake, *One Nation under God*.

72. "Zitkala-Ša in the *Atlantic Monthly*."

73. U.S. Senate, *Peyote*, 107.

74. Ibid, 63. Zitkala-Ša, during her testimony, attacked Mooney in return, challenging his authority as an ethnologist who claimed to know the Indians better than they know themselves. She said that ethnologists experienced only what the peyotists wanted them to experience. Building on a different source of authority, she continued; "I have been a schoolteacher for too long not to know that when I have a class recite for a visitor, immediately the air is charged with a certain restraint. That is human nature. When the Indians know that an ethnologist is visiting and intends to write everything down, they naturally cannot help feeling restrained and do not do what they are in the habit of doing" (ibid., 124).

75. Batker, *Reforming Fictions*, 31.

76. Qtd in Cutter, "Zitkala-Ša's Autobiographical Writings," 35.

77. For more information Bonnin's political career, see Willard, "The First Amendment," and "Zitkala-Ša"; also Hertzberg, *American Indian Identity*; Johnson and Wilson, "Gertrude Simmons Bonnin"; and Rappaport, *Flight of Red Bird*.

78. See Wilson, *Ohiyesa*, 184–93. Eastman and his wife, a staunch assimilationist, were separated by August 1921, after thirty years of marriage. Though Eastman continued to work on literary projects, he never published after he and his wife parted. See also Carol Clark, "A Cross-Cultural Collaboration."

79. Zitkala-Ša, *American Indian Stories*, 99.

80. Warrior, *Tribal Secrets*, xviii–xix.

81. Ibid., 8.

82. Ibid.

CHAPTER 5

1. Womack, *Red on Red*, 6.

2. Ibid.

3. Hoxie, *A Final Promise*, 243.

4. Ibid., 244.

5. Cook–Lynn, *Wallace Stegner*, 83.

6. Allen, *Voice of the Turtle*, 12–13.

7. See Chavkin and Chavkin, *Conversations with Louise Erdrich*, 64, 76, 80, 158. Of course, BIA boarding schools from the 1950s to the present bear little resemblance to Carlisle. The Haskell Indian Institute is today home to Haskell Indian University, which houses a program in American Indian Studies, while Sherman serves more as a school for troubled teenagers. Erdrich claimed, in a 1987 interview, that "the boarding schools have finally started serving a positive purpose. . . . They're finally schools that can take in children who have nowhere else to go" (ibid., 95). Although Erdrich and other contemporary writers have not personally experienced the darkest elements of these assimilative institutions, they are well aware of the history of cultural genocide perpetrated in the schools.

8. See Momaday, *The Names*, for more autobiographical information.

9. Allen, *Voice of the Turtle*, 13.

10. McNickle, *The Surrounded*, 273.

11. Ibid., 297.

12. Chavkin and Chavkin, *Conversations with Louise Erdrich*, 96.

13. Erdrich, *Jacklight*.

14. Ibid.

15. Lomawaima, *They Called It Prarie Light*, 98–99.

16. See Talayesva, *Sun Chief*; Daklugie's story in Ball, *Indeh*; Qoyawayma, *No Turning Back*; Mourning Dove, *Mourning Dove*; Sekaquaptewa, *Me and Mine*; Snake, *Reuben Snake*; and Horne and McBeth, *Essie's Story*. Others include Shaw, *A Pima Past*; Yava, *Big Falling Snow*; and Johnston, *Indian School Days*.

17. Qtd. in Chavkin and Chavkin, *Conversations with Louise Erdrich*, 96.

18. Shanley, "'Born from the Need to Say,'" 3.

19. Womack, *Red on Red*, 11.

20. Chavkin and Chavkin, *Conversations with Louise Erdrich*, 154–55.

21. Erdrich, *Tracks*, 226.

22. Trafzer, *Blue Dawn, Red Earth*, 4.

23. Allen, *Voice of the Turtle*, 72. Diné is the name the people call themselves, though many know them as Navajo. Tapahonso uses both terms.

24. Tapahonso, *Sáani: Dahataal*, 80–82.

25. Tapahonso states in an interview: "About three years ago I saw that girl Cathy, the one who used to walk to the cemetery, and we were talking about that. And I asked her, 'Do you remember that?' She said, 'I remember it vaguely, but,' she said, 'I thought it was a dream.' And I said, 'No, you used to walk over there'" (Breinig and Lösch 122).

26. For more information about the concept of *hózhó* and other elements of Navajo philosophy, see Witherspoon in *Language and Art in the Navajo Universe*, who explicitly discusses Navajo philosophy in terms of language.

27. Tapahonso, *Sáani: Dahataal*, xi.

28. Ibid., xii.

29. Ibid.

30. Ibid., 81.

31. All quotations in this paragraph are from ibid., 80.

32. Kluckhohn explains the use of powder: in the "classic Witchery Way . . . a preparation (usually called 'poison' by English speaking informants) is made of the flesh of corpses. The flesh of children and especially twin children is preferred . . . when this 'corpse poison' is ground into powder it 'looks like pollen.' It may be dropped into a hogan from the smoke hole, placed in the nose or mouth of a sleeping victim or blown from furrowed sticks into the face of someone in a large crowd" (*Navaho Witchcraft*, 25). Gary Witherspoon explains that witchcraft, part of the world from its inception, is "an important source of *hóchxó* that must be brought under control and reversed or neutralized"; *Hóchxó* is the opposite of *hózhó*—"the evil, the disorderly, and the ugly" (*Language and Art*, 34, 39–40). Barre Toelken demonstrates the connection between Western educational practices and witchcraft in his "Life

and Death in the Navajo Coyote Tales." Tapahonso is making this connection, too, clearly working within the Navajo worldview to explain the evil of the boarding schools.

33. Breinig and Lösch, "Luci Tapahonso," 122.

34. Allen, *Song of the Turtle*, 72.

35. Ibid.

36. Tapahonso, *Sáani: Dahataal*, 83.

37. Momaday wrote *The Indolent Boys* in the early 1990s when he was commissioned by director Geeta Hanagar and the Harvard University Native American Program. A staged reading of the play was performed at Harvard in February 1992 (and that is the text used here). In 1994, the play was performed at New York's Syracuse Stage. Since then, there have been several performances of the play, most significantly the Southwest Repertory Theater's 2002 production and the 2003 production at the Autry Museum's Wells Fargo Theatre in Los Angeles. See <http://www.buffalotrust.org> for more information.

38. For more on the Indian civil rights struggle, including AIM and the Red Power movement, see Josephy, Nagel, and Johnson, *Red Power*; Johnson, *American Indian Activism*; and Smith and Warrior, *Like a Hurricane*.

39. Momaday, *The Indolent Boys*, v.

40. Mooney, *Calendar History*, 146.

41. Ibid.

42. Ibid., 145.

43. Qtd. in ibid., 376.

44. Ibid., 145.

45. Momaday, "Poetics and Politics," 4–5. "Poetics and Politics" was a graduate seminar and coordinated series of lectures offered at the University of Arizona in 1992. The .pdf file of the transcript of Momaday's roundtable discussion with seminar participants can be found on-line at the "Poetics and Politics" web page hosted by the University of Arizona.

46. Ibid., 5.

47. This previously unpublished short story has been made available in Zitkala-Ša, *Dreams and Thunder*, 93–96.

48. Huntsman, "Native American Theatre," 370.

49. Momaday, who received his PhD in English at Stanford University in 1963, published his dissertation on the poems of Frederick Goddard Tuckerman and received a Guggenheim Fellowship in 1966 to study the poems of Emily Dickinson and transcendental literature in Amherst, Massachusetts (Schubnell, *Conversations with N. Scott Momaday*, xx). He is, therefore, quite conversant with Western literary conventions. He has also frequently asserted his knowledge of the Kiowa oral tradition. He writes in the introduction to *Man Made of Words*: "My father told me stories from the Kiowa oral tradition even before I could talk. Those stories became permanent in my mind, the nourishment of my imagination for the whole of my life. They are among the most valuable gifts that I have ever been given" (8).

50. Huntsman, "Native American Theatre," 371.

51. Momaday, *Indolent Boys*, iv. Further references to this work will be given parenthetically in the text.

52. Boyd, *Kiowa Voices, vol. 1*, 13.

53. Huntsman, "Native American Theatre," 359.

54. While Momaday's version of the story closely follows the information provided in Mooney's ethnographic study of the Kiowa calendars, it contrasts with another published version of the event. Alice Marriott, in *The Ten Grandmothers*, her 1945 history of the Kiowa, states that the stories contained in her work "may be taken as an eye-witness account of the event related" (xi). And yet, her version of "the winter the boys froze to death," which she titles simply "Running Away," portrays the incident in a significantly different manner from Momaday. She presents the runaways as young troublemakers with a history of bad behavior, denies that they were beaten, and tells the story from the point of view of a "good student" who criticizes the actions of the runaways.

55. For more on runaways and the dangers they faced, see Bell, "Telling Stories out of School."

56. Zitkala-Ša, *American Indian Stories*, 99. Zitkala-Ša's "Search for Bear Claws" ends with a similar statement: "There under the snow blanket they found the runaway school boy's body. Little Bear Claws was gone away where boarding schools can no more torture" (*Dreams and Thunder*, 96).

57. Weaver, "From I-Hermeneutics to We-Hermeneutics," 22.

58. For the "Soft-hearted Sioux," see Zitkala-Ša, *American Indian Stories*, 109–25.

59. For the Kiowa mythology, see, for example, Momaday, *The Way to Rainy Mountain*, 20–21

60. See Mooney, *The Ghost-Dance Religion*, for more on Kiowa participation in this movement. The Kiowa continued to dance long after Wounded Knee, as did other southern tribes, such as the Hualapi, Chemehuevi, and others; see Silko, *Gardens in the Dunes*.

61. Momaday, *The Names*, 25.

62. Ibid.

63. Qtd. in Nagel, *American Indian Ethnic Renewal*, 116.

64. Ibid.

65. See <http://www.buffalotrust.org> for more information. With the goal of opening several study centers and assisting tribes with the repatriation of objects of cultural patrimony and sacred items, the Buffalo Trust seeks to support tribal self–determination on a number of levels.

66. See <http://www.buffalotrust.org/indolent.htm> for more information. The Buffalo Trust has structured performances of the play as fundraising events to support the activities and mission of the organization.

67. Weaver, *That the People Might Live*, xiii.

68. This information comes from Geiogamah's history of NATE, in his introduction to *Stories of Our Way*, 3.

69. Ibid.

70. Ibid., vii.

71. Ibid., 5.

72. Pinazzi, "The Theater of Hanay Geiogamah," 187.

73. See the "Songs for *Coon Cons Coyote*," in Geiogamah and Darby, eds. *Stories of Our Way*, 147–54. The full text of the play is reprinted in this anthology.

74. Pinazzi, "The Theater of Hanay Geiogamah," 187.

75. Qtd. in Lincoln, *Indi'n Humor*, 328.

76. Ibid.

77. Huntsman, Introduction to Geiogamah, *New Native American Drama*, xvii. This is a collection of three of Geiogamah's plays, and further references to this work will be given parenthetically in the text.

78. Lincoln, *Indi'n Humor*, 335

79. Ibid.

80. Ibid., 168.

81. Pinazzi, "The Theater of Hanay Geiogamah," 184.

82. Lincoln, *Indi'n Humor*, 332.

83. Ibid., 336.

84. Many nineteenth-century novels include the motif of the young American making a grand tour of Europe to gain a cultural education. In Henry James's novella *Daisy Miller* (1878), one of the best known of these works, both Daisy, the prototypical American Girl, and her suitor, Winterbourne, confront Western cultural and educational norms as they travel throughout Europe. Silko is actively drawing on such narratives in her depiction of Indigo's travels in *Gardens in the Dunes*.

85. Shanley, "'Born from the Need to Say,'" 3.

86. Cook-Lynn, *Wallace Stegner*, 79; Cook-Lynn, *Anti-Indianism*, 35; Cook-Lynn, *Wallace Stegner*, 84.

87. Cook-Lynn, *Anti-Indianism*, 35.

88. Cheah and Robbins, *Cosmopolitics*, 2.

89. Arnold, *Conversations with Leslie Marmon Silko*, 172.

90. Ibid., 173.

91. Silko, *Gardens in the Dunes*, 15. Further references to this work will be given parenthetically in the text.

92. Silko may, in fact, have had McNickle in mind while working on *Gardens*. McNickle's 1954 novel, *Runner in the Sun*, features a protagonist named Salt (just as Indigo's sister is named Sister Salt), who is sent on a long journey to bring back something that will avert an unknown, but anticipated, disaster. Lawrence Towner explains in the Afterword to McNickle's *The Surrounded*: "He brings back, almost by accident, a new breed of corn, along with experience about the world outside, and wisdom, so that in the end his people 'lived in peace and supported one another'" (McNickle, *Surrounded*, 305). Though McNickle's novel is set before Indian-white contact, his story resonates with Silko's.

93. Momaday, *Man Made of Words*, 16.

94. See, for example, Henderson, "Between a Rock and a Sacred Place," A3, which reports on the Confederate Tribes of Grand Ronde's efforts to repatriate the Willamette meteor (known to them as Sky Person, or Tamanamas in Chinook). The Oregon tribes view the meteor as a sacred being and used it in ceremonials, until the meteor was taken to New York's American Museum of Natural History in the early years of the twentieth century, where it is currently displayed as "a relic of our solar system." Should the tribes establish their claim to the meteor under the Native American Graves Protection and Repatriation Act (NAGPRA), other native groups, such as the Inuit, may also gain repatriation of other sacred meteors as objects of cultural patrimony.

95. See the reviews of *Gardens*, however, that appear to miss this point, over-simplifying the novel by viewing it as an examination of two diametrically opposed worlds. See especially, Ruta, "Dances with Ghosts," 31. The title of Ruta's review is an indicator that she has approached Silko's work looking for simplistic, Hollywood Indians à la *Dances with Wolves*.

96. For more on Mormon participation in the Ghost Dance, see Barney, *Mormons, Indians, and the Ghost Dance Religion of 1890*.

97. Although Aunt Bronwyn is described as an American who has "gone native" in England, her Celtic name suggests her affinity with Celtic victims of British colonialism. As such, Indigo's relationship with Aunt Bronwyn constitutes a pan-tribal connection. Aunt Bronwyn's name also connects her to the Celtic goddess Branwyn, whose name means "fair bosom," perhaps suggesting that Aunt Bronwyn represents a nurturing whiteness.

98. Nagel, *American Indian Ethnic Renewal*, 114.

99. Shanley, "'Born from the Need to Say,'" 4.

CONCLUSION

1. Lomawaima, "Tribal Sovereigns," 2, 12.

2. Leap, *American Indian English*, 162.

3. Zitkala-Ša, *American Indian Stories*, 39–51.

4. Tohe, *No Parole Today*, 29.

5. Ibid., 26.

6. Ibid., 28, 26.

7. Ibid., 27.

8. See Chapter 1 of this work, and Silko's *Storyteller*.

9. Gates, *The Signifying Monkey*, xxviii.

10. Warrior, *Tribal Secrets*, xvi.

11. The most complete history of the Canadian Indian residential schools can be found in Miller, *Shingwauk's Vision*.

12. IRSRC, "Indian Residential School Statistics." <http://www.irsr-rqpi.gc.ca/english/statistics.html>.

13. IRSRC, "Statistics" <http://www.irsr–rqpi.gc.ca/English/statistics.asp>. The most frequent allegation is fiduciary duty, at 98 percent. Claims of sexual abuse also play a very significant role in the Canadian suits, with 65 percent of claimants charging their educators with sexual assault.

14. Oskaboose, "Residential Schools—30 Years Later."

15. See, for example, the Indian Residential School Survivors Society web page at <http://www.prsp.bc.ca>. The society's newsletter, called the *Survivors' Journey*, publishes survivors' poetry and narratives about their school experiences.

16. Qtd. in Craven, "Judicial Findings."

17. Ibid.

18. Ibid.

19. Tohe, *No Parole Today*, 47.

Bibliography

NEWSPAPERS

Anishinabe Enamiad. Monthly newspaper. Harbor Springs, MI. March 1896–February 1903.

The Arrow. Weekly newspaper. Carlisle Indian School Press, Carlisle, PA. 1904–1908. Continued under the name *Carlisle Arrow*, 1908–1917.

The Indian Helper. Weekly newspaper. Carlisle Indian School Press, Carlisle, PA. 1885–1900.

The Red Man. Newspaper, frequency varies. Carlisle Indian School Press, Carlisle, PA. 1888–1900 and 1909–1917.

The Red Man and Helper. Weekly newspaper. Carlisle Indian School Press, Carlisle, PA. 1900–1904.

OTHER PUBLICATIONS

Aberle, David. *Peyote Religion among the Navajo*. Norman: University of Oklahoma Press, 1991.

Adams, David Wallace. *Education for Extinction: American Indians and the Boarding School Experience, 1875–1928*. Lawrence: University Press of Kansas, 1995.

Ahern, Wilbert H. "'The Returned Indians': Hampton Institute and Its Indian Alumni, 1879–1893." *Journal of Ethnic Studies* 10.4 (December 1983): 101–24.

Allen, Paula Gunn. Email to the author. July 11, 1999.

———. *The Sacred Hoop*. Boston: Beacon, 1986.

Allen, Paula Gunn, ed. *Song of the Turtle: American Indian Literature, 1974–1994*. New York: Ballantine/One World, 1996.

———. *Voice of the Turtle: American Indian Literature, 1900–1970*. New York: Ballantine/One World, 1994.

Andrews, William L., Frances Smith Foster, Trudier Harris, eds. *The Oxford Companion to African American Literature*. New York: Oxford University Press, 1997.

Archuleta, Margaret L., Brenda J. Child, and K. Tsianina Lomawaima, eds. *Away from Home: American Indian Boarding School Experiences, 1879–2000*. Phoenix: Heard Museum, 2000.

Arnold, Ellen L., ed. *Conversations with Leslie Marmon Silko*. Jackson: University of Mississippi Press, 2000.

Babcock, Barbara. "'Maids of Palastine': Pueblo Pots, Potters, and the Politics of Representation." In *Art and the Native American: Perceptions, Reality, and Influence*, ed. Mary Louise Elliot Krumrine and Susan C. Scott. University Park, PA; Department of Art History, Penn State University, 2001.

Baerreis, David A. Forward to La Flesche, *The Middle Five*. Lincoln: University of Nebraska Press, 1978.

Bailey, Garrick A. *The Osage and the Invisible World: From the Works of Francis La Flesche*. Norman: University of Oklahoma Press, 1995.

Bakhtin, M. M. *Speech Genres and Other Late Essays*. Translated by V. McGee. Austin: University of Texas Press, 1986.

Ball, Eve. *Indeh: An Apache Odyssey*. Norman: University of Oklahoma Press, 1988.

Barney, Garold D. *Mormons, Indians, and the Ghost Dance Religion of 1890*. Lanham, MD: University Press of America, 1986.

Batker, Carol J. *Reforming Fictions: Native, African, and Jewish Women's Literature and Journalism in the Progressive Era*. New York: Columbia University Press, 2000.

Bell, Genevieve. "Telling Stories out of School: Remembering the Carlisle Indian Industrial School, 1879–1918." PhD dissertation, Stanford University, 1998.

Berkhofer, Robert F., Jr. *The White Man's Indian: Images of the American Indian from Columbus to the Present*. New York: Alfred A. Knopf, 1978.

Bernardin, Susan. "The Lessons of a Sentimental Education: Zitkala-Ša's Autobiographical Narratives." *Western American Literature* 32.3 (Fall 1997): 212–38.

Bieder, Robert. *Science Encounters the Indian, 1820–1880*. Norman: University of Oklahoma Press, 1986.

Blaine, Martha Royce. *Pawnee Passage, 1870–1875*. Norman: University of Oklahoma Press, 1990.

Boyd, Maurice. *Kiowa Voices Vol. 1: Ceremonial Dance, Ritual and Song*. Fort Worth: Texas Christian University Press, 1981.

———. *Kiowa Voices Vol. 2: Myths, Legends, and Folktales*. Fort Worth: Texas Christian University Press, 1983.

"Boys, boys . . ." *Indian Helper*, September 7, 1888, 3.

Breinig, Helmbrecht, and Klaus Lösch. "Luci Tapahonso." In *Interviews with Nine American Writers*, ed. Wolfgang Binder and Helmbrecht Breinig, 112–23. Hanover: Wesleyan University Press and the University Press of New England, 1995.

Bronson, Ruth Muskrat. *Indians Are People, Too*. New York: Friendship, 1944.

Brown, Dee. *Bury My Heart at Wounded Knee*. New York: Holt, Rinehart and Winston, 1970.

Brumble, H. David. *American Indian Autobiography.* Berkeley: University of California Press, 1988.

Bruner, Edward. "Ethnography as Narrative." In *The Anthropology of Experience,* ed. V. W. Turner and E. M. Bruner, 139–55. Urbana: University of Illinois Press, 1986.

Burgess, Marianna. "Among the Dakotas." *Indian Helper,* August 12, 1887, 1.

———. "How an Indian Girl Might Tell Her Own Story if She Had the Chance." *Indian Helper,* September 20, 1889, 1, 4.

———. "Off to the Pacific Coast." *Red Man and Helper,* August 28, 1903, 1.

———, [as Embe]. *Stiya: A Carlisle Indian Girl at Home.* Cambridge: Riverside, 1891.

"Captain Pratt vs the *Anishinabe Enamiad.*" *Anishinabe Enamiad* (March 1898): n.p.

Carlson, David J. "'Indian for a While': Charles Eastman's *Indian Boyhood* and the Discourse of Allotment." *American Indian Quarterly* 25.4 (Fall 2001): 604–25.

Carr, Darryl. "The American Indian as Prototype: Charles Eastman's Endorsement of the Boy Scouts Movement." Unpublished paper presented at the American Studies Association Conference, Montreal, Quebec, October 1999.

Chavkin, Allan, and Nancy Feyl Chavkin. *Conversations with Louise Erdrich and Michael Dorris.* Literary Conversations Series. Jackson: University Press of Mississippi, 1994.

Cheah, Pheng, and Bruce Robbins, eds. *Cosmopolitics: Thinking and Feeling beyond the Nation.* Minneapolis: University of Minnesota Press, 1998.

Child, Brenda J. *Boarding School Seasons: American Indian Families, 1900–1940.* Nebraska: University of Nebraska Press, 1998.

Clark, Carol Lea. "Charles A. Eastman (Ohiyesa) and Elaine Goodale Eastman: A Cross-Cultural Collaboration." *Tulsa Studies in Women's Literature* 13.2 (Autumn 1994): 271–80.

Clark, Jerry E., and Martha Ellen Webb. "Susette and Susan La Flesche: Reformer and Missionary." In *Being and Becoming Indian: Biographical Studies of North American Frontiers,* ed. James A. Clifton, 137–59. Chicago: Dorsey, 1989.

Clifton, James A. *The Invented Indian: Cultural Fictions and Government Policies.* New Brunswick, NJ: Transaction, 1990.

Cobb, Amanda J. *Listening to Our Grandmothers' Stories: The Bloomfield Academy for Chickasaw Females, 1852–1949.* Lincoln: University of Nebraska Press, 2000.

Coleman, Michael. *American Indian Children at School, 1850–1930.* Jackson: University Press of Mississippi, 1993.

Cook, Jessie W. "The Representative Indian." *The Outlook* 65.1 (May 5, 1900): 80–83. (Reprinted in *Red Man and Helper* (June 1900): 3.

Cook-Lynn, Elizabeth. *Anti-Indianism in Modern America: A Voice from Tatekeya's Earth.* Urbana: University of Illinois Press, 2001.

———. *Why I Can't Read Wallace Stegner and Other Essays: A Tribal Voice.* Madison: University of Wisconsin Press, 1996.

Craven, James M. "Judicial Findings from the Inter-tribal Tribunal on Residential Schools in Canada." July 14, 1998. On-line article at <http://sisis.nativeweb.org/resschool/tribunal.htm>.

Cutter, Martha J. "Zitkala-Ša's Autobiographical Writings: The Problems of a Canonical Search for Language and Identity." *MELUS* 19.1 (March 1994): 31–44.

DeCora, Angel. "Angel DeCora—An Autobiography." *Red Man* (March 1911): 279–80, 285.

"Dedication of the Susie Reyos Marmon Elementary School, March 11, 1990." Carlisle Barracks Library, vertical file, "Students."

Deloria, Ella Cara. *Waterlily.* Lincoln: University of Nebraska Press, 1988.

Deloria, Philip. *Playing Indian.* New Haven: Yale University Press, 1998.

"Dennison Wheelock." Notes. Carlisle Barracks Library, vertical file, "Students."

Duran, Eduardo, and Bonnie Duran. *Native American Postcolonial Psychology.* Albany: SUNY Press, 1995.

Eastman, Charles Alexander. *From the Deep Woods to Civilization.* 1916. Lincoln: University of Nebraska Press, 1977.

———. *Indian Boyhood.* 1902. Lincoln: University of Nebraska Press, 1991.

———. *The Soul of the Indian: An Interpretation.* 1911. Lincoln: University of Nebraska Press, 1980.

Eastman, Elaine Goodale. *Pratt, the Red Man's Moses.* Norman: University of Oklahoma Press, 1935.

———. *Sister to the Sioux: The Memoirs of Elaine Goodale Eastman, 1885–1891.* Edited by Kay Graber. Pioneer Heritage Series, vol. 7. Lincoln: University of Nebraska Press, 1978.

Ellis, Clyde. *To Change Them Forever: Indian Education at the Rainy Mountain Boarding School, 1893–1920.* Norman: University of Oklahoma Press, 1996.

Erdrich, Louise. *The Bingo Palace.* New York: HarperCollins, 1994.

———. *Jacklight.* New York: Holt, 1984.

———. *Love Medicine.* 2nd ed. New York: HarperCollins, 1993.

———. *Tracks.* New York: Harper/Perennial, 1988.

Fisher, Dexter [Alice Poindexter Fisher]. *The Transformation of Tradition: A Study of Zitkala-Ša and Mourning Dove, Two Transitional American Indian Writers.* PhD dissertation, City University of New York, 1979; Ann Arbor, MI: University Microfilms International, no. 80–66440.

———. "Zitkala-Ša: The Evolution of a Writer." In Zitkala-Ša, *American Indian Stories,* v–xx. 1921. Lincoln: University of Nebraska Press, 1985.

Fletcher, Alice, and Francis La Flesche. "The Omaha Tribe." In *Twenty-seventh Annual Report of the Bureau of American Ethnology, 1905–1906.* Report of the Chief W. H. Holmes, 15–655. Washington: GPO, 1911.

———. *The Omaha Tribe.* Vol. 1. Lincoln: University of Nebraska Press, 1972.

Foot, Richard. "Canadian Churches Face $500-million Liability [for] Residential School Abuse." *National Post Online* December 18, 1999. <http://nationalpost.com/story.asp?f=991218/155585.html>.

Foucault, Michel. *Discipline and Punish: The Birth of the Prison.* Translated by Alan Sheridan. 2nd ed. New York: Vintage, 1995.

Franklin, Benjamin. *The Autobiography, 1771–89*. New York: Vintage Books/Library of America, 1990.

Freire, Paulo. *Pedagogy of the Oppressed*. New York: Continuum, 1998.

"From Home Letters." *Indian Helper*, March 16, 1888, 4.

Gates, Henry Louis, Jr. *The Signifying Monkey: A Theory of African-American Literary Criticism*. New York: Oxford University Press, 1988.

Geiogamah, Hanay. "Introduction: The New American Indian Theater." In *Stories Of Our Way: An Anthology of American Indian Plays,* ed. Hanay Geiogamah and Jay T. Darby, 1–6. Los Angeles: UCLA American Indian Studies Center, 1999.

————. *New Native American Drama: Three Plays*. Norman: University of Oklahoma Press, 1980.

Geiogamah, Hanay, and Jaye T. Darby, eds. *American Indian Theater in Performance: A Reader*. Los Angeles: UCLA American Indian Studies Center, 2000.

————. *Stories of Our Way: An Anthology of American Indian Plays*. Los Angeles: UCLA American Indian Studies Center, 1999.

Gilcreast, Everett Arthur. *Richard Henry Pratt and American Indian Policy, 1877–1906. A Study of the Assimilation Movement*. PhD dissertation, Yale University, 1967, Ann Arbor, MI: University Microfilms International..

Gilman, Carolyn, and Mary Jane Schneider. *The Way to Independence: Memories of a Hidatsa Indian Family, 1840–1920*. Minnesota Historical Society Museum Exhibit Series 3. St. Paul: Minnesota Historical Society Press, 1987.

Grammer, Maurine. "Laguna Matriarch Dies at age 110." Carlisle Barricks Library, vertical file, "Students."

Graulich, Melody, ed. *"Yellow Woman"/ Leslie Marmon Silko*. New Brunswick: Rutgers University Press, 1993.

Green, Norma Kidd. *Iron Eye's Family: The Children of Joseph La Flesche*. Lincoln: University of Nebraska Press, 1969.

Hafen, P. Jane. "A Cultural Duet: Zitkala-Ša and *The Sun Dance Opera*." *Great Plains Quarterly* 18.2 (Spring 1998): 102–11.

————. "Introduction." In Zitkala-Ša, *Dreams and Thunder: Stories, Poems, and the Sun Dance Opera*, xiii–xxiv. Lincoln: University of Nebraska Press, 2001.

Haig-Brown, Celia. *Resistance and Renewal: Surviving the Indian Residential School*. Vancouver, BC: Arsenal Pulp Press, 1991.

Hailmann, W. N. *Report of the Superintendent of Indian Schools*. Washington, D.C.: GPO, 1895.

————. *Report of the Superintendent of Indian Schools*. Washington, D.C.: GPO, 1897.

Harjo, Joy, and Gloria Bird, eds. *Reinventing the Enemy's Language: Contemporary Native Women's Writings of North America*. New York: W.W. Norton, 1997.

Heath, Sally Ann. *The Development of Native American Theatre Companies in the Continental United States*. PhD disserttion, University of Colorado, Boulder, 1995. University Microfilms International, no. 9620629.

Heflin, Ruth. *I Remain Alive: The Sioux Literary Renaissance*. Syracuse: Syracuse University Press, 2000.

Henderson, Diedtra. "Between a Rock and a Sacred Place." *Boston Globe,* January 12, 2000, A3.

Hertzberg, Hazel. *The Search for an American Indian Identity: Modern Pan-Indian Movements.* Syracuse: Syracuse University Press, 1971.

Hittman, Michael. *Wovoka and the Ghost Dance.* Lincoln: University of Nebraska Press, 1997.

"Home Difficulties of a Young Indian Girl." *Indian Helper,* September 16, 1887, 1, 4, September 30, 1887, 1, 4, and October 8, 1887, 1, 4.

Horne, Esther Burnett, and Sally McBeth. *Essie's Story: The Life and Legacy of a Shoshone Teacher.* Lincoln: University of Nebraska Press, 1998.

Hoxie, Frederick. "Exploring a Cultural Borderland: Native American Journeys of Discovery." In *American Nations: Encounters in Indian Country, 1850–Present,* ed. Hoxie, Peter C. Mancall, and James H. Merrell, 265–87. New York: Routledge, 2001.

———. *A Final Promise: The Campaign to Assimilate the Indians, 1880–1920.* Lincoln: University of Nebraska Press, 1984.

Hoxie, Frederick, ed. *Encyclopedia of North American Indians: Native American History, Culture and Life from Paleo-Indians to the Present.* Boston and New York: Houghton Mifflin, 1996.

Huntsman, Jeffrey. "Native American Theatre." In *Ethnic Theatre in the United States,* ed. Maxine Schwartz Seller. Westport, CT: Greenwood, 1983.

"Hurrah for the Printer." *Indian Helper,* February 7, 1890, 4.

Hyde, George E. *The Pawnee Indians.* Norman: University of Oklahoma Press, 1974.

———. *A Sioux Chronicle.* Norman: University of Oklahoma Press, 1956.

"Indian Boys at School; Review of *The Middle Five,* by Francis La Flesche." *Red Man and Helper,* August 21, 1900.

"Indian Residential Schools Survivors' Society." <http://www.prsp.bc.ca>.

"An Indian Year." *Red Man and Helper,* July 13, 1900, n.p.

IRSRC (Indian Residential Schools Resolution Canada), "Indian Residential School Statistics." <http://www.irsr-rqpi.gc.ca/english/statistics.html>.

———. "Statistics." <http://www.irsr-rqpi.gc.ca/English/statistics.asp>.

Iverson, Peter. *Carlos Montezuma and the Changing World of American Indians.* Albuquerque: University of New Mexico Press, 1982.

James, Henry. *Daisy Miller.* 1878. New York: Penguin, 1986.

Johnson, David L., and Raymond Wilson. "Gertrude Simmons Bonnin, 1876–1938: 'Americanize the First American'." *American Indian Quarterly* 12 (December 1988): 27–40.

Johnson, Troy, ed. *American Indian Activism: Alcatraz to the Longest Walk.* Urbana: University of Illinois Press, 1997.

Johnston, Basil H. *Indian School Days.* Norman: University of Oklahoma Press, 1989.

Josephy, Alvin M., Jr. *500 National: An Illustrated History of North American Indians.* New York: Alfred A. Knopf, 1994.

Josephy, Alvin M., Jr., Joane Nagel, and Troy Johnson, eds. *Red Power: The American Indian's Right for Freedom.* 2nd ed. Lincoln: University of Nebraska Press, 1999.

Katanski, Amelia. "Victory Songs: The Transformation of the Indian School Band from Assimilative Tool to Marker of Identity." Unpublished essay presented at the American Studies Association Conference, Montreal, Quebec, October 1999.

Kluckhohn, Clyde. *Navajo Witchcraft*. Boston: Beacon, 1944.

Konishi, N. "What He Would Have Said." *Indian Helper*, October 22, 1897, 1.

Kroskrity, Paul V. *Language, History, and Identity: Ethnolinguistic Studies of the Arizona Tewa*. Tucson and London: University of Arizona Press, 1993.

Krupat, Arnold. "The Dialogic of Silko's *Storyteller*." In Grasslich, *"Yellow Woman,"* 185–200.

———. *For Those Who Come After: A Study of Native American Autobiography*. Berkeley and Los Angeles: University of California Press, 1985.

Krupat, Arnold, ed. *Native American Autobiography: An Anthology*. Madison: University of Wisconsin Press, 1994.

La Flesche, Francis. *Ke-ma-ha: The Omaha Stories of Francis La Flesche*. Edited with introduction by James W. Parins and Daniel F. Littlefield. Lincoln: University of Nebraska Press, 1995.

———. *The Middle Five: Indian Schoolboys of the Omaha Tribe*. 1900. Lincoln: University of Nebraska Press, 1978.

———. "The Osage Tribe: Rite of the Wa-xo'-be." *Forty-fifth Annual Report of the Bureau of American Ethnology, 1927–1928*. Washington: GPO, 1930.

Landis, Barbara. "Carlisle Indian Industrial School." On-line web page <http://www.epix.net/~landis/main.html>.

———. "Carlisle Indian Industrial School History." On-line web page, <http://www.rootsweb.com/~pacumber/ciihist2.htm>.

Leap, William L. *American Indian English*. Salt Lake City: University of Utah Press, 1993.

Liberty, Margot. "Francis La Flesche: The Osage Odyssey." In *American Indian Intellectuals*, ed. Margot Liberty, 45–59. Proceedings of the American Ethnological Society, 1976. St. Paul: West, 1978.

———. "Native American Informants': The Contribution of Francis La Flesche." In *American Anthropology: The Early Years*, ed. John V. Murra, 99–110. St Paul: West, 1978.

Lincoln, Kenneth. *Indi'n Humor: Bicultural Play in Native America*. New York: Oxford University Press, 1993.

———. *Native American Renaissance*. Berkeley: University of California Press, 1983.

Lindsey, Donal F. *Indians at Hampton Institute, 1877–1923*. Urbana: University of Illinois Press, 1995.

Littlefield, Daniel F., Jr. "Catholics, 'Krauts,' and (Later) 'Commies': Conspiracy Theorists and Indian Affairs, 1890–1940." Unpublished essay.

———. Conversation. July 17, 1999.

Littlefield, Daniel F., Jr., and James Parins. *American Indian and Alaska Native Newspapers and Periodicals*. Westport, CT: Greenwood, 1984.

———. Introduction to Francis La Flesche, *Ke-ma-ha*. Lincoln: University of Nebraska Press, 1995.

Lomawaima, K. Tsianina. *They Called It Prairie Light: The Story of Chilocco Indian School*. Lincoln: University of Nebraska Press, 1994.

———. "Tribal Sovereigns: Reframing Research in American Indian Education." *Harvard Educational Review* 70.1 (Spring 2000): 1–21.

Lyons, Scott Richard. "Rhetorical Sovereignty: What Do American Indians Want from Writing?" *College Composition and Communication* 51.3 (February 2000): 447–68.

M.L.F., So Bethlehem, PA. Letter. *Red Man* (March 1890): 5.

Malmsheimer, Lonna M. "'Imitation White Man': Images of Transformation at the Carlisle Indian School." *Studies in Visual Communication* (September 1985): 54–75.

Mark, Joan. "Francis La Flesche: The American Indian as Anthropologist." *ISIS* 73 (1982): 497–510.

———. *A Stranger in Her Native Land: Alice Fletcher and the American Indians*. Lincoln: University of Nebraska Press, 1988.

Marr, Carolyn J. "Making Oneself: Use of Photographs by Native Americans of the Southern Northwest Coast." *American Indian Culture and Research Journal* 20.3 (1996): 51–64.

Marriott, Alice. *The Ten Grandmothers*. Norman: University of Oklahoma Press, 1945.

McBeth, Sally J. *Ethnic Identity and the Boarding School Experience of West-Central Oklahoma American Indians*. Lanham, NY: University Press of America, 1983.

McFee, Malcolm. "The 150% Man, a Product of Blackfeet Acculturation." *American Anthropologist* 70 (December 1968): 1096–103.

McNickle, D'Arcy. *Runner in the Sun: A Story of Indian Maize*. Albuquerque: University of New Mexico Press, 1987.

———. *The Surrounded*. Afterword by Lawrence W. Towner. 1936. Albuquerque: University of New Mexico Press, 1992.

Mihesuah, Devon. *American Indians: Stereotypes and Realities*. Atlanta, GA: Clarity, 1996.

———. *Cultivating the Rosebuds: The Education of Women at the Cherokee Female Seminary, 1851–1909*. Urbana: University of Illinois Press, 1998.

Miller, J. R. *Shingwauk's Vision: A History of Native Residential Schools*. Toronto: University of Toronto Press, 1996.

Milner, Clyde A. III. *With Good Intentions: Quaker Work among the Pawnees, Otos, and Omahas in the 1870s*. Lincoln: University of Nebraska Press, 1982.

Momaday, N. Scott. *The Indolent Boys*. Unpublished play. 1994.

———. *The Man Made of Words*. New York: St. Martin, 1997.

———. *The Names: A Memoir*. Sun Tracks American Indian Literary Series 16. Tucson: University of Arizona Press, 1976.

———. "Poetics and Politics." March 30, 1992. On-line at <*http://www.coh.arizona.edu/english/poetics/momaday/momaday_top.html*>.

———. *The Way to Rainy Mountain*. Albuquerque: University of New Mexico Press, 1969.

Montezuma, Carlos. "An Apache. To the Students of Carlisle Indian School." *Indian Helper,* October 14, 1887, 1, 4.

―――. Correspondence with Zitkala-Ša. The Papers of Carlos Montezuma, MD. Wilmington, DE: Scholarly Resources, 1983. Nine microfilm reels.

Mooney, James. *Calendar History of the Kiowa Indians.* Washington, D.C.: Smithsonian Institution, 1979.

―――. *The Ghost-Dance Religion and the Sioux Outbreak of 1890.* Abridged, with an introduction by Anthony F. C. Wallace. Chicago: University of Chicago Press, 1965.

Morgan, Lewis Henry. *Ancient Society.* Foreword by Elisabeth Tooker. Classics of Anthropology. Tucson: University of Arizona Press, 1985.

Morgan, Thomas. "Which Should Have the Best Chance for Education: Indian Boys or Girls?" *Indian Helper,* January 17, 1890, 4.

Morrow, Mary Frances. Correspondence with author, July 15, 1999.

Mourning Dove. *Mourning Dove: A Salishan Autobiography.* Edited by Jay Miller. Lincoln: University of Nebraska Press, 1990.

"Mr. See-All." *Indian Helper,* October 22, 1897, 4.

Murray, David. *Forked Tongues: Speech, Writing, and Representation in North American Indian Texts.* Bloomington: Indiana University Press, 1991.

Nagel, Joane. *American Indian Ethnic Renewal: Red Power and the Resurgence of Identity and Culture.* New York: Oxford University Press, 1996.

Noriega, Jorge. "American Indian Education in the United States: Indoctrination for Subordination into Colonialism." In *The State of Native America,* ed. M. Annette Jaimes, 371–402. Race and Resistance Series. Boston: South End Press, 1992.

Okker, Patricia. "Native American Literatures and the Canon: The Case of Zitkala-Ša." In *American Realism and the Canon,* ed. T. Quirk and G. Scharnhorst, 87–101. Newark: University of Delaware Press, 1994.

Olson, James C. *Red Cloud and the Sioux Problem.* Lincoln: University of Nebraska Press, 1965.

Oskaboose, Gilbert. "Residential Schools—30 Years Later." On-line article at <http://firstnations.com/oskaboose/residential-schools.htm>.

"Our World." "Indian Department," *Southern Workman* (February 1885): 20.

Parks, Douglas R., and Raymond J. DeMallie. "Plains Indian Native Literatures." In *American Indian Persistence and Resurgence,* ed. Karl Kroeber, 106–48. Durham: Duke University Press, 1994.

Peterson, Erik. "'An Indian . . . an American': Ethnicity, Assimilation and Balance in Charles Eastman's *From the Deep Woods to Civilization.*" In *Early Native American Writing: New Critical Essays,* ed. Helen Jaskoski. Cambridge: Cambridge University Press, 1996.

Picotte, Agnes. Introduction. In Zitkala-Ša, *Old Indian Legends,* xi–xvii. Lincoln: University of Nebraska Press, 1985.

Pinazzi, Annamaria. "The Theater of Hanay Geiogamah." In *American Indian Theater in Performance: A Reader.* Los Angeles: UCLA American Indian Studies Center, 2000.

Powell, Malea. "Rhetorics of Survivance: How American Indians Use Writing." *College Composition and Communication* 53.3 (February 2002): 396–434.

Pratt, Richard Henry. *Battlefield and Classroom: Four Decades With the American Indian.* Edited by Robert M. Utley. New Haven: Yale University Press, 1964.

"Press Comments on the Band." *Red Man* (April 1900): 8.

"Promoted." *The Arrow,* October 13, 1904, n.p.

Prucha, Francis Paul. *Americanizing the American Indians: Writings by the "Friends of the Indian," 1880–1900.* Cambridge: Harvard University Press, 1973.

Public Broadcasting Service (PBS). *In the White Man's Image.* The American Experience series. Series editor Llewellyn Smith, writer and producer Christine Lesiak. National American Broadcasting Corporation and Nebraska Educational Television Network, 1992. 60 min. documentary.

Qoyawayma, Polingaysi. *No Turning Back: A Hopi Indian Woman's Struggle to Live in Two Worlds.* As told to Vada F. Carlson. Albuquerque: University of New Mexico Press, 1964.

Ramsey, Jarold. "Francis La Flesche's 'The Song of Flying Crow' and the Limits of Ethnography." In *American Indian Persistence and Resurgence,* ed. Karl Kroeber. Durham: Duke University Press, 1994.

Rappaport, Doreen. *The Flight of Red Bird: The Life of Zitkala-Ša.* New York: Dial, 1997.

Reese, Debbie, et al. "A Critical Review of Ann Rinaldi's *My Heart Is on the Ground: The Diary of Nannie Little Rose, a Sioux Girl.*" *Oyate Online,* August 30, 1999, at <http://www.oyate.org/avoid/myheart.html>.

Rice, Julian. *Lakota Storytelling: Black Elk, Ella Deloria, and Frank Fools Crow.* New York: Peter Lang, 1989.

Rinaldi, Ann. *My Heart Is on the Ground: The Diary of Nannie Little Rose, a Sioux Girl.* Dear America Series 12. New York: Scholastic, 1999.

Riney, Scott. *The Rapid City Indian School, 1898–1933.* Norman: University of Oklahoma Press, 1999.

Ruoff, A. LaVonne Brown. "Ritual and Renewal: Keres Traditions in Leslie Silko's 'Yellow Woman.'" In Graulich, *"Yellow Woman,"* 69–82.

Ruta, Suzanne. "Dances with Ghosts." Review of Silko's *Gardens in the Dunes. New York Times,* April 18, 1999, section 7, page 31.

Sarris, Greg. *Keeping Slug Woman Alive: A Holistic Approach to American Indian Texts.* Berkeley and Los Angeles: University of California Press, 1993.

"School Days of an Indian Girl." *Red Man* (February 1900): 8.

Schubnell, Matthias. *Conversations with N. Scott Momaday.* Literary Conversations Series. Jackson: University Press of Mississippi, 1997.

Schutt, Amy C. "Reading in Community: The Auditory Text in Moravian Missions to Native Americans." Unpublished paper presented at SHARP Conference, Madison, Wisconsin, July 15–18, 1999.

Sekaquaptewa, Helen. *Me and Mine: The Life Story of Helen Sekaquaptewa.* As told to Louise Udall. Tucson: University of Arizona Press, 1969.

Shanley, Kathryn W. "'Born from the Need to Say': Boundaries and Sovereignties in Native American Literary and Cultural Studies." *Paradoxa* 15 (2001): 3–16.

———. "'Writing Indian': American Indian Literature and the Future of Native American Studies." In *Studying Native America: Problems and Prospects*, ed. Russell Thornton. Madison: University Wisconsin Press, 1998.

Shaw, Anna Moore. *A Pima Past*. Tucson: University of Arizona Press, 1974.

Silko, Leslie Marmon. *Ceremony*. New York: Penguin, 1977.

———. *Gardens in the Dunes*. New York: Simon and Schuster, 1999.

———. *Storyteller*. New York: Arcade, 1981.

———. *Yellow Woman and a Beauty of the Spirit: Essays on Native American Life Today*. New York: Touchstone/Simon and Schuster, 1997.

"The Sioux Bill: Will the Indians Be Cheated If They Sign the Act?" *Indian Helper*, September 7, 1888, 2.

Smith, Huston, and Reuben Snake, eds. *One Nation under God: The Triumph of the Native American Church*. Santa Fe: Clear Light, 1996.

Smith, Jeanne. "'A Second Tongue': The Trickster's Voice in the Works of Zitkala-Ša." In *Tricksterism in Turn of the Century American Literature*, ed. Elizabeth Ammons. Hanover, NH: University Press of New England, 1994.

Smith, Paul Chaat, and Robert Allen Warrior. *Like a Hurricane: The Indian Movement from Alcatraz to Wounded Knee*. New York: New Press, 1996.

Smith, Sherry L. "Francis LaFlesche and the World of Letters." *American Indian Quarterly* 25.4 (Fall 2001): 579–603.

Snake, Reuben. *Reuben Snake: Your Humble Serpent*. As told to Jay C. Fikes. Santa Fe: Clear Light, 1996.

"'Soft-hearted Sioux' Morally Bad." *Red Man and Helper* 12 (April 1901): 1.

"Song of the Printer." *Indian Helper*, May 19, 1899, 1.

Spack, Ruth. *America's Second Tongue: American Indian Education and the Ownership of English, 1860–1900*. Lincoln: University of Nebraska Press, 2002.

———."Dis/Engagement: Zitkala-Ša's Letters to Carlos Montezuma, 1901–1902." *MELUS* 26.1 (Spring 2001): 172–204.

———. "Re-visioning Sioux Women: Zitkala-Ša's Revolutionary *American Indian Stories*." *Legacy* 14.1 (1997): 25–42.

Standing Bear, Luther. *My People, the Sioux*. 1928. Lincoln: University of Nebraska Press, 1975.

Stewart, Omer C. *Peyote Religion: A History*. Norman: University of Oklahoma Press, 1987.

Stocking, George W., Jr. *Race, Culture, and Evolution*. Chicago: University of Chicago Press, 1968.

Stoltz, Marguerite Bigler. *The Dove always Cried: Narratives of Indian School Life with Stories by Her Pupils*. Blacksburg, VA: Pocahontas, 1994.

Stowe, Harriet Beecher. *Uncle Tom's Cabin*. New York: Norton, 1993.

Susag, Dorothea M. "Zitkala-Ša (Gertrude Simmons Bonnin): A Power(full) Literary Voice." *SAIL* 5.3 (Fall 1993): 3–24.

Swann, Brian, and Arnold Krupat, eds. *Recovering the Word: Essays on Native American Literature*. Los Angeles: University of California Press, 1987.

Talayesva, Don C. *Sun Chief: The Autobiography of a Hopi Indian*. Edited by Leo W. Simmons. Institute of Human Relations. New Haven: Yale University Press, 1942.

Tapahonso, Luci. *Sáanii Dahataal, the Women Are Singing: Poems and Stories*. Sun Tracks American Indian Literary Series 23. Tucson: University of Arizona Press, 1993.

Toelken, Barre. "Life and Death in the Navajo Coyote Tales." In *Recovering the Word*, ed. Brian Swann and Arnold Krupat. Berkeley and Los Angeles: University of California Press, 1987.

Tohe, Laura. *No Parole Today*. Albuquerque: West End Press, 1999.

Tompkins, Jane. *Sensational Designs: The Cultural Work of American Fiction 1790–1860*. New York: Oxford University Press, 1986.

Trafzer, Clifford E. *Blue Dawn, Red Earth: New Native American Storytellers*. New York: Anchor Books, 1996.

Trennert, Robert A., Jr. *The Phoenix Indian School: Forced Assimilation in Arizona, 1891–1935*. Norman: University of Oklahoma Press, 1988.

Trevithick, Scott R. "Native Residential Schooling in Canada: A Review of Literature." *Canadian Journal of Native Studies* 18.1 (1998): 49–86.

"Two Carlisle Boys at Pine Ridge Talk Over the Sioux Bill." *Indian Helper*, August 31, 1888, 1, 4.

U.S. Congress. Hearings before the Joint Commission to Investigate Indian Affairs, *Carlisle Indian School*. 63rd Cong., 2nd sess., 1914.

———. Senate. *Peyote: Hearings before a Subcommittee of the Committee on Indian Affairs*. Washington: GPO, 1918.

———. Secretary of the Interior. "Education of Indian Children in Certain Schools." 55th Cong., 2nd sess. Senate Doc. no. 136 (serial set 3599), 1898.

"Untitled ['The Band-stand commands . . .']." *Indian Helper*, March 9, 1888, 2.

Utley, Robert M. *The Last Days of the Sioux Nation*. New Haven: Yale University Press, 1963.

Walsman, Carl. *Word Dance: The Language of Native American Culture*. New York: Facts on File, 1994.

Warrior, Robert Allen. *Tribal Secrets: Recovering American Indian Intellectual Traditions*. Minneapolis: University of Minnesota Press, 1995.

Washburn, Wilcomb E. *The American Indian and the United States*. Vol. 4. New York: Random House, 1973.

Weaver, Jace. "From I-Hermeneutics to We-Hermeneutics: Native Americans and the Post-Colonial." In *Native American Religious Identity: Unforgotten Gods*, ed. Jace Weaver. Maryknoll, NY: Orbis, 1998.

———. *That the People Might Live: Native American Literatures and Native American Community*. New York: Oxford University Press, 1997.

Wexler, Laura. "Tender Violence: Literary Eavesdropping, Domestic Fiction, and Educational Reform." In *The Culture of Sentiment: Race, Gender, and Sentimentality in Nineteenth-Century America*, ed. Shirley Samuels, 9–38. New York: Oxford University Press, 1992.

"What Our Pupils Think about the Order from the Indian Department at Washington Prohibiting the Teaching of Indian Languages in Indian Schools." *Morning Star* (December 1887): 8.

"What Uncle Joe Has to Say." *Anishinabe Enamiad* (October, 1899): n.p.

Wheelock, Dennison. "Is It Right for the Government to Stop the Teaching of Indian Languages in Reservation Schools?" *Indian Helper*, November 18, 1887, 1.

White, Richard. *The Middle Ground*. Cambridge: Cambridge University Press, 1991.

"Who Is that Man-on-the-Band-stand?" *Indian Helper*, November 29, 1889, 1.

Willard, William. "The First Amendment, Anglo–Conformity, and American Indian Religious Freedom." *Wicazo-Sa Review* 7.1 (Spring 1991): 26–30.

———. "Zitkala-Ša: A Woman Who Would Be Heard." *Wicazo-Sa Review* 1.1 (Spring 1985): 11–16.

Williams, Robert. "Documents of Barbarism: The Contemporary Legacy of European Racism and Colonialism in the Narrative Traditions of Federal Indian Law." *Arizona Law Review* 31 (1989): 237–78.

Wilson, Raymond. *Ohiyesa: Charles Eastman, Santee Sioux*. Urbana: University of Illinois Press, 1983.

Witherspoon, Gary. *Language and Art in the Navajo Universe*. Ann Arbor: University of Michigan Press, 1977.

Witmer, Linda F. *The Indian Industrial School, Carlisle, Pennsylvania, 1879–1918*. Carlisle: Cumberland County Historical Society, 1993.

Womack, Craig S. *Red on Red: Native American Literary Separatism*. Minneapolis: University of Minnesota Press, 1999.

Wong, Hertha Dawn. *Sending My Heart Back across the Years: Tradition and Innovation in Native American Autobiography*. New York: Oxford University Press, 1992.

Yabe, Kazushi. "Balancing Realities: A Study in Navajo Philosophy and Peyotism." Master's thesis, UCLA, 1998.

Yava, Albert. *Big Falling Snow: A Tewa-Hopi Indian's Life and Times and the History and Traditions of His People*. New York: Crown, 1978.

Zitkala-Ša. *American Indian Stories*. 1921. Lincoln: University of Nebraska Press, 1985.

———. *Dreams and Thunder: Stories, Poems, and The Sun Dance Opera*. Lincoln: University of Nebraska Press, 2001.

———. *Iktomi and the Ducks and Other Sioux Stories*. Lincoln: University of Nebraska Press, 2004.

———. Letter to the editor. *Red Man*, April 1900.

———. *Old Indian Legends*. Illustrated by Angel de Cora. 1901. Lincoln: University of Nebraska Press, 1985.

"Zitkala-Ša in the *Atlantic Monthly*." *Red Man and Helper* (June 1900): n.p.

Index

Many Lightnings. *See* Eastman, Jacob
Marmon, Henry C. (Silko's "Grandpa
Hank"), 20, 23, 166
Marmon, Lee (Silko's father), 24
Marmon, Maria Anaya (Silko's "Grandma
A'mooh"), 20, 22–23, 67, 89, 166;
response to *Stiya*, 80–82
Marmon, Susie Reyos (Silko's "Aunt Susie"),
20–23, 67, 89, 166, 219, 225n5; response
to *Stiya*, 80–82
McNickle, D'Arcy: *Runner in the Sun*,
252n92; *Surrounded*, 168, 205
Medicine Wheel: Bighorn Medicine Wheel,
183, 190; in *Indolent Boys*, 183–84
*Middle Five: Indian Schoolboys of the Omaha
Tribe* (La Flesche), 17, 96, 119, 148;
excerpted and reviewed in *Red Man and
Helper*, 99–102; publication history, 98;
repertoire of identities in, 103; student
resistance in, 106–108
Middle ground, 17, 95, 105, 163, 206,
239n25; in Momaday's writing, 182; in
Tapahonso's writing, 176
Momaday, Al, 193
Momaday, N. Scott, 167, 217, 250n49; as
activist, 193; and Buffalo Trust, 194;
Indolent Boys, 18, 178, 179–94, 214, 250n37;
Names, 193; portrayal of mother, 193; on
silence, 14
Montezuma, Carlos, 15, 228n55, 231nn26–27;
in *Indian Helper*, 58, 70, 83; as "represen-
tative Indian," 38, 96; and Zitkala-Ša,
161–62
Mooney, James, 163, 180
Morgan, Lewis Henry, 31–32, 77, 226n24;
Ancient Society, 31
Morgan, Thomas J., 34; on educating
Indian girls, 77
Morning Star (newspaper), 88
Mourning Dove, 170
"Mr. See-All," 54, 56, 104. *See also* Disci-
plinary power; *Indian Helper*
*My Heart Is On the Ground: The Diary of
Nannie Little Rose, a Sioux Girl. See*
Rinaldi, Ann
Mysterious Medicine (Eastman's uncle),
146

Names (Momaday), 193
Napawat, Martha, 72
Native American Church. *See* Peyotism
Native American Theater Ensemble
(NATE), 195–96
Natwawa, Mary, 72, 235n83

Navajo-Land Outdoor Theater, 195
No Parole Today (Tohe), 3, 6, 12, 221

Occupation of Wounded Knee (1973). *See*
Wounded Knee, 1973 Occupation of
Ohiyesa. *See* Eastman, Charles Alexander
Omaha Tribe (Fletcher), 97, 110
"Our World," 83–84

Pan-Indianism, 8, 9, 18, 28, 130, 146;
activism, 162–63, 178, 194; in boarding-
school narratives, 169–70, 172; and
boarding-school repertoire, 181; use of
English and, 129, 133; in *Foghorn*,
194–201; in *Gardens in the Dunes*, 211;
intertribal marriage and, 193; literary
tradition, 161, 219; Native American
Church and, 111; schools as marker of
identity, 9, 192, 201, 236n94
Panopticon, 55. *See also* Boarding-school
newspapers, as rhetorical panopticon;
Foucault, Michel; Man-on-the-Band-
stand
Paper Indians, 16, 83, 85, 94, 115, 217;
antithesis of, 189; definition, 47; and
Indian Helper, 59–65, 89, 90, 92; musical
equivalent, 91; student resistance
against, 123
Peace Commission (1868), 35
Peyotism, 110–11, 162–64, 240n39, 248n74
Photography: at Carlisle, 23, 39; and
Marmon family, 23–25, 29; in *Stiya*, 67,
72; and student writing, 89, 99, 102, 120,
123
Pine Ridge Reservation, S.Dak., 61–62, 132,
140–44
Pocahontas, 194, 197
Pratt, Richard Henry, 3, 15, 23, 85, 96, 167,
235n85; conflict with Catholic mission
schools, 226n29; educational experiment
at Ft. Marion, 5, 188; educational philosophy, 32; Francis La Flesche and, 98–102,
111, 131; Ghost Dance and, 68; Man-on-
the-Band-stand and, 54, 57; memoir
(*Battlefield and Classroom*), 5; peyotism
and, 111; returned students and, 69;
school newspapers and, 47; Sioux Bill
and, 62–63; Zitkala-Ša and, 98, 115, 119,
123–29, 131
Presbyterian Mission School (Omaha
Agency), 102
Project HOOP, 195

Qoyawayma, Polingaysi, 170

274